AF576966

Haitian Creole Newspaper Reader

Kate Howe

with the assistance of
Lyonel Desmarattes

Dunwoody Press
1990

All questions and inquiries should be directed to:

Dunwoody Press, P.O. Box 1825, Wheaton, MD, 20915

First Edition: 1990
Printed and bound in the United States of America
Library of Congress Catalog Number: 90-80442
ISBN: 0-931-745-59-4

Table of Contents

The Forty-Two Selections

Translations of the Selections

Table of Contents

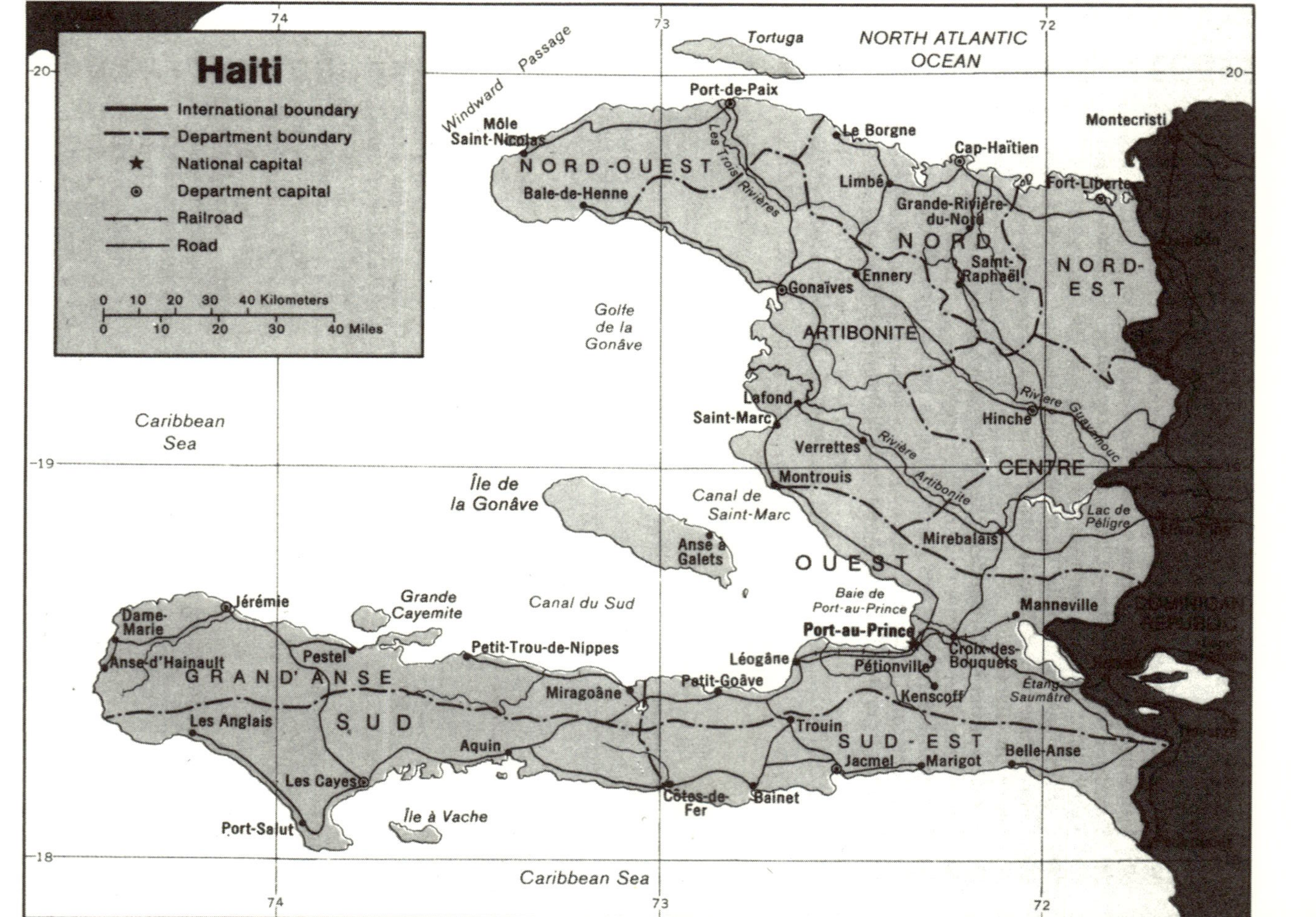
Haiti
International boundary
Department boundary
National capital
Department capital
Railroad
Road
0 10 20 30 40 Kilometers
0 10 20 30 40 Miles
NORTH ATLANTIC OCEAN
Tortuga
Windward Passage
Caribbean Sea
Golfe de la Gonâve
Île de la Gonâve
Canal de Saint-Marc
Canal du Sud
Baie de Port-au-Prince
Grande Cayemite
Île à Vache
Caribbean Sea
NORD-OUEST
NORD
NORD-EST
ARTIBONITE
CENTRE
OUEST
GRAND'ANSE
SUD
SUD-EST
Port-de-Paix
Môle Saint-Nicolas
Bale-de-Henne
Les Trois Rivières
Le Borgne
Limbé
Cap-Haïtien
Montecristi
Fort-Liberté
Grande-Rivière-du-Nord
Saint-Raphaël
Ennery
Gonaïves
Lafond
Saint-Marc
Verrettes
Rivière Artibonite
Rivière Guayamouc
Hinche
Montrouis
Mirebalais
Lac de Péligre
Anse à Galets
Manneville
Port-au-Prince
Croix-des-Bouquets
Pétionville
Kenscoff
Étang Saumâtre
Léogâne
Petit-Goâve
Miragoâne
Petit-Trou-de-Nippes
Jérémie
Dame-Marie
Anse-d'Hainault
Pestel
Les Anglais
Les Cayes
Port-Salut
Aquin
Côtes-de-Fer
Bainet
Trouin
Jacmel
Marigot
Belle-Anse
74
73
72
20
19
18

Preface

This reader follows the same basic format as others in the Newspaper Reader series published by Dunwoody Press, with the difference that most of the reading selections herein are transcriptions of radio broadcasts rather than newspaper articles. The book is intended to provide students of Haitian Creole who already have some knowledge of the language with further practice in reading on a wide variety of topics, thus also increasing their familiarity with some aspects of Haitian life, in the broadest sense. The texts vary in difficulty from elementary to advanced, with the majority ranging from 2 to 3+ on the US Government Interagency Language Roundtable scale. All the texts were originally produced by native Haitian Creole speakers for native Haitian Creole speakers.

Those reading selections transcribed from radio broadcasts were recorded in Haiti between 7 and 25 November 1988. Three selections are samples of graffiti found in the slums of La Saline, and one is a political slogan on a main street in the Pacot neighborhood of the capital. The remainder are articles or letters reproduced with the kind permission of the weekly newspaper, *Haïti Progrès.*

Tapes are available of all the selections: those radio broadcasts which are clear enough are in the original, some have been re-recorded to ensure clarity. The selections from *Haïti Progrès* have also been included on the tapes, read by a native speaker.

I have followed the IPN *(Institut de Pédagogie National)* spelling system, as exemplified in the *Diksyonè Otograf Kreyòl Ayisyen* (see bibliography), for the transcription of the radio broadcasts. This system is explained in the chapter on Spelling and Pronunciation. I have reproduced the newspaper texts as they appeared in *Haïti Progrès*, including any typographical or other errors and variations in spelling as they occurred in the original. Editing of the radio transcriptions has been kept to a minimum: three periods within square brackets indicate that a portion of the text has been omitted, either because of lack of clarity in the recording, or because the newsreader has repeated a portion, or corrected an error. Variation in pronunciation, and use of Gallicisms (either as calques or direct borrowings) are common in Haitian Creole, particularly in urban dialects; I have tried to remain faithful to the original, as this is the reality of language use in Haiti, and the student who is not aware of both factors will have unnecessary problems when confronted with a native speaker.

The order of the selections reflects their relative complexity on two counts: grammatical structure and amount of "world knowledge" regarding Haiti, past and present, required to make sense of the content of each selection. This means that selections dealing with the same or related topics are not necessarily presented together; cross-references are given in the notes.

The vocabulary list below each selection contains new items only (or a new meaning for an item already introduced elsewhere). Some words may require different translations according to context; the lists give the context-specific meaning, but if the word is common with a more basic sense, that sense is also given. Parts of speech are given when the English gloss is ambiguous in this respect, otherwise they are omitted. Strictly speaking, these lists should be called 'lexicons', as they contain not only 'words' in the usual sense, but also grammatical markers, and idioms. An alphabetized general glossary is given at the end of the book.

The notes after the vocabulary lists are intended to clarify the Creole texts. Thus, additional information on grammar and vocabulary is included, and also information required for full comprehension of the content.

An asterisk next to an entry in the vocabulary list or in the notes indicates that that item is treated in the Reference Grammar.

The English translations of the texts have been kept as literal as possible, to assist the user in following the original structure. See the introduction to the translations section for details.

The Reference Grammar does not purport to be complete, but rather addresses the most basic structures of the language, and specifically those which occur in the selections. Although it is assumed that users of this reader have already completed an introductory course in Haitian Creole, it is hoped that someone with no previous knowledge of the language, after studying the Reference Grammar, will also be able to learn enough to read the selections.

It is recommended that the user read through the Reference Grammar and the explanation of the spelling and pronunciation before starting to work with the selections.

As there is considerable confusion among non-specialists as to the meaning of the term 'creole', and also the linguistic situation in Haiti, two short chapters address the fundamental aspects of these questions.

Finally, a bibliography suggests further reading in several areas of the language, as well as the history and culture of Haiti. It is by no means exhaustive. Many of the works cited have excellent bibliographies, which users can refer to for topics of personal interest.

Grateful acknowledgement is due to Lyonel Desmarattes, my first teacher of Haitian Creole, and patient, careful, and demanding assistant at all stages of research and writing; also to Bernard Théotise for many hours of fruitful discussion in and about Haitian Creole. Bryant Freeman has, throughout the project, given generously of his time, knowledge and enthusiasm. I would also like to thank Jim Stone, R.David Zorc, John D. Murphy, and Pamela Johnstone-Moguet for their helpful comments at various stages of the project. Thanks are also due to John E. Joseph, Evelyn McClave, Vivian Noble, George Oliver, Richard Howe, and Colin Jones for their advice on and editing of the Reference Grammar and the chapters on Haitian Creole and Creoles and Pidgins, and to Monique Wong for discussions and opinions on linguistic matters.

In Haiti, I would like to thank Carrié Paultre, Roger Désir, Yves Déjean, Pradel Pompilus, Pierre Vernet, Madame St Lot, Mssrs. Belizaire and Charles of the Institut de Pédagogie National, Bob Alerte, Michel St Lot, Emerante de Pradines and Justin Jackson for their time and assistance, and the staff at the Hotel Oloffson and my

Haitian friends for their patience in teaching me more about Haiti and Haitian Creole.

Last but certainly not least, thanks to Frédérique Schutt-Ainé for transcribing the tapes, and to Steve Bladey for overall formatting.

K.H.
Washington DC
December 1990

Abbreviations

adj.	adjective
adv.	adverb
[+ant]	[+anterior]
attr.	attributive
COMPL	complementizer
CONJ	conjuction
COP	copula
def. det.	definite determiner
DEM	demonstrative
DET	definite determiner singular
DETPL	definite determiner plural
Eng.	English
fem.	feminine
Fr.	French
HC	Haitian Creole
interj.	interjection
[interr]	interrogative marker
[+irr]	[+irrealis]
lit.	literally
loc.	locative
masc.	masculine
n.	noun
NEG	negative marker
NP	noun phrase
POSS	possessive
PREP	preposition
[+prog]	[+progressive]
Q	question marker
RELPRO	relative pronoun
Sp.	Spanish
sth.	something
subj.	subject
TMA	Tense Mode Aspect
var.	variant
vb.	verb
VP	verb phrase
1s	first person singular
2s	second person singular
3s	third person singular
1/2p	participants in discourse
3p	nonparticipants/third person plural

Language in Haiti

What is Haitian Creole?

The only language all Haitians have in common is Haitian Creole (also called 'Haitian' or, amongst Haitians, just 'Creole'). French is also used in Haiti, but it is estimated that only 8-10% of Haitians know French well enough to use it comfortably in any situation; moreover, about 80% of the population is functionally or totally illiterate, in either language.

Haitian Creole is not a deviant of French, but a member of a class of languages known as 'creoles'; more specifically it is one of a subgroup of creoles known as 'French creoles' or 'French-based creoles' because the majority of the vocabulary, or lexicon, is taken from French. French is therefore referred to as the *lexifier* language of the French creoles. Other French-based creoles are: Mauritian Creole, spoken on the island of Mauritius; Seychellois Creole, spoken in the Seychelles; and Louisiana Creole, spoken in Louisiana, USA. There are other groups of creole languages whose lexifier languages are English, Spanish, Dutch, or Portuguese, and which came into being with European colonial expansion (see below).

Vocabulary is the most arbitrary part of any language, and also the most susceptible to change. As an illustration, consider how English takes many words from other languages. The following sentence is largely made up of French words:

The coup d'état of the élite forced the avant-garde and the engagés to rendezvous.

Note that the original French meaning of **rendezvous** is a verb in the imperative; within French this has come to mean also *meeting*. English has taken this noun, and made it a verb again, but with English form, not the original French infinitive (**se rendre**). However, no-one would argue that this sentence is not a sentence of English.

A similar phenomenon occurs in Haitian Creole. It is estimated that approximately 80% of Haitian Creole vocabulary is French-derived, but the words do not necessarily have the same meaning, or even the same form or function, as in French. Some nouns remain nouns, but their meaning might become restricted or expanded, e.g. HC **blan** *foreigner* < Fr. **blanc** *white*; HC **nèg** *man, guy* < Fr. **nègre** *negro*. An adjective that has retained its meaning and its function, but changed its form, is HC **ti** *little* < Fr. **petit** *little*. The Haitian Creole preverbal marker used to indicate anteriority is **te** < Fr. **été** *been* or **était** *was*; part of the meaning has been retained, but the form and the function have both changed.

The structure of Haitian Creole, however, is quite different from French, and this is why it cannot be considered a dialect or variety of French. Structurally, creole languages have more in common with other creoles than they do with their respective lexifier languages.

Status of Haitian Creole

French was declared the official language of the country in the constitution of 1918, which made the use of French obligatory in public service. Not until 1964 was a modification introduced allowing monolinguals (i.e. non-francophones) to use Creole for any official purpose. In 1979, a presidential decree allowed the use of Creole in the schools, both as the medium of teaching and as an object of study. Until then, French had been the language of instruction, even though most of the students knew no French, and many of the teachers themselves spoke it badly.

Finally, in the latest constitution (1987), Creole was given official recognition:

> *"All Haitians are united by a common language, Creole. Creole and French are the official languages of the Republic"*
>
> [Author's Translation]

Nonetheless, French continues to be the language of social prestige. Haiti is dominated by a bilingual francophone élite, who have access to the prestige language, which until recently was used almost exclusively in all areas of public life -- political discourse, newspapers and other publications, legal documents, and as the medium of education. The vast majority of the population, however, is made up of monolingual creolophones. A small percentage of these creolophones are somewhat literate, thanks to some state schooling, radio literacy programs, and missionary schools, but they do not have enough mastery to function at any useful level.

Although there is a tradition of writing in Haitian Creole among some of the 'creolizing' members of the educated classes, only very recently has it become a written language in any meaningful sense. The long-term neglect of the language has meant that there are no 'official' grammar rules, such as those informing English or French. The student should always keep in mind that in the case of Haitian Creole, the rule is basically "If a native Creole speaker says it, it's OK". However, there are outside influences that affect an individual's use of language, and there is a difference between, for example, the Creole spoken by a bilingual Haitian living in Port-au-Prince, a monolingual semiliterate living in Port-au-Prince, and a monolingual, illiterate peasant from the interior. In any case, one should remember that variation in pronunciation and grammar occur in all languages, written or not, codified or not.

The Concept of Diglossia

Diglossia is a linguistic situation in which two varieties of a language, or two different languages, are used, but each variety or language has its specific functions within the society. For the Haitian élite there is diglossia between French and Creole. French, as noted above, is used in most public situations, in formal private contact, and with children (to ensure that they grow up knowing French); Creole is reserved for use in the family, when speaking with servants and obvious monolinguals, for *vodou* ceremonies, and with close friends.

The Creole Continuum and Decreolization

The idea of a continuum was introduced into creole studies to explain the 'shades of grey' in Jamaica between the 'radical' creole spoken there (the basilect) and standard Jamaican English (the acrolect). This situation holds for any creole language that is in contact with its lexifier language. City dwellers, who usually have more contact with the lexifier, speak a more acrolectal variety, while country dwellers, living in a more homogeneous linguistic community, are more conservative in their speech. The term 'decreolization' describes the process that brings the creole closer to its lexifier language.

Perception of Creole in Haiti

Because of such social factors, many Haitians, including well-educated ones, think that Creole is a non-language. It is not unusual to hear a Haitian say that Creole 'has no grammar', for example. In fact, some well-educated Haitians feel that they do not have a native language at all; while apparently fluent in both French and Creole (and often English and Spanish), they nevertheless say that they are not able to express themselves completely in any language.

Foreigners in Haiti should not be surprised, then, at the educated Haitians' apparent reluctance to speak Creole with them. Some might be insulted by a foreigner's using Creole with them because of the low prestige of the language; for others, however, the problem may simply be that the habits of diglossia are difficult to break, and closer acquaintance with the individual will gradually remove this barrier to the use of Creole.

Norm and Standardization of Creole

This said, however, the education reform of 1979 (now being implemented), and the more frequent use of Creole on the radio, television, in the newspapers, and for literary and intellectual endeavours, will have some important effects on the language. Creole will grow in status, it will be used in more and more circumstances, and its very form will undergo modification.
We can see in Haitian Creole the three types of change identified by Joseph (1983) as preceding standardization:

1. change in function, as Creole supplants French in many areas of communication, gradually undoing the diglossia situation of the Haitian élite.

2. change in form, necessary to accommodate new topics of conversation, as the functions expand.

These two types of change will result in the creation of new words and also of new styles to fill the expanded communicative need.

3. change in status, which is a concomitant of the above two changes.

This, as Joseph points out, will result in the Creole language variety of the intellectual élite becoming the basis for the norm.

Standardization can be either deliberate or unconscious. If we take Chaudenson's definition of norm to be the "the usage of the dominant social group" (Chaudenson 1989:62, author's translation), then certainly no deliberate and concerted effort is necessary. For Haitian Creole, the dominant social group is composed of the 'creolizing' intellectuals, journalists (radio and newspapers), and the church.

If we look at the three most obvious sources of change in Haitian Creole, we find that there is occasion for both deliberate and unconscious changes to take hold:

- French influence will continue and even intensify as bilinguals introduce more and more Gallicisms (words and expressions taken from French) into Creole. This is particularly true of radio announcers, who often translate from French texts as they are talking, and journalists, who likewise usually work under severe time constraints, and so do not give much attention to using 'pure' Creole. In addition, the attitude persists in many quarters that the more French the language sounds, the better.

- Conscious internal neologisms will grow in number as speakers seeking to avoid borrowing from French turn to Creole possibilities, coining new words and expressions from native Creole elements.

- Normal internal change (unconscious) will continue. All languages are continually evolving over time; writing and standardization cannot stop this evolution, although they slow it. It is possible that some changes could be the result of French influence initially, and then become 'self-powered', taking their own direction within Creole.

So far, few steps have been taken towards establishing any kind of official norm for Haitian Creole, although the writing system has been standardized, and is widely used in publications.

Nevertheless, as the norm is taken from the usage of those with high prestige, the use of the standard textbooks now being published for use in the schools, along with other publications and media use of Creole, means that even if it is not official or codified, a norm will emerge and spread.

However, at least for some time to come, theory and practice in Haiti are likely to diverge. By law, education is available to all, but the reality is still too few teachers and too few school buildings. Students lack the money to buy materials, and many are often kept at home to work. On the other hand, most people throughout Haiti have some access to radio.

It is possible then, that until standardization is complete, two norms will emerge. The first would be a spoken norm, influenced mainly by radio. As new terms are introduced for situations not previously widely discussed in Creole, dialect levelling will take place to a certain extent: all dialects will share the new vocabulary, and pronunciation differences may be reduced as well. The second would initially be a written norm, emerging from formal education using the standard texts, and from further reading of texts written by the intellectual élite. This would probably be a more widespread levelling, involving not only vocabulary but, more important (from the perspective of linguistic structure), the syntax of Haitian Creole.

The student of Haitian Creole, then, should not be surprised to find Haitians with a knowledge of French interspersing their Creole speech with French words or expressions -- or, conversely, to hear the occasional Creole phrase or sentence in the middle of a conversation or speech in French.

Pidgin and Creole Languages

As we saw above, there is a class of languages known as 'creoles'. Linguists also recognize a related class of languages known as 'pidgins', and often the two classes are referred to and studied together as 'pidgin and creole languages'.

My purpose here is not to give a full survey of the history and present state of pidgin and creole studies. However, I believe that it is important for anyone dealing with a creole language to have a basic understanding of some of the issues involved, including the linguistic and social status of these languages. (The bibliography includes works concerning theoretical and social issues, for the benefit of those who wish to pursue the matter further.)

I shall begin with a couple of brief definitions. This, unfortunately, is not as easy as it may seem. While linguists agree that there are such things as pidgin and creole languages, there is little consensus as to just what they are. Different definitions take into account structural questions, sociological questions, and historical questions, sometimes combining all three.

With this caveat, I propose the following general definitions:

Pidgin: a 'contact' language used for restricted purposes, such as trade, between people who share no other common language, and also presumably between slaves with different native languages. Pidgins have no native speakers: they are reduced languages, lacking such features as plural marking for nouns, tense marking for verbs, and mechanisms for clause subordination.

Creole: usually considered to be a 'nativized' pidgin, or a pidgin that has 'acquired' native speakers. In the case of Haitian, this definition presumes that the slaves brought to Haiti used a pidgin for general communication (both with other slaves of different native languages and with the French masters). Their children picked up this pidgin, but in the process 'expanded' it to meet their communicative needs - wider than those of their parents using the pidgin for restricted purposes. The children, 'nativizing' the pidgin, found means of expressing the plural, tenses, sentential complements, relative clauses, etc. Most linguists agree that a creole is the result of some catastrophic break with the earlier generation's native speech community.

There are, however, certain languages that present problems for these broad definitions, for example, those that are less reduced than 'true' pidgins, but have no native speakers.

For the past thirty years or so, the study of pidgins and creoles has been gaining momentum in the fields of theoretical linguistics, historical linguistics, and sociolinguistics.

With the exception of such pioneering figures as Hugo Schuchardt (1842-1927), most linguists of the 19th and early 20th centuries regarded pidgin and creole languages as unworthy of serious attention, merely degenerate versions of their European lexical source languages (French, English, Spanish, Portuguese, Dutch). Some took this view as further proof of the "intellectual inferiority" of pidgin and creole speakers (reflecting ideas then current on white superiority). An example is this late 19th century comment on Samoan Pidgin English:

> *It is a corrupted form of English mixed with many morsels from other languages, and it is adapted to the mentality of the natives; therefore, words tend to be simply concatenated, and conjugation and declension are avoided.*
>
> (Mühlhäusler 83:32-33, quoting Baessler 1895:23-24)

Recently, linguists have recognized creoles as complete, autonomous languages, and have turned to examining them for crucial evidence in support of various theories of language genesis and evolution, variation, acquisition, and so on.

Creole Genesis Theories

It was formerly commonplace to consider Haitian Creole a Romance language, more specifically a dialect of French. Few now subscribe to this view. One objection is that it implies a historical continuity, when in fact, as mentioned above, it is now assumed that creoles are the result of some catastrophic break with the pidgin speakers' native language community.
The positions which have received most attention and sparked the most debate are the following:

Monogenesis: Creoles arose from a common Portuguese-based pidgin, spoken by sailors, which was later 'relexified' (i.e. words from French, English, etc., were substituted for the original Portuguese vocabulary). This would seem to explain the remarkable structural similarity between at least the European-based creoles. Some of the objections to the monogenesis theory are:

- if creoles arose from some single lingua franca, how is it that so many different languages with almost identical syntax emerged from this 'parent' tongue. ('Daughter' languages do not usually display such close similarities, because the substratum languages -- the original native languages of persons who acquire the 'parent' or upon whom it is imposed -- affect syntax and morphology, as well as lexicon. Consider the history of the Romance 'daughters' of the 'parent' Latin.)

- Juba Arabic, a creole language spoken in southern Sudan, with no Romance language influence, nevertheless has a verb system almost identical to that of other creoles.

Substratum: Creoles are a mixture of European lexicon with a fusion of syntax from the various African languages spoken by the slaves. However, for many creoles, the possibility of their having such a 'fusion' as their substratum is implausible for both historical and linguistic reasons.

Universal Grammar (exemplified by Chomskyan theory) and the Language Bioprogram Hypothesis (proposed by Bickerton): While differing in details, both theories hold that the language faculty is innate, and that all languages are structurally and semantically the same at an abstract level. Linguists subscribing to one or other theory believe that creole languages, being the 'youngest' languages (most did not exist before European trade and colonial expansion), are the closest reflection of this innate faculty available for study.

These theories of precisely how creoles have come to exist continue to be hotly debated. Arguments and counterarguments can be found for each. It is possible that the truth is somewhere in the middle -- language universals account for some features, while substratum influence accounts for others. As samples of the developmental stages of the creoles are fragmentary and often unscientifically recorded, it is unlikely that this question will be resolved with the methods of investigation currently available to linguists.

Spelling and Pronunciation

The spelling system used throughout this book is that of the IPN (Institut de Pédagogie National), as used in the *Diksyonè Otograf Kreyòl Ayisyen*† (DOKA). Below is a list of the letters used, in the order followed in the DOKA, with an example of a Haitian word for each one, and the closest English equivalent where possible. Where English has no sound corresponding to the Haitian, an explanation of the physical production is given, with examples from other languages; this is intended merely as a reminder and guide, as it is assumed the student has already completed basic studies of Haitian, including pronunciation.

a	**a**k	**a**nd
b	**b**a	as in English
ch	**ch**ak	**sh**oe
d	**d**at	as in English
e	**e**ta	d**a**te, without the **y** glide
f	**f**ini	as in English
g	**g**out	**g**as, never as in Eng. **g**in, nor Fr. **g**ens
h	**h**ing**h**ang	as in English
i	**i**maj	b**ee**
j	**j**i	Eng. 's' in mea**s**ure
k	**k**at	as in English
l	**l**iv	as in English
m	**m**ache	as in English
n	**n**aje	as in English
o	**o**fri	b**oa**t, without the 'w' glide
p	**p**ri	as in English
r	**r**ele, o**r**al	in initial position, pronounced with tongue further back and with stronger aspiration than in English; similar to a forceful 'h', with tongue close to back of roof of mouth; cf. Parisian pronunciation of *Paris*. In medial position, similar to English.
s	**s**ik	**s**ea, never as in boy**s**
t	pi**t**i	as in English
u	**u**it	similar to English 'w' in **w**eek, with lips more rounded and tensed
v	**v**eye	as in English
w	**w**i	as in English
y	**y**en**y**en ba**y**	in initial and medial position, as in English **y**es; in final position, as in bo**y**, never as in happ**y**
z	**z**am	as in English

† For full references of works cited in this book, see bibliography

Nasal Vowels

Haitian has three commonly occurring nasal vowels, nasal **a**, **e** and **o**; these are represented by **an**, **en** and **on**, in final position, or followed by another consonant or the semiconsonants **w** and **y**, and correspond to the French **an/am**, **in/im**, and **on/om** respectively. In addition, there is a nasal **ou**, which occurs only in a few words, the most notable of which is one variant of the singular indefinite determiner, **youn***.

Oral Vowel + 'n' sound

When an oral vowel is followed by an 'n' sound, in order to show the non-nasalization of the vowel by the following 'n' letter, the following conventions are used:

written accent:	àn, èn, òn
repetition of nasal consonant:	jwenn
vowel after nasal consonant:	enèji

Nasal Vowel + 'n' sound

The 'n' letter is doubled, the first 'n' indicating the nasalization of the preceding vowel, the second representing the 'n' that is pronounced, e.g. **kabann**, **konprann**.

NB. Unfortunately, the system also allows for V+ 'n' letter x 2 to indicate non-nasalization (see above, **jwenn**); the pronunciation (nasalization or non-nasalization) must therefore be learned for each individual word.
This inconsistency within the system allows for alternative spellings of some words, e.g. **jenn/jèn**.

Other uses of written accents

The grave accent (`) is used to show the 'open' quality of e and o; è is similar to English **e**dge; ò is similar to English f**o**rt.

N.B. There is no special letter to represent the sound of French si**gn**er. This is written **y**, e.g. si**y**en.

How to use the alphabetical listings

In the present work, the order in which the alphabet is presented on the previous page is the order of alphabetical listings. However, students should be aware that some authors use a slightly different ordering, e.g. e>è>en.

Reference Grammar

This grammar of Haitian Creole does not attempt to cover all aspects of the syntax, let alone to address in any detail the problem of variation. Its purpose is to serve as a reminder of and reference for the main points of the language. The notes following each reading selection point out where the text diverges from the analysis given here. Each point and the examples illustrating them have been carefully checked with a native speaker.

Introduction

Haitian Creole (HC) has no inflectional morphology, that is, affixes that signal such grammatical distinctions as singular and plural for nouns, or tense, mode and aspect for verbs. This means that most words never change their form, grammatical distinctions being shown by the use of markers, e.g.:

liv **la**
book [singular definite marker]
the book

liv **yo**
book [plural marker]
the books

Tidjo **ap** kriye
Tidjo [progressive marker] cry
Tidjo is crying [1]

It is the syntax, or the order in which the words of a sentence are put together, which bears the burden of signaling the grammatical relations between the words. For example, the order for a declarative sentence is: subject - verb - (indirect object) - (direct object), or S - V- (IO) - (O), e.g.:

Tidjo kriye
Tidjo cry
Tidjo cries

Jan wè Mari
John see Mary
John sees Mary

Wobè ba li senk goud[2]
Robert give 3s five gourde
Robert gives her/him five gourdes

Possession is shown by placing the 'possessor' immediately after the thing possessed, e.g.

kay	Anita
house	Anita
Anita's	*house*

1. Personal markers

1.1. Forms

In HC, the grammatical persons, singular and plural, are as follows:

Singular			**Plural**		
full form	short form		full form	short form	
mwen	**m**	*1s*	**nou**	**n**	*1/2p 'participants'*
ou	**w**	*2s*			
li (ni)[3]	**l (n)**	*3s*	**yo**	**y**	*3p 'nonparticipants'*

In the singular, there are three persons, as in English; note that in the plural, however, there are only two. The first, **nou**, corresponds to both *we* and *you(pl)*, and therefore can be said to refer to more than one person, at least one of whom is a participant in the conversation. The other, **yo**, refers to more than one person or thing, not participants in the conversation.[4]

HC uses **ou, yo**, or **moun** *(people)* for the impersonal *you, they* or *people*.

1.2. Choice of forms

The choice of full or short form is determined by stylistic considerations and by which sounds come before or after (the phonetic environment):

m, l, n (from **nou**) cannot occur after a phrase final consonant, or between two consonants.

y can only appear before a vowel, e.g.: **y** ap grandi *they are growing up.*

w can only occur before or after a vowel, e.g.: **w** a pati demen *you will leave tomorrow*, mwen wè **w** *I see you.*

Full forms are required:

i) after the copula **se**, e.g. se **mwen** *it's me.*

ii) after the negative **pa**, e.g. pa **nou** *not us/you(pl).*

iii) after a monosyllabic preposition, except possessive **pa** [5], e.g. pou **mwen** *for me* [6] but pa **m** *mine.*

iv) before **menm**, emphatic marker, *self*, e.g. **nou** menm *ourselves.*

Short forms are preferable before the verb markers **ap, a.**

1.3. Use of personal markers

These same forms are used for all cases of the pronoun, and also as the possessive adjective:

1.3.1. Subject

mwen	pral	nan	mache
1s	be-going	PREP	market

I am going to the market.

nou	pale	kreyòl
1/2p	speak	Creole
we/you(pl)	*speak*	*Creole*

y	ap	grandi
3p	[+prog]	grow-up

they are growing (up)

mwen	konnen	**li**	Ø [7]	malad
1s	know	3s	COP	ill

I know s/he is ill

1.3.2. Direct object

yo	rele	**m**	Mari
3p	call	1s	Mary

they call me Mary (= My name is Mary)

koute	**l**
listen-to	3s

listen to her/him/it

1.3.3. Indirect object

ban **m** liv yo
give 1s book DETPL
give me the books

1.3.4. Object of preposition

ak **nou**
with 1/2p
with us/you(pl)

pou **mwen**
for 1s
for me

1.3.5. Possessive adjective

liv **mwen**
book 1s
my book

manman n(i)
mother 3s
his/her mother

1.3.5.1. The possessive marker **pa**

Note that the possessive marker **pa** exists, equivalent in English to the stressed possessive adjective or possessive adjective followed by *own*, or the possessive pronoun, e.g.:

peyi pa nou
country POSS 1/2p
our/your(pl) own country

liv la Ø pa li
book DET COP POSS 3s
the book is hers/his

2. Determiners

2.1. The indefinite determiner

The indefinite marker in HC is **yon**[8] *a*; there is no plural form:

yon liv	liv
a book	*(some) books*

When English *some* indicates *some as opposed to others*, the prenominal form **dè/de** is used, e.g.:

gen	**de**	fwa	m	pa[9]	konprann	ni
there-are	some	time	1s	NEG	understand	3s

there are times I do not understand her/him (but there are times I do)

2.2. The definite determiner

2.2.1. Singular

This has several forms, conditioned by the preceding sound, and follows the noun phrase (NP) it determines:

after a non-nasal consonant:	**la**	e.g.: tab **la** *the table*
after an oral vowel:	**a**	e.g.: peyi **a** *the country*
after a nasal consonant:	**lan/nan**[10]	e.g.: kabann **lan/nan** *the bed.* moun **lan/nan** *the person*
after a nasal vowel, or after a nasal consonant+**i**:	**an**	e.g.: gason **an** *the man* zanmi **an** *the friend*

These forms correspond roughly to the English *the* before singular nouns.[11]

2.2.2. Plural

In all cases:	**yo**	e.g. tab **yo** *the tables* or tab la **yo** *the tables*

Because **yo** can attach to a noun alone or can follow the various forms of the singular definite determiner, it has been analyzed as denoting simply 'plural'; in the second example above, **la** would be analyzed as denoting 'definite', **yo** as denoting 'plural'.

2.3. Use of definite and indefinite determiners

2.3.1. Zero realization of determiner

Sometimes, where in English one would find *a* or *the*, HC has nothing but the bare noun.

2.3.2. Use of definite determiner with clauses

The definite determiner can be used in HC to determine a whole clause. This use cannot easily be translated into English, and, if expressed at all, must be done so by paraphrase or explanation, e.g.:

(m	vle	ou	fini)	[sa	w	ap	fè	la]	**a**
(1s	want	2s	finish)	pro	2s	[+prog]	do	there	DET

(I want you to finish) what you are doing (right now)

N.B. The definite determiner can also be placed at the end of a relative clause. See 7.

2.4. The demonstrative determiner

HC does not distinguish, as English does, between a thing near to the speaker *(this, these)* as opposed to a thing near to the hearer, or near to neither *(that, those)*. In HC the word **sa** is placed after the noun and before the definite determiner, to signify *this/that* or *these/those:*

liv **sa** a
book DEM DET
this/that book

liv **sa** yo
book DEM DETPL
these/those books

As **sa** ends with an oral vowel, the form of the singular definite determiner is always **a**.

An alternative form of the demonstrative, **sila**, is also found. There is no difference in meaning, e.g. liv **sila** a/yo.

3. Adjectives

3.1. Postnominal adjectives

The majority of adjectives in HC come after the noun they modify, and most have one form only:

lang **kreyòl** la
language Creole DET
the Creole language

lang **kreyòl** yo
language Creole DETPL
the Creole languages

fi **entèlijan**
woman intelligent
intelligent woman

gason **entèlijan**
man intelligent
intelligent man

3.2. Prenominal adjectives

Some adjectives come before the noun they modify:

ansyen	*former*	bon	*good*
ti	*little*	gwo	*big*
gran	*big, tall*	sèl	*only*
kokennchenn	*huge*	move	*bad*
vye	*old*	bèl	*beautiful, nice*

e.g.:

youn **gran** kay
a big house
a big house

youn **move** jou
a bad day
a bad day

3.3. Masculine and feminine forms

Some adjectives of nationality referring to persons have both a masculine and feminine form:

masculine	**feminine**	
ayisyen	ayisyèn	*Haitian*
ameriken	amerikèn	*(North) American*
angle	anglèz	*English*
franse	fransèz	*French*
kanadyen	kanadyèn	*Canadian*

4. Verbs

As there is no inflectional morphology in HC, the verb has only one form[12], which is used for the infinitive (*to do*), for the present participle (*I am doing*), the past participle (*I have done*) and the past participle used as an adjective (*I am annoyed*); information regarding tense, mode, and aspect is provided either by means of verbal markers, or by the use of catenative verbs, and information regarding person is provided by the subject noun or pronoun. The tense, mode and aspect (TMA) markers always occur in fixed order, before the verb they modify[13], and may be combined to give complex meanings.

4.1. Forms of TMA markers

Tense	Mode	Aspect
[± anterior]	[± irrealis]	[± progressive]
te	**a/va/ava/**	**ap/ape**

e.g.:

m	**te**	ekri
1s	[+ant]	write

I wrote

m	**a**	ekri
1s	[+irr]	write

I will write

m	**ap**	ekri
1s	[+prog]	write

I am writing

4.2. Combinations of TMA markers[14]

[+ant] + [+irr] = conditional

te + **a** = **ta**

e.g.:

li	**ta**	renmen	sòti
3s	[+ant +irr]	like	go-out

s/he would like to go out

[+ant] + [prog] = imperfective

te + **ap** = **tap**

e.g.:

nou	**tap**	dòmi	lè	li	rive
1/2p	[+ant +prog]	sleep	when	3s	arrived

we/you(pl) were sleeping when s/he arrived

4.3. Use of TMA markers

English or French speakers should be wary of making too rigid translations for these markers, as they correspond to somewhat different divisions of TMA from their native languages. Tense in HC, rather than being the more familiar division between 'past' and 'present', reflects [±anterior]: that is, relevant to the time established as the reference point in discourse, which is, of course, not necessarily the 'present'. The modal marker [±irrealis] is used with verbs referring to unrealized conditions. It presents somewhat less of a translation problem, as it corresponds fairly closely to the *will/shall* of the English 'future', or to the 'present used as future' e.g. *he leaves tomorrow*. The aspect marker distinguishes [±progressive], i.e. whether the action is in the process of being done, relevant to the time reference of the discourse. (Note that often the translation of [+progressive] is best rendered in English by *will*. [15])

Verbs are divided into two basic types, stative and nonstative; stative verbs include those of cognition and desire, and nonstative verbs include verbs of action, perception and process. TMA markers may be applied to both kinds of verbs; in general, stative verbs with no marker are interpreted as present, and nonstative verbs with no marker are interpreted as recent past, or the 'general present' (i.e. nonpunctual), as in English *he writes books, I work in Port-au-Prince,* depending on context. (In this sense, English 'present' and HC 'unmarked' might be said to coincide, except that English cannot refer backwards in time, while HC can).

Zero marked verbs:

nou	vle	ale	nan	sinema
1/2p	want	go	PREP	cinema

we want to go to the cinema

m	ekri	anpil	atik
1s	write	many	article

I wrote/write many articles

4.4. Other means of expressing aspect and mode

4.4.1. Aspect

Catenative verbs are used to express aspects other than progressive:

koumanse/kòmanse	*begin (doing/to do)*
fèk	*have just (done)*
sot/sòt	*have just (done)*
fin	*have (done)* (perfective)
pral	*be going (to do)*
konn	*be in the habit of (doing), usually (do)*

e.g.:

m	**fèk**	rive
1s	have-just	arrive

I have just arrived

yo	**pral**	sòti
3p	be-going	go-out

they are going to go out

4.4.2. Mode

Catenative verbs are used to express mode other than irrealis:

dwe/do[16]	*have (to do)*
gen pou	*have (to do)*
sètoblije/oblije/blije	*have (to do)*
se	*have (to do)*
fèt pou	*should/ought (to do)*
kapab/kap/kab/ka	*be able (to do)*
vle	*want (to do)*
bezwen	*want (to do)*
mèt	*may (do)*
pito	*would rather (do), prefer (to do)*
annik	*just (do)*
ann/annou	*let's (do)*
pinga	*DON'T (do)* (emphatic negative imperative)
fòk/fò (+ subject + verb)	*it is necessary (for subject to do)*
se pou (+subject + verb)	*(subject) should/ought (to do)*
kite (+subject + verb)	*let (subject) do*
fè (+subject + verb)	*make (subject) do, cause (subject) to do*
pito (+ subject +verb)	*(subject) had better (do)*

e.g.:

ou fèt pou vini
2s should come

you should come

or

you have to come

ann ale
let's go

let's go

TMA markers may be used with catenative verbs where semantically appropriate, e.g.:

yo **te** **konn** fè l
3p [+ant] be-in-habit-of do it

they used to do it

4.5. Verb phrase

The verb phrase (VP) contains: minimally, the main verb, as in English *John [VP runs]*; the main verb with any auxiliaries (and in English, any endings), as in *John [VP is running]*; or the main verb, any auxiliaries and endings, and any arguments[17] of the verb, as in *John [VP had given the letter to Mary] three days before.*

4.5.1. Intransitive verbs

The VP contains the verb with any markers, and any arguments requiring a preposition:

Wobè	**(ap/te** ...)	**kouri**
Robert	(+prog/+ant)	run

Robert (is run(ning)/ran) runs

yo	**sòti**	**nan**	**mòn**
3p	come-out	PREP	hill

they came out of the hills

4.5.2. Transitive verbs

A transitive VP contains the verb, any verb markers, and the direct object of the verb, that is, the argument which follows the verb directly, with no intervening preposition; transitive verbs have only one argument:

Pyè	**ap**	**manje**	**pwason**
Pierre	[+prog]	eat	fish

Pierre is eating fish

4.5.3. Ditransitive verbs

A ditransitive verb is one that has two arguments, so the VP contains the verb plus any verb markers, and the two arguments. In HC, there are two kinds of ditransitives:

4.5.3.1. Word order ditransitives

This is a small class of verbs whose two arguments are both direct in the sense that neither are preceded by a preposition; it is the fixed order of the two NP objects which determines their function, the first being the 'beneficiary' (usually equivalent to English *to* or *for*), the second being the direct object proper:

Tidjo	bay	**Mari**	**youn**	**flè**
Tidjo	give	Mary	a	flower

Tidjo gave Mary a flower/Tidjo gave a flower to Mary

Jan	pase	**mwen**	**liv**	**li**
John	pass	me	book	3s

John passed me his book/John passed his book to me

di	**mwen**	**ni**
tell	1s	3s

tell it to me

4.5.3.2. Preposition-marked ditransitives

The second kind of ditransitive is that which takes a direct object and an object preceded by a preposition, e.g.:

li	wete	**kòb**	**nan**	**pòch**	**li**
3s	take-out	money	PREP	pocket	3s

s/he took some money out of her/his pocket

yo	pran	**manje**	**a**	**nan**	**men**	**timoun**	**yo**
3p	take	food	DET	PREP	hand	child	DETPL

they take the food from the children

N.B. Many verbs which in English take an indirect object (preceded by *to*) in addition to a direct object require a special construction in HC, known as serial verbs. See 4.9.2.

4.6. Short forms of verbs

Some HC verbs have both a full and a short form; those used in the short form sometimes have a different meaning, being used as aspectual or modal catenative verbs (see 4.4.), although both forms can be found with both meanings. Examples are:

konnen	*know*
soti/sòti	*go/come out*
fini	*finish*
vini	*come*
konn	*be in the habit of*
sot/sòt	*have just*
fin	*have* (perfective)
vin	*become, get + adj.*

Other verbs with short forms, with no change in meaning:

genyen/gen	*have; there is/are*
(a)prale/pral	*be going*
kapab/kap/kab/ka	*be able*
ale/al	*go*
rete/ret	*stay, remain*

The short forms are not used in phrase final position.

4.7. 'Irregular' verbs

4.7.1. The verb **bay**

The verb *to give* in HC has three possible forms: **bay**, **ba**, and **ban**; **bay** is the basic form, **ba** is used before the pronouns **ou (w)**, **li**, and **yo**; **ban** is used before those beginning with a nasal consonant, i.e., **m(wen)** and **n(ou)**.

4.7.2. The verb **prale**

The verb **prale** or **aprale** *be going* (short form **pral**) is 'irregular' in that it cannot take the anterior marker **te**; to express the meaning *was going* the particle **ta** is used, e.g.:

li	**ta**	**pral**	pati	yè
3s	[+ ant + irr]	be-going	leave	yesterday

s/he was going to leave yesterday

4.8. The copula

The copula in HC, corresponding to English *to be* when used to link two concepts, has three possible realizations: Ø (zero), **se**, and **ye**.

4.8.1. Copula = Ø

HC does not express the copula in declarative sentences that have as their complement adjectival or adverbial phrases, e.g.:

liv	la	Ø	jòn
book	DET	COP	yellow

the book is yellow

timoun	yo	Ø	lakay
child	DETPL	COP	home

the children are at home

pi fò	agwonòm	pa	Ø	avèk	zotobre	sa	yo
majority	agronomist	NEG	COP	with	bigshot	DEM	DETPL

the majority of agronomists are not with those bigshots (i.e. on their side)

li	te	Ø	an	Ayiti
3s	[+ant]	COP	in	Haiti

s/he was in Haiti

4.8.2. Copula = **se**

4.8.2.1. NP complement

se is used when the complement is a noun phrase (NP), e.g.:

Chal	**se**	ekriven
Charles	COP	writer

Charles is a writer

N.B. When negation or TMA markers occur, **se** is optional, but note that if **se** is used, it precedes NEG and TMA markers, e.g.:

Chal	se/Ø	**te**	ekriven
Charles	COP	[+ant]	writer

Charles was a writer

Chal	se/Ø	**pa**	ekriven
Charles	COP	NEG	writer

Charles is not a writer

4.8.2.2. NP complement of relative clause

se is optional in a relative clause with NP complement, e.g.:

Chal,	ki	se/Ø	ekriven,	pa	vini
Charles	RELPRO	COP	writer	NEG	come

Charles, who is a writer, did not come

4.8.2.3. Copula with no semantic subject

se is used when there is no semantic subject, i.e. when the 'dummy' subject *it* is used in English, e.g.:

se	mwen
COP	me

it is me

se	posib
COP	possible

it is possible

4.8.2.4. Reduplication with **se**

se is also used in a construction known as reduplication, which serves to emphasize the element reduplicated, e.g.:

se	kouri	m	ap	kouri
COP	run	1s	[+prog]	run

I am really running

or

I am really in a hurry

se	kontan	li	Ø	kontan
COP	happy	3s	COP	happy

s/he is really happy

4.8.3. Copula = **ye**

The form **ye** is used in cases where a grammatical operation involving movement of an element of the clause results in a zero-copula being 'stranded' in clause-final position, or, more precisely, before the 'gap' left by the moved element, e.g.:

4.8.3.1. Direct questions

m	Ø	la
1s	COP	there

I am well

but:

ki jan	ou	**ye** ______?
how	2s	COP ______?

how are you?

li	te	Ø	lekòl
3s	[+ant]	COP	school

s/he was at school

but:

ki kote	li	te	**ye** ______?
where	3s	[+ant]	COP ______?

where was s/he?

Exceptions: in questions with **kote, konbyen** (asking price), and **pou ki (moun)** (=*whose*), **ye** may be omitted with unmarked verbs only:

pou ki moun	liv	la	Ø?
whose	book	DET	COP

whose book is it?

but:

pou ki moun	liv	la	te	**ye**?
whose	book	DET	[+ant]	COP

whose book was it?

4.8.3.2. Indirect questions

Indirect questions have the same structure as direct questions, therefore **ye** is required for the 'stranded' copula, e.g.:

m	pa	konnen	ki moun	li	**ye**
1s	NEG	know	who	3s	COP

I don't know who s/he is

For details on content question formation in HC, see 8.2.

4.8.3.3. Clefting

To emphasize an NP, HC has recourse to an operation known as clefting: two clauses are formed by moving the NP to be emphasized to second position after **se**. If this leaves the original copula in final position it is realized as **ye**, e.g.:

se	yon	ekriven	Chal	**ye**
COP	a	writer	Charles	COP

Charles is a writer

For more examples of clefting, see 13.2.

4.9. Prepositions, arguments and serial verbs

4.9.1. Prepositions

HC does not make extensive use of prepositions, and often uses word order or a special kind of verbal construction known as serialization (see 4.9.2.) where English and French use a preposition. The most common HC prepositions are:

nan	*in, out of*	sou	*on*
pou	*for*	de	*of* (NOT possessive *of*), *about*
anba	*under*		
anwo	*above*	avè/avèk/ak	*with*
anvan	*before*	deyè	*behind*
apre	*after*	devan	*in front of*
jouk/jous/jouska	*until*	san	*without*

It is notoriously hard to give an exact meaning for prepositions in another language, as the correspondence is rarely one-to-one. The student should note uses not corresponding to English, e.g. **nan** means *in* or *out of* or *among* etc. depending on the context.

HC can use verbs for the equivalent of 'from ... till ... ':

sòti	jedi	**rive**	dimanch
come-out	Thursday	arrive	Sunday

from Thursday till Sunday

4.9.2. Serial verbs

As we saw above, (4.5.), all verbs except true intransitives take one or more arguments in English. HC, however, has very few verbs that can take more than one argument, and in order to convey the same meaning and express the same number of arguments per clause as, for example, English, HC resorts to a construction known as serialization.

4.9.2.1. Serial verbs expressing beneficiary arguments

The clearest examples of serial verbs are those that correspond to verbs taking both a direct and an indirect object (= beneficiary) in English (other than **pase, bay** and **di**, see 4.5.3.1.), e.g.:

Pòl	**voye**	yon	kado	**bay**	Emi
Paul	send	a	present	give	Amy

Paul sent a present to Amy

zanmi	yo	**pote**	rad	**bay**	timoun	yo
friends	DETPL	bring	clothes	give	children	DETPL

the friends brought clothes for the children

4.9.2.2. Serial verbs expressing transitive verb plus adverbial meaning

Another important use of serial verbs is to express the equivalent of English transitive 'verb + adverb' constructions. The HC second verb has semantic features in common with the English adverb, e.g.:

li	**pote**	kado	a	**tounen**
3s	bring	present	DET	return

she brought the present back

yo	**mennen**	bèt	yo	**vini**
they	lead	animal	DETPL	come

they brought the animals (in)

4.9.2.3. Serial verbs expressing intransitive verb plus adverbial meaning

Finally, serial verbs are used to express intransitive actions, which also often correspond to English 'verb + adverb' or 'verb + preposition', e.g.:

li	**tounen**	**vini**
3s	return	come

he came back

yo	**kouri**	**desann**	**al**	anba	pye	figye	a
3s	run	descend	go	under	tree	fig	DET

they ran down to under the fig-tree

4.10. Subjectless verbs

HC has a small number of verbs that have no overt subject pronoun; they correspond to English verbs with a 'dummy' subject (*it* or *there*). These are the most common:

se	*it is*	genyen/gen	*there is/are*
genlè	*it seems*	sanble	*it seems*
fòk/fò	*it is necessary*	rete	*there remain/s*
pito	*it is preferable*		

e.g.:

gen	anpil	timoun	nan	machin	lan
there-are	many	child	PREP	car	DET

there are many children in the car

pito	ou	tounen	demen
it-is-preferable	2s	return	tomorrow

you had better come back tomorrow

fò	m	ale
it-is-necessary	1s	go

I must go

4.11. Reflexive verbs

Reflexive verbs are not common in HC; when they do occur, there are three possibilities for the form of the reflexive pronoun; the usual personal marker, **tèt + personal marker**, or **kò + personal marker**, e.g.:

li	sakrifye	**l**[18]
3s	sacrifice	3s

s/he sacrificed herself/himself or
s/he made sacrifices (i.e. in order to achieve something)

m	poze	**tèt**	**mwen**	keksyon
1s	pose	head	1s	question

I ask myself questions or
I wonder

yo	kraze	**kò**	**yo**
3p	smash	body	3p

they tire themselves out

4.12. The passive

As HC has no verbal morphology, there is no special form to indicate a passive meaning, which must be understood from the context, e.g.:

trafik	la	**bloke**	nèt
traffic	DET	block	completely

the traffic is completely blocked

While there is still discussion[19] as to which kinds of verbs may be passive in HC, it seems that they should be those whose meaning implies some kind of effect on the patient argument (i.e. the direct object of the verb in its active use, or the subject of the verb in its passive use). However, counterexamples to this 'rule' are not uncommon; whether this is due to new usage based on French (which allows different kinds of verbs to be passivized) is not yet clear.

Strictly speaking, the agent of a passive verb is not expressed, although, due to French influence, one occasionally finds an agentive phrase (with **pa**, from French **par**).

4.12.1. Exception: **fè**

An exception to the rule of verbs having no passive morphology is the verb **fè** *do, make; give birth;* when this is used with a passive meaning, the form **fèt** is always used, e.g.:

y	ap	**fè**	grèv
3p	[+prog]	do	strike

they are striking

masak	la	te	**fèt**
massacre	DET	[+ant]	done

the massacre was done

fi	a	**fè**	yon tigason	
woman	DET	give-birth	a	boy

the woman has given birth to a boy

frè	m	te	**fèt**	nan	lane 58
brother	1s	[+ant]	born	PREP	year 58

my brother was born in 58

5. Negation

5.1. Simple verb negation

To negate a verb in HC, the negative marker **pa** is placed immediately before the verb, or before the TMA marker preceding the verb:

m	**pa**	wè	l
1s	NEG	see	3s

I don't see it

li	**pa**t	byen
3s	NEG + [+ant]	well

s/he wasn't well

Note: When **pa** is followed by **ap** or **te**, they are contracted into **pap** and **pat** respectively.

5.2. Negation of coordinate NP

To negate a coordinate NP, **pa ... ni ... ni ...**is used, e.g.:

m	**pa**	renmen	**ni**	lèt	**ni**	kafe
1s	NEG	like	CONJ	milk	CONJ	coffee

I do not like either milk or coffee

or

I like neither milk nor coffee

5.3. Other negations

Never is expressed by **pa janm**:

nou	**pap**	**janm**	bliye	l
1/2p	NEG + [+prog]	never	forget	3s

we/you(pl) will never forget it

No longer is expressed by **pa ... ankò**

li	**pa**	vini	**ankò**
3s	NEG	come	any-more

he no longer comes

Nothing is expressed by **pa ... anyen**:

nou	**pa**	vle	**anyen**
1/2p	NEG	want	nothing

we/you(pl) want nothing

or

we/you(pl) do not want anything

No + noun, *not any* ... (emphatic) is expressed by **pa ... okenn/ankenn**:

yo	**pat**	ba	li	**okenn**	rezon	pou	sa
3p	NEG + [+ant]	give	3s	no	reason	for	that

they gave her/him no reason for that

Nobody is expressed by **pa ... pèsonn**

pa gen **pèsonn** ki vle fè l
NEG there-is no-one RELPRO want do 3s
there is nobody who wants to do it

Not yet is expressed by **poko/ponko/panko** (see DOKA for other variants):

li **poko** vini
3s not-yet come
s/he hasn't come yet

Exception: negative words (and TMA markers) follow the copula **se**, e.g.:

se **pat** li
COP NEG + [+ant] 3s
it wasn't her/him

5.4. Negative words in subject position

When a negative word is the subject of a clause, the negative marker **pa** must occur before the verb, e.g.:

anyen **pap** fèt
nothing NEG + [+prog] done
nothing is being done

pèsonn **pa** vini
nobody NEG come
nobody came

6. Noun phrase

6.1. Simple NPs

The simplest form of the NP consists of the head (main) noun, which can be a proper noun, a pronoun, or a common noun without a determiner:

Wobè kouri
Robert run
Robert runs

m pral lekòl
1s be-going school
I'm going to school

Fiyèt	Lalo	konn	manje	**timoun**
Fiyèt	Lalo	be-in-habit-of	eat	child

Fiyèt Lalo[20] *is in the habit of eating children*

6.2. Complex NPs

As we saw above, the head noun can be followed by a definite determiner (2.2.) or a personal marker (1.3.5.), or preceded by the indefinite determiner (2.1.):

tab la	liv mwen	yon pòt
table DET	book 1s	a door
the table	*my book*	*a door*

The head noun may be modified by an adjective:

yon	**bèl**	kay
a	pretty	house

a pretty house

by another noun or noun phrase (often indicating the possessor):

gouvènman	**boujwazi**	a
government	bourgeoisie	DET

the government of the bourgeoisie

avni	**lit**	**yo**	a
future	struggle	3p	DET

the future of their struggle

Tousen	Louvèti	se	te	papa	**Izaak**
Toussaint	Louverture	COP	[+ant]	father	Isaac

Toussaint Louverture was the father of Isaac

or by a clause:

liv	**mwen**	**te**	**achte**	**Ozetazini**	an
book	1s	[+ant]	buy	in-the-United-States	DET

the book I bought in the United States

tout	ofisye	e	souzofisye	**ki**	**te**	**reponn**	**prezan**	yo[21]
all	officer	and	NCO	RELPRO	[+ant]	answer	present	DETPL

all the officers and NCOs who were present

Note that in the above examples the definite determiner is placed at the end of the complete NP, not immediately after the head noun.

7. Restrictive relative clauses

Restrictive relative clauses are a kind of modifier of a noun or noun phrase, serving to define further the NP they modify, e.g.:

Etidyan	**yo**	pa	vini.	**Etidyan**	**yo**	rete	nan
student	DETPL	NEG	come.	student	DETPL	live	PREP

sant	vil	la.
center	town	DET

The students did not come. The students live in the center of town.

Etidyan	**ki**	rete	nan	sant	vil	la	**yo**
student	RELPRO	live	PREP	center	town	DET	DETPL
pa	vini						
NEG	come						

The students who live in the center of town did not come.

This means that there are other students who do not live in the center of town -- and maybe they came.

A restrictive relative clause can be formed when two clauses give information about an element common to both; in HC the second mention of the element is either

- changed into the relative pronoun and placed clause-initially
- deleted
- changed into a personal marker

The whole relative clause is then embedded in the first clause. (Note the use of the definite determiner at the end of the whole NP, i.e. the head noun + relative clause.)

Which strategy is used depends on the position to be relativized:

7.1. Position relativized

7.1.1. Subject

If the position to be relativized is the subject, HC uses the relative pronoun **ki**, e.g.:

Liv	**la**	Ø	wouj.	**Liv**	**la**	Ø	sou	tab	la.
book	DET	COP	red.	book	DET	COP	on	table	DET

The book is red. The book is on the table.

> Liv **ki** Ø sou tab la Ø wouj.
> book RELPRO COP on table DET COP red.
The book which is on the table is red.

7.1.2. Direct object

If the position to be relativized is the direct object, HC deletes the second occurrence of the NP, e.g.:

Liv la Ø wouj. Mwen achte **liv la**.
book DET COP red. 1s buy book DET.
The book is red. I bought the book.

> **Liv Ø** mwen achte a Ø wouj.
> book RELPRO[22] 1s buy DET COP red.
>*The book (which/that) I bought is red.*

7.1.3. Indirect object

To relativize the indirect object (= beneficiary argument, see 4.5.3.1.), HC deletes the second occurrence, as for the direct object position, e.g.:

Timoun lan se elèv. Li bay **timoun lan** yon liv.
child DET COP student. 3s give child DET a book.
The child is a student. S/he gave the child a book.

> **Timoun Ø** li bay yon liv **la** se elèv.
> child RELPRO 3s give a book DET COP student.
> *The child s/he gave a book to is a student.*

7.1.4. Object of preposition

To form a relative clause from the object of a preposition, the second clause is embedded as is (with a personal marker replacing the second mention of the NP) after the NP to which it relates, e.g.:

Timoun lan Ø lekòl. Mwen pote liv pou **timoun lan**.
child DET COP at-school. 1s bring book for child DET.
The child is at school. I brought a book for the child.

> **Timoun** mwen pote liv pou **li a** Ø lekòl.
> child 1s bring book for 3s DET COP at-school.
> *The child I brought a book for is at school.*

7.1.5. Locative

To relativize a locative phrase, the relative pronoun **kote** is used; the second occurrence of the locative is deleted, e.g.:

Li manje **nan** **otel** **la**. Ou rete **nan** **otel** **la**.
3s eat PREP hotel DET 2s live PREP hotel DET
S/he eats in the hotel. You live in the hotel.

> Li manje **nan** **otel** **kote** ou rete **a**
> 3s eat PREP hotel RELPRO 2s live DET
> *S/he eats in the hotel where you live.*

8. Questions

8.1. Yes/No questions

Yes/No questions are those which require confirmation or negation only, not further information. In HC, this type of question is signaled either by rising intonation, or by the interrogative marker **èske** in phrase initial position, e.g.

w ap vini?
2s [+prog] come
are you coming?

èske li pati?
Q 3s leave
did s/he leave?
or
has s/he left?

8. 2. Content questions

These are questions that request further information, and are introduced in HC by phrases, the choice of which is dictated by the function of the element being questioned. The basic structure of most of these phrases is the same:

ki NP (ki)
[interr] NP (subj relpro)

That is, each phrase is introduced by the interrogative marker **ki** followed by the NP about which information is being requested (i.e. person, thing, place, etc.), and, if that NP is the subject of the following verb, the subject relative pronoun **ki** must be used. (Interrogative **ki** and subject relative pronoun **ki**, while having the same form, should not be regarded as being the same word, as they function in quite different ways[23].)

8.2.1. Direct questions

e.g.:

ki	**liv**	**ki**	enterese	w?
[interr]	book	[SUBJ.RELPRO]	interest	2s

which book interests you?

ki	**liv**	**Ø**	y	ap	achte?
[interr]	book	RELPRO	3p	[+prog]	buy

which book are they buying?

This same structure is used for the HC equivalent of English interrogative pronouns, e.g.:

ki moun (ki)[24]	*who*	*(+ subj)?*
ki bagay (ki)	*what*	*(+subj)?*
(ki)[25] sa (ki)	*what*	*(+subj)?*
(ki) kote (ki)	*where*	*(+subj)?*
ki bò (ki)	*where*	*(+subj)?*
ki lè (ki)	*when*	*(+subj)?*
ki jan (ki)	*how*	*(+subj)?*

Exceptions:

konbyen	*how much/many?*
kouman/kòman	*how?*

e.g.:

ki	**moun**	**ki**	dòmi	isit?
[interr]	person	[SUBJ. RELPRO]	sleep	here

who sleeps here?

(ki)	**sa**	**Ø**	li	vle?
[interr]	pro	RELPRO	3s	want

what does s/he want?

ki	**jan**	**Ø**	yo	fè	l?
[interr]	manner	RELPRO	3p	do	3s

how do they do it?

or:

kouman	yo	fè	l?
how	3p	do	3s

how do they do it?

The same form is used for the NP object of preposition, with the preposition occurring before the interrogative phrase, e.g.:

ak ki moun	*with whom/who ... with?*
ak ki sa	*with what/what ... with?*

e.g.:

ak	**ki**	**moun**	yo	pati?
PREP	[interr]	person	3p	leave

who did they leave with?

Note the parallel formation of:

poukisa	*why?*
(= pou ki sa)	

and: pou ki moun *whose?*

e.g.:

pou	**ki**	**moun**	liv	la	(ye)[26]?
PREP	[interr]	person	book	DET	COP

whose book is it?

Note that in HC these question phrases do not entail any change of word order, other than fronting of the question word if it is not the subject.

8.2.2. Indirect questions

Indirect questions are formed in exactly the same way as direct questions, and require only a change in verb marking or personal marker, if applicable, e.g.:

poukisa	**w**	**ap**	kriye?
why	2s	[+ prog]	cry

why are you crying?

but:

yo	**te**	mande	poukisa	**li**	**tap**	kriye?
3p	[+ant]	ask	why	3s	[+ ant + prog]	cry

they asked why s/he was crying.

9. Non-restrictive relative clauses

There are several types of non-restrictive relative clauses, some of which are:

9.1. Peripheral non-restrictive relative clauses

A peripheral non-restrictive relative clause merely gives additional, non-essential information about the noun it relates to, without limiting it in any way, e.g.:

Etidyan	**yo,**	ki	rete	nan	sant	vil	la,	pa	vini
student	DETPL	RELPRO	live	PREP	center	town	DET	NEG	come

The students, who live in the center of town, did not come.

This example means that all the students (to whom reference has already been made, or who are the only students in the universe of discourse) live in the center of town (c.f. the similar example in 7.).

9.2. Constituent non-restrictive relative clauses

This type takes the place of a constituent of the main clause, such as subject or object, e.g.:

9.2.1. Subject

sa	**ki** [27]	**te**	**pase**	**a**	Ø	pa	klè
pro	SUBJ.RELPRO	[+ant]	happen	DET	COP	NEG	clear

what happened is not clear

9.2.2. Object

m	kwe	**sa**	**Ø**	**ou**	**di**	**a**
1s	believe	pro	RELPRO	2s	say	DET

I believe what you say

m	konnen	**ki**	**lè**	**y**	**ap**	**rive**
1s	know	[interr]	time	3p	[+prog]	arrive

I know what time they are arriving

Note that **ki sa (ki)** and **ki jan** drop the **ki [interr]** in this type of clause.

10. Comparison

HC expresses three degrees of comparison for adjectives:

10.1. More

kay	sa	a	**pi**	bèl	**pase**	lòt	yo
house	DEM	DET	more	pretty	pass	other	DETPL

this house is prettier than the others

10.2. Less

kay	sa	a	**mwen**	bèl	**pase**	lòt	yo
house	DEM	DET	less	pretty	pass	other	DETPL

this house is less pretty than the others

10.3. Same

kay	sa	a	bèl	**tankou**	lòt	yo
house	DEM	DET	pretty	like	other	DETPL

this house is as pretty as the others

Note: **tankou** is often shortened to **kou**
The same construction is used for comparison of adverbs.

10.4. Comparison of quantity
The word **plis** *more* or **mwens** *less* is followed immediately by **pase**, e.g.:

plis	**pase**	san	blese
more	pass	100	wound

more than 100 wounded

ou	manje	**mwens**	**pase**	mwen
2s	eat	less	pass	1s

you eat less than I (do)

11. The complementizer **pou**

11.1. Complement of adjective
Complements of adjectives are introduced by **pou**, e.g.:

li	fasil	**pou**	l	vann	liv
3s	easy	COMPL	3s	sell	book

it is easy for her/him to sell books

11.2. The **pou** relative

The HC equivalent of the so-called 'infinitival relative' of English requires **pou**, e.g.:

li	gen	youn	liv	**pou**	l	vann
3s	has	a	book	COMPL	3s	sell

s/he has a book to sell

Note that this is not the same meaning as a 'normal' relative; compare, e.g.:

m	gen	youn	liv	**pou**	l	vann
1s	have	a	book	COMPL	3s	sell

I have a book for her/him to sell

with:

m	gen	youn	liv	Ø	li	vann
1s	have	a	book	RELPRO	3s	sell

I have a book (that) s/he sold

11.3. Complement of verb

Some verbs can take **pou** to introduce the complement, e.g.:

deside	*decide*
di	*tell*
konseye	*advise*
mande	*ask*
pwomèt	*promise*
swete	*wish*
vle	*want*

e.g.:

m	mande	l	**pou**	l	vann	liv
1s	ask	3s	COMPL	3s	sell	book

I asked her/him to sell books

m	swete	**pou**	l	vann	liv
1s	hope	COMPL	3s	sell	book

I wish (that) s/he sold books

or

I would like her/him to sell books

The above verbs can also take complements without **pou**; note that the verbs **espere** *hope* and **regrete** *regret* never take **pou**.

11.4. Complement of preposition

pou is also found, optionally, after prepositions introducing clauses, e.g.:

anvan	**pou**	moun	sa	a	rive	Pòtoprens
before	COMPL	person	DEM	DET	arrive	P-au-P

zanmi	li	gentan	pati
friend	3s	already	leave

before that person arrived in Port-au-Prince her/his friend had already left

11.5. Zero complementizer

In HC, after certain verbs, the complementizer is zero, e.g.:

m	konnen	Ø	li	vann	liv
1s	know	COMPL	3s	sell	book

I know s/he sells books

m	kwè	Ø	li	vann	liv
1s	believe	COMPL	3s	sell	book

I believe s/he sells books

N.B. The use of **ke** as a complementizer where basilectal HC has none (Ø) is becoming more widespread.

12. Time

12.1. Asking the time

To ask the time of day in HC, one can say:

ki	lè	li	ye?
[interr]	hour	3s	COP

what time is it?

or:

ki	lè	li	fè?
[interr]	hour	3s	make

what time is it?

or:

ki	lè	ou	genyen?
[interr]	hour	2s	have

what time do you have?

12.2. Giving the time

12.2.1. On the hour

The answer for each hour must be learned separately, as HC has here borrowed very directly from French, involving French-based liaison between the number and **è**, *hour*:

li (fè) -

inè	*one o'clock*	uitè	*eight o'clock*
dezè	*two* "	nevè	*nine* "
twazè	*three* "	dizè	*ten* "
katrè	*four* "	onzè	*eleven* "
senkè	*five* "	midi	*noon*
sizè	*six* "	minui	*midnight*
setè	*seven* "		

12.2.2. Past the hour

'Minutes past the hour' is expressed by putting the number immediately after the hour, e.g.:

li dezè **senk**
3s two-o'clock five
it is five past two

'A quarter past' is expressed:

li senkè **eka**
3s five-o'clock and-quarter
it is quarter past five

'Half past' is expressed:

li midi **edmi**
3s noon and-half
it is half past midday

12.2.3. To the hour

'Minutes to the hour' is expressed:

li twazè **mwen dis**
3s three-o'clock less ten
it is ten to three

'A quarter to' is expressed:

li	sizè	**mwen/mwenn**	**ka**
3s	six-o'clock	less	quarter

it is quarter to six

13. Emphasis

13.1. Reduplication

13.1.1. Reduplication with **se**

See 4.8.2.4.

13.1.2. **Ala** + reduplication of adjective

Another construction using reduplication emphasizes an adjective, introduced by **ala**, e.g.:

ala	**bèl**	ou	**bèl**!
EMPH	pretty	2s	pretty

how pretty you are!

13.1.3. Reduplication of verb

Reduplication of a verb expresses the idea *as soon as...*, e.g.:

vini	ou	**vini,**	n	ap	koumanse
come	2s	come	1/2p	[+prog]	begin

as soon as you come, we will begin

or

when you come, we will begin

13.1.4. Reduplication of adverb

Simple repetition of an adverb serves as emphasis of that element, e.g.:

yo	mennen	li	**prese**	**prese**	nan	dispensè	a
3p	take	3s	quickly	quickly	PREP	clinic	DET

they took her/him as quickly as possible to the clinic

13.2. Clefting

As seen in 4.8.3.3., sentences may be clefted to emphasize an element. This operation involves making two clauses from one, with the element to be emphasized immediately following **se**, and the remainder of the sentence becoming a relative clause, e.g.:

se	Chal	ki	Ø	ekriven
COP	Charles	RELPRO	COP	writer

it is Charles who is a writer

or

Charles is a writer

se	anba	tonèl	elèv	yo	travay
COP	PREP	bower	student	DETPL	work

the students work under a bower

13.3. Left-dislocation

An operation known as left-dislocation (as the element to be emphasized is moved to the left, i.e., to the beginning of the clause) can also be used; note that the dislocated item does not leave a 'gap' in the sense used above (4.8.3.), as a coreferential pronoun is used, e .g.:

mizè	**sa**	**yo,**	fò	n	pa	kache	**yo**
misery	DEM	DET	it-is-necessary	1/2p	NEG	hide	them

these miseries we must not hide (them)

jounalis	**la,**	**li**	te	vle	fè	youn	repotaj
journalist	DET,		3s	[+ant]	want	make	a report

the journalist wanted to make a report

13.4. Emphasizing a whole clause

HC can also emphasize a whole clause, not just single elements of the clause, e. g.:

ala	nou	ta	engra!
EMPH	1/2p	[+ant +irr]	ungrateful

how ungrateful we would be!

Another construction sometimes heard is:

se	**ke**	li	pa	vle
COP	COMPL	3s	NEG	want

s/he does not want to

Reference Grammar Notes

1 Note that English requires a change in the form of the main verb, which is in fact redundant, as the progressive aspect is already signaled by the use of *is* before the main verb. In contrast, HC is characteristically a low redundancy language.

2 Haitian currency: 5 gourdes = US$ 1.00.

3 **ni**, or the short from **n**, is used after a nasal vowel or a nasal consonant by many speakers.

4 For a fuller semantic analysis of the plural personal pronouns, see Howe (1989).

5 See 1.3.5.1.

6 After **pou** as a complementizer, however, the short form may be used e.g.: **pou m pati** (see 11).

7 For zero copula, see 4.8.1.

8 The variant forms **you/youn/oun/on/ou/gnou** also occur.

9 For negative forms, see 5.

10 **nan** is a variant of **lan**, parallel to **ni/li**.

11 There is still no satisfactory analysis of the use of definite determiners in Haitian.

12 The exceptions being **bay** *to give*, (4.7.1.) and the equivalent of the copula (= *to be)*, (4.8.); however, these variations of form are governed by the phonetic environment (**bay**) or structural considerations (copula), not grammatical distinctions. For **fè** *to make, do; to give birth to*, see 4.12.

13 Except for copula **se**; see 4.8.2.

14 Other combinations are possible; these are the most common.

15 for a fuller discussion of HC TMA markers, see Spears 1990.

16 **do** is used more after **te** and **ta.**

17 An argument of a verb is here defined as any NP, other than the subject, which is essential to the verb, though not necessarily expressed, e.g., all transitive verbs by definition have a direct object, and all ditransitives have a direct and an indirect object, e.g., 'give **something** to **someone**'. Adverbials of time and manner are not part of the VP.

18 This is in fact ambiguous, as it could refer to another person, i.e. *s/he sacrificed her/him*

19 See Winford (1988).

20 Fiyèt Lalo is an ogress. It also refers to a female **tonton makout** (see reading Selections)

21 For relative clauses, see 7.

22 The question of whether this position is to be considered an 'empty' relative pronoun slot or a complementizer slot is under debate; furthermore, **ke** is found more and more frequently in this position. For pedagogical clarity, I have kept the structural description parallel to the English equivalent.

23 My motivation for referring to this subject **ki** as a relative pronoun is too long to include in a work of this scope. Adequate treatment would entail discussion of complementizers and general strategies for forming questions and require postulating a deleted-copula cleft sentence. For details, see Howe 1991.

24 One also finds the phrase **ki lès moun (ki)**, etc.

25 **(ki) sa (ki)** and **(ki) kote** can optionally drop the interrogative marker **ki**, but the subject marker **ki** is still obligatory.

26 Note that in this structure, the use of the copula is optional, if and only if the verb is unmarked for TMA.

27 **sa ki** is also used for *the person who / those who*, as in **sa ki pa vini lekòl pa aprann** *the person who / those who do[es] not come[s] to school do[es] not learn.*

The Forty-Two Selections

Selection One

Egzamen Bakaloreya

Atansyon, atansyon, ou menm ki pa pase lan egzamen bakaloreya[1] ane sa a, ale kounyeya nan Sant Fòmasyon Kretyèn[2] Dayiti, mande youn demi bous. Sant Fòmasyon Kretyèn Dayiti chita[3] nan Riyèl Kretyen, Enpas Fransis, nimewo katòz. Pou tout enfòmasyon, telefonnen senk swasant sis trann[4] twa, senk swasant sis trann twa, Sant Fòmasyon Kretyèn Dayiti.

Vocabulary

atansyon	attention
ou*	2s personal marker
menm*	emphatic marker with personal marker.
ki*	who (rel. pro.)
pa*	not (verb negation)
pase	pass (vb.)
lan*	in (var. of **nan***)
egzamen	examination
bakaloreya	baccalaureate
ane	year
sa a*	this
ale	go
kounyeya	now
nan*	in, to
sant	center
fòmasyon	training
kretyen	Christian
Dayiti	of Haiti
mande	ask (for)
youn*	a
demi	half
bous	scholarship, grant
chita	be situated
riyèl	little street
enpas	dead-end street
nimewo	number
katòz	fourteen
pou	for
tout	all
enfòmasyon	information
telefonnen	telephone (vb.)
senk	five
swasant	sixty
sis	six
trann	thirty
twa	three

Notes

1 **bakaloreya** in Haiti, this is the diploma conferred on completion of High School, not university.

2 **Kretyèn** this is in the fem. form, usually reserved for humans*; here, the newscaster has read the original French name (which has the fem. form) with HC pronunciation.

3 **chita** the usual word for *sit*; also used for location of buildings or organizations.

4 **trann** variation of **trant** *thirty*, occurring before consonant of following number, e.g. **trann de, trann twa**.

Selection Two

Remèsiman

KOLFA (Konbit[1] pou Liberasyon Fanm Ayisyèn) ap voye you gwo kout chapo remèsiman bay[2] tout zanmi, òganizasyon, laprès pale ak ekri ki te ede nou reyisi sware fanm nan dimanch 13 mas 88 nan Klara Baton[3]. Ansanm ansanm, n a ka rive kaba lenjistis.

Pou KOLFA
Ketlin Moyiz

Vocabulary

remèsiman	thanks	ak	and
konbit	collective work group	ekri	write
liberasyon	liberation	te*	verb marker [+anterior]
fanm	woman	ede	help (vb.)
ayisyèn*	Haitian (fem.)	nou*	1/2p personal marker
ap*	verb marker [+progressive]	reyisi	make success of
voye	send	sware	evening
you*	a	dimanch	Sunday
gwo	big	mas	March
kout	denotes action involving following noun	ansanm	together
		n*	1/2p personal marker
chapo	hat	ka*	be able, can
bay*	give	rive	manage (to do sth.), succeed in (doing something)
zanmi	friend		
òganizasyon	organization	kaba	end (vb.)
laprès	media, press	lenjistis	injustice
pale	speak, talk		

Notes

1 **Konbit** in the traditional sense, a group of people who get together to do one specific task, such as dig or sow a field, build a house, etc. This is the normal practice in the Haitian countryside when the work involved would be too much for one person or family. By extension, **konbit** now can mean *association* or *union*.

2 **voye ... bay** serial construction*; translate **bay** here as *to* (indirect object).

3 **Klara Baton** Clara Barton High School in Brooklyn, NY.

Selection Three

Libreri Louvèti

W ap jwenn tout kalite liv sou Ayiti an kreyòl, franse, panyòl, angle. Liv pou edikasyon bileng ak alfabetizasyon. W ap jwenn tou plak, tep ak tout jounal ayisyen

1502 Nostrand Avenue
Ant Church & Snyder Ave
Tel: (718) 469 2295

Ouvè chak jou de 10 zè a 9 vè[1]

Vocabulary

libreri	bookstore	edikasyon	education
Louvèti	Louverture	bileng	bilingual
w*	2s personal marker	alfabetizasyon	literacy
jwenn	find (vb.)	tou	also, too
kalite	kind (n.)	plak	record, disk
liv	book	tep	tape (n.)
sou*	about, on	jounal	newspaper
Ayiti	Haiti	ayisyen	Haitian
an	in (followed by language name)	ant	between
		ouvè	open
kreyòl	Creole	chak	every, each
franse	French	jou	day
panyòl	Spanish (language); person from Dominican Republic	de*	from
		a	to
angle	English		

Notes

1 **10 zè a 9 vè** this is pronounced **dizè a nevè***.

Selection Four

Kou fòmasyon medikal

Jèn fi, jèn gason, tande. Aprann youn metye pou lavi ou, enskri ou depi jodi a nan kou fòmasyon oksilyè enfimyè polivalan ki gen syèj li nan lopital Sen Jilbè de Nefontèn[1], Chemen dè Dal[2] katreven de (82)[3]. Kèlkeswa laj ou, ou ka vin youn bon oksilyè medikal ak oun diplòm valab ki gen siyati youn seri teknisyen konpetan, ki fè prèv yo nan anpil gwo ensititsyon nan peyi a; epi tou, se sèl lekòl prive kote etidyan tou jwenn lopital pou fè pratik. Plis etidyan an fè pratik, se plis l ap vin pi fò nan branch la. Si ou vle rete lontan nan youn djob poutèt konpetans ou, ale enskri ou san kè sote lan kou fòmasyon oksilyè medikal lan lopital Sen Jilbè, Chemen dè Dal katreven de (82).

Vocabulary

jèn	young	siyati	signature
fi	woman	seri	series, some
gason	man	teknisyen	technician
tande	hear	konpetan	qualified
aprann	learn	fè prèv li	prove oneself
metye	profession	yo*	3p personal marker
lavi	living, livelihood, life	anpil	many
enskri	register (vb.)	gwo	important
depi	from (in time expressions)	enstitisyon	institution
jodi a	today	peyi	country
kou	course, class	a*	the
oksilyè	assistant	epi	and
enfimyè	nurse	se*	be
polivalan	general	sèl*	only (adj.)
gen*	have	lekòl	school
syèj	head office	prive	private
li*	3s personal marker	kote*	where
lopital	hospital	etidyan	student
katreven	eighty	fè	do, make
de	two	pratik	practice (n.)
kèlkeswa	whatever	plis	(the) more
laj	age	an*	the
vin*	become	pi (+ adj.)*	more (= adj.), adj. + -er
bon*	good	fò	good (at doing sth.)
medikal	medical	branch	area, branch
oun*	a	si	if
diplòm	diploma	vle*	want
valab	valuable	rete*	stay, remain

lontan	a long time	san	without
djob	job	kè	heart
poutèt	because of (prep.)	sote	jump (vb.)
konpetans	proficiency	kè sote	fear (n.)

Notes

1 Fr.: Saint Gilbert de Neufontaine.

2 Fr.: Chemin des Dalles.

3 I have followed the usual practice of writing the numerals in parenthesis after the spelling.

Selection Five

Avi ESP

ESP reyafime avi talè a -- ESP ki nan lokal Radyo Karayib. Enstiti Siperyè Pwofesyonèl mande tout moun ki enskri yo[1] -- tout elèv ki abitye vin lekòl, kou sekretarya, daktilografi, resepsyonis, kou de kontabilite[2] -- pou yo vin lan kou nòmalman jodi a.[3] Donk n ap jwenn taksi deyò a pou nou vini e sa k pa vle pran taksi gen dwa vin a pye, kòm dabitid paske nou konsyan ke[4] elèv la sakrifye l[5] pou l jwenn ti tchotcho a[6] pou l bay chak mwa. Nou pa ta renmen pèdi youn kou paske li pap pwofitab pou elèv la. Alò, nou mande tout elèv yo vin nan kou daktilografi, sekretarya, kontabilite, resepsyonis etc. jounalis.

Y[7] ap tann tout elèv jodi a, lekòl ap fonksyone nòmalman tout lajounen. Se Enstiti a ki siyen.

Vocabulary

reyafime	reaffirm, confirm
avi	notice (n.)
talè a	a short time ago, just now
lokal	premises, headquarters
radyo	radio
Karayib	Caribbean
enstiti	institute
siperyè	higher
pwofesyonèl	professional
moun	person
tout moun	everyone
elèv	pupil
abitye + vb.	usually + vb., be in the habit of + vb.
sekretarya	secretariat
daktilografi	typing
resepsyonis	receptionist
kontabilite	accounting
pou*	complementizer
nòmalman	normally
donk	for, in that case
taksi	taxi
deyò a	outside
vini	come
e	and
sa	that, those (pronoun)
sa k(i)*	those who
pran	take
gen dwa	can, be able
vin*	come
pye	foot
a pye	on foot
kòm	like, as
dabitid	usually
kòm dabitid	as usual
paske	because
konsyan	aware
ke*	that (compl.)
sakrifye	sacrifice
ti	little
tchotcho	money (small amount, earned with difficulty)
mwa	month
ta*	verb marker [+anterior +irrealis]
renmen	like (vb.)
pèdi	lose
pap*	negative marker + verb marker [+ progressive]
pwofitab	advantageous, profitable
alò	so
jounalis	journalism
y*	3p personal marker

tann	expect, wait for	lajounen	day, daytime
fonksyone	function (vb.)	siyen	sign (vb.)

Notes

1 **tout moun ... yo** note the position of the definite determiner after the relative clause*.

2 **kou de kontabilite** use of **de** here is a translation from the French; note it is not used in **kou sekretarya** etc.

3 **pou yo vin ... jodi a** a nation-wide general strike was called for 21 November 1988. See also Selections 9, 10, 11, 23, 32, 33, 42.

4 **ke** the use of **ke** as a complementizer* is becoming more widespread.

5 **sakrifye l** reflexive verb: *sacrifice himself**.

6 **tchotcho** note that this word is also a euphemism for *penis*.

7 **y** the announcer has finished reading the notice in the name of the ESP, and now changes to the 3p marker, from 1/2p marker (= *we*)

Selection Six

Zafè fatra

Sa k ap pase konsa a[1] nan lari Pòtoprens[2] ? Eben, zafè fatra[3] toujou ap fè pale de li. Prèske tout kote ou pase nan kwen peyi a ou rankontre youn pil fatra avèk dlo sal ladann[4].

Tout semèn pase an wo, tout moun ap rele anmwe pou zafè fatra a, e vrèman li te youn jan diminye. Kounyeya nou wè li kòmanse repran chè ankò, kidonk moun yo voye youn kout rèl nan zòrèy moun meri yo, moun ki konsène sou zafè fatra a pou fè on[5] jan pou yo, pase sante a deja pa fin kòdyòm nan peyi a, vwa si[6] gen fatra avèk dlo, mouch, vè, k ap sikile bò kote moun.

Vocabulary

sa k*	what
pase	happen
konsa	thus, like this
lari	street
eben	well (introducing sentence)
zafè	matter, affair
fatra	trash
toujou	still
prèske	almost
tout kote	everywhere
kwen	corner
rankontre	find
pil	pile (n.)
avèk	with
dlo	water
sal	dirty (adj.)
ladan	in, inside
semèn	week
semèn pase an wo	week before last
rele	call (vb.)
anmwe	help (as exclamation)
vrèman	really
jan (with **yon**)	a little
diminye	diminished
wè	see
kòmanse	begin
repran	take (on) again
chè	flesh
repran chè	get bigger
ankò	again
kidonk	so
rèl	shout (n.)
zòrèy	ear
meri	townhall
konsène	responsible (for sth.)
on*	a
fè on jan pou	solve the problem for, do something for, help
pase	because (var. of **paske**)
sante	health
deja	already
pa fin kòdyòm	not to be right, the way it should be
vwa si	you can imagine what it's like if..
mouch	fly (n.)
vè	maggot
k*	which
sikile	move around
bò kote	near

Notes

1 **konsa a** the def. det. here signifies *particular thing*. **konsa**, lit. *thus*; here it has sense of: *So, what's happening ...* .

2 **Pòtoprens** Port-au-Prince, capital of Haiti.

3 **zafè fatra** the problem of piles of rotting trash in the streets is perennial; the official excuses vary. There have been reports of neighborhood groups cleaning the streets themselves, only to have unidentified individuals come and dump new piles of trash in the recently cleaned streets.

4 **ladann** prep. + **n(l)**, *in it*.

5 **fè on** in rapid speech, Haitians usually run together the 'e' and the nasal 'o' sounds ('fon'); this also happens frequently with **se on**, ('son'), **gen on** ('gon'), etc.

6 **vwa si** more normally **ale vwa si**; the sense is: *you can imagine what it's like with all this too*, i.e. it's even worse.

Selection Seven

Sapen natirèl

Nou genyen Asosyasyon pou Lit kont Ewozyon avèk Reyabilitasyon Total[1] Anviwonman ki voye di nan epòk Nwèl la konn gen anpil fanmi ki bezwen fè ti bèbèl lakay yo, mete ti ab de Nwèl[2] ki fèt avèk sapen natirèl. Eben [...] ALERTE[3] di varyete sapen sa a ou jwenn sèlman isit nan Ayiti avèk Kiba, donk, li merite pou nou pwoteje l. ALERTE sijere bay[4] komèsan yo ak tout enterese sou zafè ab de Nwèl yo, pou komèsan yo mete sou mache a ab de Nwèl sentetik avèk youn pri ke tout moun kapab achte pou semèn desanm nan[5]. ALERTE oblije fè chwa sa a pou moun yo pou yo kapab mete ab de Nwèl sentetik lakay yo, e li di tou ke ab de Nwèl sentetik la li[6] konsève tout frechè li, li pa vin jòn, li pa sal kay la e ou kapab sèvi avè l chak ane, ou pap bezwen depanse tout tan ankò.

Vocabulary

genyen*	have	merite	deserve
asosyasyon	association	pwoteje	protect
lit	fight, struggle (n.)	sijere	suggest
kont	against	komèsan	merchant, shopkeeper
ewozyon	erosion	enterese	concerned (in, with)
reyabilitasyon	rehabilitation	mache	market
anviwonman	environment	sentetik	synthetic, artificial
di	say	pri	price
epòk	period, time	kapab*	be able, can
Nwèl	Christmas	achte	buy (vb.)
konn + vb.*	vb. + usually, often	desanm	December
fanmi	family	chwa	choice
bezwen*	want	konsève	keep, conserve
bèbèl	decorations	frechè	freshness
lakay	at home, in the house of	jòn	yellow
mete	put	sal	dirty (vb.)
ab de Nwèl	Christmas tree	sèvi	use (vb.)
fèt*	made	avè	with
sapen	fir tree	sèvi avè yon bagay	to use something
natirèl	natural	bezwen*	need (vb.)
varyete	kind, variety	depanse	spend (money)
sèlman	only (adv.)	tan	time
isit	here	pa ... ankò*	no longer, not ... any more
Kiba	Cuba		

Notes

1 **total** in HC means *first-rate*; this title is translated directly from the French, in which **total** means the same as its English cognate.

2 **ab de Nwèl** This is a direct borrowing from the Fr. **arbre de Noël**; the normal word for *tree* in HC is **pye bwa.**

3 **ALERTE** Fr. acronym: **Association pour la Lutte contre l'Erosion et pour la Réhabilitation Totale de l'Environnement**, *Association for the Fight against Erosion and for the Total Rehabilitation of the Environment.* The problem of soil erosion, a concomitant of deforestation, is extreme in Haiti. See also Selections 8, 41.

4 **sijere bay** serial verb construction*: *suggest to ...* .

5 **semèn desanm nan** meaning, of course, the holiday week in December.

6 **ab de Nwèl sentetik la, li** left-dislocation for emphasis*.

Selection Eight

Deklarasyon ANDAH

Gen *Association Nationale des Agronomes Haïtiens*[1] ki fè soti you deklarasyon ki di:

Douvan deblozay ki genyen nan Damyen[2] depi pase you mwa, e sitou

douvan lòbèy ki te pete le disèt novanm nan[3], ant Minis Agrikilti a avèk gwo chabrak nan Ministè a,

alòske poko gen anyen ki janm di sou gwo pwoblèm fondalnatal k ap ravaje agrikilti peyi a tankou pwoblèm kochon[4], pwoblèm tè[5], pwoblèm rebwazman[6], dlo[7], kontrebann[8] k ap fini ak kondisyon nasyonal la, kondisyon [...] travay teknisyen yo sou teren an,

devan sitirasyon sa a, nou menm ANDAH[9] (Asosyasyon Nasyonal Agwopwofesyonèl Ayisyen), nou vle fè tout moun konnen, premyèman sa k ap pase la, pa genyen anyen a revwa[10] ak pwoblèm agrikilti peyi a.

Dezyèmman, pi fò agwonòm ak lòt moun k ap travay nan Ministè Agrikilti, pa avèk ni younn ni lòt gwoup nan zotobre sa yo k ap goumen [...] pou pòs ak lajan.

Twazyèmman, atitid zotobre sa yo ap sal tout pwofesyonèl ayisyen douvan figi peyi a ak lòt peyi k ap gade l.

Pou lonè pwofesyon an ak tout pwofesyonèl ayisyen yo, pou respè peyi a, nou menm, manm ANDAH, nou mande pou Minis la, direktè jeneral la ak direktè jeneral adjwen an bay demisyon yo san pèdi tan, prese prese, e nou mande tou pou otorite ki konsène yo pran mezi prese prese pa sèlman pou chanje moun[11], men sitou pou reyòganize[12] Ministè a.

ANDAH mande tout agwonòm, tout pwofesyonèl k ap travay nan agrikilti, tout etidyan fakilte agwonomi, tout gwoupman ak òganizasyon peyizan, pou yo mobilize yo [...] jouk tan nou jwenn youn solisyon nètalkole pou fè Ministè Agrikilti vini[13] sèvi tout bon vre agrikilti peyi a.

Pou direksyon nasyonal la ANDAH a, se Maks Astre, Jeral Matiren, Jan Klod Amede, Pol Dirè, Antoni Dabe e Ari Laprich ki pase paraf[14] yo.

Vocabulary

fè soti*	put out, publish (causative)	depi	for (period of time in past), since
deklarasyon	statement		
douvan	before, faced with	pase	more than (+ number)
deblozay	violent quarrel	sitou	especially
		lòbèy	quarrel, disagreement

pete	break out, burst
disèt	seventeen
novanm	November
minis	minister
agrikilti	agriculture
gwo chabrak	bigshot
ministè	ministry
alòske	whereas, while
poko*	still not
anyen*	nothing, not ... anything
janm*	never, not ... ever
pwoblèm	problem
fondalnatal	profound, basic
ravaje	ravage
tankou	such as, like
kochon	pig
tè	land (n.)
rebwazman	reforestation
kontrebann	contraband
fini ak	ruin (vb.)
kondisyon	condition
nasyonal	national
travay	work (n. and vb.)
teren	field
sitirasyon	situation
agwopwofesyonèl	agroprofessional
konnen	know
premyèman	firstly
genyen ...	
a revwa ak	to have ... to do with
dezyèmman	secondly
pi fò	majority
agwonòm	agronomist
lòt	other
ni ... ni	and, both ... and
pa ... ni ... ni*	not ... either ... or

younn	one (pron.)
gwoup	group
zotobre	bigshot
goumen	fight (vb.)
pòs	position, post
lajan	money
twazyèmman	thirdly
atitid	attitude
figi	face
gade	look at
lonè	honor
respè	respect (n.)
manm	member
direktè	director
jeneral	general
adjwen	assistant
demisyon	resignation
pèdi tan	waste time
prese	in a hurry
prese prese*	as quickly as possible
otorite	authority
mezi	measure
chanje	change (vb.)
men	but
reyòganize	reorganize
fakilte	faculty (university)
gwoupman	group
peyizan	peasant
mobilize	mobilize
jouk	until
solisyon	solution
nètalkole	definitively, totally
tout bon vre	truly
direksyon	leadership
paraf	mark, signature

Notes

1 **Association Nationale des Agronomes Haïtiens** Fr.: *National Association of Haitian Agronomists.*

2 **Damyen** Suburb of Port-au-Prince where the Department of Agriculture building is located.

3 **le disèt ...** **le** is French definite determiner, and tautological here.

4 **pwoblèm kochon** the small black 'creole' pigs were exterminated in an effort to eradicate African swine fever; see Selections 13, 40.

5 **pwoblèm tè** there are constantly disputes over land ownership and use; see Dupuy (1989).

6 **pwoblèm rebwazman** deforestation is one of Haiti's major problems, affecting rainfall, underground water supplies, and soil, which, with few trees to anchor it, washes away with each rainfall. See Selections 7, 41.

7 **dlo** uncontaminated drinking water is available to few people in Haiti. Also, rainfall diminishes with the disappearance of trees, which also keep springs running under their roots.

8 **kontrebann** contraband goods, particularly food, aggravate the Haitian producers' poverty. An example is the so-called 'Miami rice', surplus rice sent or bought from the US, which is sold at under-market prices. This has led to the financial ruin, and subsequent displacement, of many rice-growers in the Artibonite plain, the major rice-growing region of Haiti.

9 **ANDAH** Fr. acronym; **Association Nationale des Agronomes Haïtiens,** *National Association of Haitian Agronomists.* Note that the name given for this organization in HC does not exactly correspond.

10 **pa genyen anyen a revwa** (almost) literal translation of the French; HC should be **pa gen oken rapò.**

11 **pou chanje moun** better with **yo** in subject position (before **chanje**).

12 **pou reyòganize** better with **yo** in subject position (before **reyòganize**).

13 **vini** i.e. *start.*

14 **paraf** not, strictly speaking, a signature, but a personal sign serving as a signature, such as initials, etc. Journalists, however, have recently started to use the word in the sense of 'signature'.

Selection Nine

Grèv nan Pòtoprens

La CATH[1] ap fè grèv la[2] pou pwoteste[3] kont tout sa k pa bon k ap dewoule nan peyi a. Se konsa jounen lendi sa a, aktivite nan divès sektè nan peyi a, nan Pòtoprens, tap fonksyone o ralanti[4]. Nan santre vil la[5] gen kèk magazen ki te ouvè; sepandan, majorite ti machann[6] yo pat vin chita arebò lari a, yo te chita lakay yo. Lekòl la pat fonksyone ditou piske tout elèv te chita lakay yo tou.

Pou transpò a, nou ka di [...] se yon ka ki fonksyone nan tout sikwi yo. Nou te remake kèk taksi ki tap sikile nan lari a tou.

Nan faktori yo, prensipalman nan pak endistriyèl la, anpil ouvriye te absan. Genyen de twa[7] faktori ki pat ouvè tou. Dapre ouvriye yo, se chofè ki travay yo ki ta kòz ouvriye vin travay; sa ap pèmèt patwon wè si ta movèz fwa ou si ta paske yo apiye grèv la ki fè si yo pa vini[8]. Yo oblije vini tou pou yo pa pèdi lajan jounen an, men sa pa vle di yo pa apiye grèv la.

Vocabulary

grèv	strike
pwoteste	protest
dewoule	happen
lendi	Monday
aktivite	activity
divès	different, various
sektè	sector
tap*	verb marker [+anterior +progressive]
o ralanti	at a slow pace
vil	town
sant vil	town center, downtown
kèk	some
magazen	store
sepandan	however
majorite	majority
machann	vendor
chita	sit, stay
arebò	on the side of
pat*	negative + verb marker [+anterior)
ditou	at all
pa ... ditou	not ... at all
piske	as, since
transpò	transportation
yon*	a
ka	quarter
sikwi	route, circuit
remake	notice (vb.)
faktori	factory
prensipalman	mainly, mostly
pak	park
endistriyèl	industrial
ouvriye	worker
absan	absent
de twa (2-3)	a few
dapre	according to
chofè	driver
kòz	reason, cause
pèmèt	allow, permit
patwon	owner, boss
fwa	faith
movèz fwa	bad faith, insincerity
apiye	support, back (vb.)
vle di	mean (vb.)

Notes

1 **La CATH** **la** is the French preposed definite article; Fr. acronym for **Centrale Autonome de Travailleurs Haïtiens**, *Autonomous Federation of Haitian Workers.*

2 **grèv la** general strike which was called for 21 November 1988. See also Selections 5, 10, 11, 23, 32, 33, 42.

3 **pou pwoteste** better with **l(i)** in subject position before **pwoteste**.

4 **o ralanti** this **o** is used in set phrases borrowed directly from French.

5 **santre vil la** HC should be **sant vil la**; this is from the Fr. **centre ville.**

6 **ti machann** in downtown Port-au-Prince the streets are lined with vendors, with wide, shallow baskets of wares (from fruit to chewing gum and toothpaste).

7 **de twa** lit. *two three.*

8 **Dapre ouvriye yo ... yo pa vini** this sentence is not well constructed. **si ta movèz fwa**, **ta** should be **se.** **ki fè si yo ...** , better without **si.**

Selection Ten

Grèv Okap

Korespondan nou nan Okap[1] fè n konnen ke grèv la, li obsève[2] nan vil sila a; lekòl yo pa fonksyone, kòmès avèk transpò piblik la prèske paralize[3]. Kiris Maksino pou detay[4]:

"Nan Okap obsèvatè yo estime reyisit grèv la a anviwon katreven kenz pou san (95%). Prèske tout magazen rete avèk pòt yo fèmen, transpò piblik la paralize. Kit se taptap[5] k ap fè Site Chovèl[6] ou byen lòt kamyonèt ki relye vil Okap avèk zòn ozanviwon yo, rive nan gwo bis Kap-Pòtoprens, tout machin sa yo rete kanpe. Se kèk grenn taksi avèk oto prive k ap vire nan vil la.

Lajounen jodi[7], lekòl pa fonksyone nan Okap, tout elèv rete chita lakay yo. Mache piblik yo pa rive reyini kòm sa dwa[8], sitou Mache Ri Twa a ki toujou chaje, jodi a machann yo pa mete pye[9]. Se prèske tout aktivite nan lavil Okap ki paralize jodi lendi venteyen novanm nan. Se te Kiris Maksino denpi[10] Okap."

Vocabulary

korespondan	correspondent
obsève	observe
sila a*	this, that
kòmès	trade, commerce
piblik	public
paralize	paralyze
detay	detail
obsèvatè	observer
estime	estimate
reyisit	success
a	at
anviwon	about, approximately
kenz	fifteen
katreven kenz	ninety five
san	hundred
pou san	percent
pòt	door
fèmen	close (vb.)
kit ... ou byen	whether ... or else
taptap	**taptap** (covered pickup truck or van, with set route and price, for urban public transportation)
site	housing development; in Haiti, often slum areas
kamyonèt	small truck (for interurban public transportation)
relye	connect, link
zòn	area, zone
ozanviwon	surrounding
rive*	including, up to (vb. used with prep. function)
bis	bus
machin	vehicle, car
kanpe	stand (still)
grenn	single unit
oto	auto (car)
vire	drive around, stroll around
reyini	meet
dwa	must, should
kòm sa dwa	as it should, properly
ri	street
chaje	full, busy
lavil	downtown (n. and loc.)
venteyen	twenty one
denpi	from, since

Notes

1 **Okap** Cape Haitian, the former capital of Saint Domingue, as Haiti was known when a French colony.

2 **grèv la, li obsève** a better construction would be: **yo obsève grèv la;** the passive interpretation* is only 'correct' in HC with a certain class of verbs, according to some linguists (for a convincing analysis, see Winford (1988)). Note also that the full noun phrase (**grèv la**) followed by a pause and then the pronoun, coreferential with the noun phrase (left-dislocation), is one way of expressing emphasis* (cf. note Selection 7).

3 **transpò piblik la ... paralize** passive reading*.

4 **pou detay** journalistic 'shorthand'. For more on the strike, see Selections 5, 9, 11, 23, 32, 33, 42.

5 **taptap** this name is taken from the adverb meaning *quickly* or *rapidly,* as in **li fè sa taptap.**

6 **Site Chovèl** an area in Cape Haitian.

7 **lajounen jodi** more correct would be **jodi a**; strictly speaking **(la)jounen jodi** means 'nowadays', **(jounen) jodi a**, 'today'.

8 **dwa** variation of **dwe***, due to Fr. influence (**doit**).

9 **pa mete pye** i.e. *did not show up.*

10 **denpi** var. of **depi**; the speaker is speaking (selfconsciously?) **Kreyòl rèk** or basilectal HC (see chapter "Language in Haiti").

Selection Eleven

Grèv nan depatman Nòdès

Nan depatman Nòdès la, nou konstate grèv la[1] reyisi a katreven di pou san (90%), espesyalman nan Fò Libète[2] ak anpil nan lòt vil nan Nòdès la. Trafik piblik la bloke nèt, tout machin piblik yo te rete kanpe nan estasyon ou byen devan pòt kay pwopriyetè yo.

Bò kote lekòl yo, ni lekòl segondè, lekòl primè, piblik ak[3] lekòl prive yo oblije fèmen pòt yo paske elèv yo pa te[4] al lekòl. Nan Fò Libète, se sèlman lekòl Kay Mè[5] ki te fonksyone jounen jodi a ak kèk grenn elèv.

Bò kote biwo leta yo, tout pòt yo te ouvè. Se konsa, yo te ap[6] fonksyone timidman ak kèk grenn anplwaye ki te al lan biwo, al fè biwo sa yo onè[7].

Vocabulary

depatman	department (geographical division)	pwopriyetè	owner
Nòdès	Northeast	bò kote	as for
konstate	find, ascertain	segondè	secondary
reyisi	be successful	primè	elementary (school)
di	ten	oblije*	have to
katreven di	ninety	biwo	office
espesyalman	especially	leta	state
trafik	traffic	timidman	timidly
bloke	block (vb.)	anplwaye	employee
nèt	totally, completely	onè	honor
estasyon	station		

Notes

1 **grèv la** strike called for 21 November 1988. See also Selections 5, 9, 10, 23, 32, 33, 42.

2 **Fò Libète** Fort Liberté, capital of the Northeast department.

3 **...piblik ak lekòl ...** **ak** should be **ni***.

4 **pa te** it is rare not to run these markers together as **pat**.

5 **Kay Mè** **mè** *religious mother*, so *convent school.*

6 **te ap** see note above on **pa te**.

7 **fè ... onè** when Haitians come to someone's home, they call out "Onè"; the reply, to welcome them, is "Respè". Here, the expression has the sense of *greeting* or *giving importance to.*

Selection Twelve

Lèt Asosyasyon Jounalis Ayisyen

Genyen yon lèt ki soti bò kote Asosyasyon Jounalis Ayisyen ke yo adrese bay Konsil Jeneral Peyi Ba ki an Ayiti, msye Wobè G. Patbèg. Asosyasyon Jounalis Ayisyen yo[1] ekri li, se pou yo kapab atire atansyon Konsil Jeneral la sou ka konfrè yo, jounalis *Haïti Observateur*[2], Rene Anjelo yo te arete nan Sen Maten, lan pati olandèz la, uit novanm ki sòt pase la a. Li te genyen avèk li kat de près[3] li, epi paspò l tou te an règ. Jounalis la, li te vle fè yon ti repotaj, pandan youn semèn, sou kominote ayisyen an nan Sen Maten. Arestasyon Rene Anjelo epi tou le fèt ke[4] yo te mete l nan prizon nan lil Sen Maten, se yon vyolasyon Konvansyon San Jose de Kostarika sou libète laprès epi tou sou akò entènasyonal nan matyè dwa vwayaj. Yo pat bay jounalis *Haïti Observateur* a okenn rezon sou atitid otorite yo nan Sen Maten. AJH[5] donk mande Konsil Jeneral la pou l kapab pote eklèsisman sou afè sila a. Yo mande tou pou l kapab entèvni bò kote reskonsab afè eksteryè nan peyi pa l la pou yo kapab respekte dwa vwayaj Ayisyen e patikilyèman jounalis yo ki an misyon nan rejyon sila a nan Karayib la. Kòm nou di w, se yon nòt ki soti bò kote Asosyasyon Jounalis Ayisyen.

Vocabulary

lèt	letter
bò kote	from
jounalis	journalist
adrese	address (vb.)
konsil	consul
Peyi Ba	Holland
msye	Mr
atire	draw, attract
ka	case
konfrè	colleague
arete	arrest (vb.)
Sen Maten	St Martin
pati	part
olandèz	Dutch
uit	eight
sòt*	have just
kat	card
près	press (n.)
paspò	passport
règ	rule (n.)
an règ	in order
repotaj	report, article
kominote	community
arestasyon	arrest (n.)
prizon	prison
lil	island
vyolasyon	violation, breach
konvansyon	convention
akò	agreement
entènasyonal	international
matyè	matter, subject
dwa	right (n.)
vwayaj	travel, journey
pa ... okenn*	none, not ... any
rezon	reason (n.)
pote	bring, carry
eklèsisman	clarification
afè	matter, business
entèvni	intervene, intercede
reskonsab	responsible
eksteryè	foreign, exterior
pa*	emphatic possessive
respekte	respect (vb.)
patikilyèman	particularly, especially
misyon	mission
rejyon	region
nòt	note

Notes

1 **yo** this **yo** is unnecessary

2 ***Haïti Observateur*** French language newspaper published in New York.

3 **kat de près** The **de** is French, *of*.

4 **le fèt ke** direct borrowing from French **le fait que** *the fact that*.

5 **AJH** Fr. acronym: **Association des Journalistes Haïtiens**, *Association of Haitian Journalists*.

Selection Thirteen

Evenman nan zòn sidès

Anbochay anbachal la[1] toujou ap rapousib[2] nan zòn sidès nan peyi a e korespondan nou nan zòn Tyòt pral ban nou plis detay sou sa avèk lòt enfòmasyon ankò nan zòn sa a:

"Zafè anbochay la ap kontinye pou pi rèd nan tout sidès peyi a, kote moun yo ap sòti tribòpabò pou y al nan Ansapit[3] kote yo gen randevou ak mesye pasè[4] yo k ap fè yo travese limit fontyè a pou y al monte machin dominiken. Dapre sa yo fè nou konnen, pasè sa yo arive touche senkant goud ayisyen pou chak tèt Ayisyen yo arive bay Dominiken yo. Lè nou te kontakte peyizan sa yo, yo te fè nou konnen sa k fè yo kite peyi a pou y al travèse nan peyi panyòl[5]: se paske apre siklòn Jilbè an[6], yo pa gen okenn moun ki pote yo okenn sekou. Ti kochon kreyòl ki te sous lavi yo[7], mesye PEPADEP[8] yo te retire l nan men yo.

Youn lòt kote nan komin Bèl Ans[9], se san ki tap koule ant de gwoup, ki se Bèl Anfòm ak Pati Pèp. Poukisa? Se paske Bèl Anfòm ki apiye Jan Erol Kazimi kòm majistra, epi Pati Pèp ki sanble ki pi manbre ki apiye mèt Bo kòm majistra kominal ki te eli lan eleksyon disèt janvye yo[10], ke pèp Bèl Ans la di se mèt Bo yo vle ki pou rete dirije yo toujou nan lakomin nan[11]. Zafè a lan men Depatman Enteryè pou l kapab al anpeche san koule nan komin Bèl Ans la.

Toujou nan awondisman Bèl Ans la, Dipi, ki youn seksyon[12] kominal nan komin Tyòt la, chèf seksyon[13] Kanòl Loti sanble ap fè peyizan yo anpil abi, kote[14] li kite mesye grandon yo[15] sèvi ak li pou regle zafè pèsonèl yo.

Peyizan k ap viv nan Dipi mande chèf seksyon Kanòl Loti pou l kase boujon l[16] k ap boujonnen paske fò l pa bliye lè bagay la mare, menm wè li pap wè[17] gwo nèg yo.

Se Jan Ejèn, Radyo Solèy, Tyòt."

Vocabulary

anbochay	recruiting, hiring
anbachal	clandestine, secret
rapousib	continue
sidès	southeast
pral*	be going
ban*	give
kontinye	continue
rèd	severe, stubborn
pou pi rèd	more severely, stubbornly
sòti*	go out, come out, leave
tribòbabò	everywhere
randevou	appointment, rendez-vous
mesye (pl.)	men, Messrs.
pasè	ferryman
travèse	cross (vb.)
fontyè	border, frontier
monte	go up, get in (vehicle)
dominiken	Dominican, of the Dominican Republic
arive	manage (to do sth.)
touche	earn
senkant	fifty
goud	gourde (Haitian currency)

tèt	head	dirije	lead, direct
lè	when	lakomin	commune (administrative district)
kontakte	contact (vb.)	enteryè	interior
kite	leave	anpeche	prevent
apre	after	awondisman	ward (administrative district)
siklòn	hurricane	seksyon	section, subdivision
sekou	help, aid (n.)	chèf	head, leader
sous	source	chèf seksyon	section chief
retire	take from	abi	abuse (n.)
men	hand (n.)	grandon	big landowner
kote	place (n.)	regle	settle
komin	commune (administrative district)	pèsonèl	personal
san	blood	viv	live (vb.)
koule	flow	kase	break (vb.)
pati	party (political)	boujon	bud (n.)
pèp	people (vs. élite)	boujonnen	bud, blossom (vb.)
poukisa*	why	fò (+ subj. + vb.)*	be necessary, must
majistra	mayor	bliye	forget
sanble*	seem	bagay	thing
manbre	have members	mare	tie, attach
mèt	Master (title for lawyer)	bagay la mare	things are difficult
kominal	of a commune	menm	even (adv.)
eli	elect (vb.)	nèg	guy
eleksyon	election		
janvye	January		

Notes

1 **anbochay anbachal la** i.e. of Haitian workers to be taken to the sugarcane plantations in the Dominican Republic (see Ferguson, 65-66, and Lemoine (1981)). See also Selections 19, 26, 40.

2 **rapousib** original meaning, *to chase after someone*; now used to mean *continue* (Fr. influence).

3 **Ansapit** Anse à Pitre

4 **pasè** *ferryman, ferry* in the sense of taking someone somewhere, not just in a ferry boat.

5 **peyi panyòl** i.e. the Dominican Republic; from Fr. **espagnole** *Spanish.*

6 **siklòn Jilbè** Hurricane Gilbert, which devastated parts of Haiti in September 1988.

7 **sous lavi yo** owning a pig is the equivalent of a savings account for a Haitian peasant; they often rely on the potential extra income for large or important expenses, such as sending their children to school. See also Selections 8, 40.

8 **PEPADEP** Fr. acronym **Projet d'Eradication de la Peste Africaine et du Développement de l'Elevage Porcin** - *Project for the Eradication of African Swine Fever and for the Development of Pig Husbandry.*

9 **Bèl Ans** Belle Anse, a town on the southern coast of Haiti, approximately 20 miles from the Dominican border.

10 **eleksyon disèt janvye yo** the date of the first elections held in Haiti since Jean Claude Duvalier's leaving the country, which were widely boycotted, and in which Leslie Manigat was elected president.

11 This sentence is lacking a main clause.

12 **ki youn seksyon** ... **se** is not required here, even though the complement is NP, as it is in a relative clause after **ki*.**

13 **chèf seksyon** rural police chief; they often exploit the local people.

14 **kote** this refers back to Dipi.

15 **grandon yo** the big landowners often exploit the smallholding peasants; the word is now sometimes used as an insult.

16 **boujon l** i.e. his budding business with the **grandon. n** would be more normal than **l** after nasal*.

17 **menm wè ...** reduplication for emphasis*.

Selection Fourteen

Anivèsè

Jodi a fè egzakteman youn ane depi ke te genyen oun ekip sanmanman[1] ki te mete dife nan youn gwo aparèy ke Radyo Limyè genyen nan plenn nan nan kote yo rele Menelas. Sa te fè ke radyo a te bèbè pandan youn bon bout tan. Li pat kapab bay enfòmasyon epi li pat kapab kenbe pwogram ke l te genyen nan tout peyi a.

Men demen ap fè en an depi ke yo te boule Mache Salomon[2], yo te eseye boule BEK[3] Pòtoprens nan[4] epi ansanm avèk presbitè nan vil Sen Mak[5]. Yo te mete tèt anba Biwo Fon Nasyonal Konsètasyon ki te genyen nan vil Ti Gwav[6].

Demen tou ap fè youn anne depi ke ansyen jeneral Klòd Remon[7] te demanti nan laprès ke li menm li te patisipe ou byen li te gen a revwa[8] avèk zak kraze brize sa yo ki te fèt nan peyi a anvan ke eleksyon ven nèf novanm nan te fini nan san pèp la[9].

Vocabulary

egzakteman	exactly	boule	burn
ekip	team	eseye	try (vb.)
sanmanman	outlaw	presbitè	rectory
dife	fire	anba	below, under, underneath
mete dife	set fire	fon	fund
aparèy	facility, apparatus	konsètasyon	unity, concert
limyè	light (n.)	anne	year
plenn	plain (flat land); rural area not far from the city	ansyen	former
bèbè	mute	demanti	deny
bout	piece of, length of	patisipe	participate
kenbe	hold, support	gen a revwa avèk	have to do with
pwogram	program	zak	act (n.)
men	here is (often not translated when introducing sentence)	kraze	smash
demen	tomorrow	brize	break (vb.)
en	one (numeral)	kraze brize	destructive
an	year	anvan	before
		nèf	nine

Notes

1 **sanmanman** lit. *without mother*; therefore, without restraining moral influence or sentiment: *scum, lowdown no-good.*

2 **Mache Salomon** covered market in Port-au-Prince.

3 **BEK Biwo Elektoral Kominal**, *Commune Electoral Bureau.*

4 **Pòtoprens nan** the definite determiner would more normally be **la** after a non-nasal consonant; the preceding **n** influences the choice of determiner form.

5 **Sen Mak** Saint Marc, a town on coast between Port-au-Prince and Gonaïves.

6 **Ti Gwav** Petit Goâve, a town southwest of Port-au-Prince.

7 **Klòd Remon** General Claude Raymond, candidate for the 1987 elections, who was disqualified for his duvalierist connections.

8 **li te gen a revwa** Fr. influence; better would be **li te gen rapò** or **li te mele**.

9 **san pèp la** a reference to the massacre on election day, 29 November 1987. See also Selections 20, 31, 38.

Selection Fifteen

Lèt APN

Pòtoprens, 4 avril 1988

Asanble Popilè Nasyonal (APN) voye yon gwo kout chapo pou tout senpatizan[1] l nan Montreal[2] ki te òganize yon soupe pou ede nou kontinye fè travay konsyantizasyon an nan mitan mas pèp la. Se avèk anpil kè kontan nou resevwa $400.00 k ap pèmèt nou reyalize kèk ti pwojè, pa ekzanp: seminè, deplasman e latriye.
Se yon bèl ekzanp konpatriyòt Kanada yo bay lòt Ayisyen ki nan lòt peyi tankou Etazini, Frans, Meksik ki dapre nou, ap swiv eksanp sa a. Se youn nan fason, nou ka pote kontribisyon nan lit pèp ayisyen an.

Yon gwo kout chapo pou gwoup *Veye Yo* ak tout lòt moun ki te patisipe nan soupe sa a. Nou di Marie Célie Agnant[3]: kenbe pa lage.

Pou APN: Lalane Jean-Robert[4]

Vocabulary

avril	April	seminè	seminar
asanble	assembly	deplasman	transportation
popilè	popular	latriye	the rest
senpatizan	sympathizer	e latriye	etc.
òganize	organise	bèl*	pretty, good
soupe	supper	konpatriyòt	compatriot
konsyantizasyon	consciousness-raising	Kanada	Canada
mitan	midst, middle	Etazini	United States
mas	mass (quantity)	Frans	France
kontan	happy, pleased	Meksik	Mexico
resevwa	receive	swiv	follow
reyalize	realize, make real	fason	way, manner
pwojè	project	kenbe	endure, stay firm
ekzanp	example	lage	give up, let go
pa ekzanp	for example		

Notes

1 **pou tout senpatizan l** **bay* tout senpatizan** (serial verb*) would be a better construction.

2 **Montreal** French spelling; HC is **Monreyal**.

3 **Marie Célie Agnant** id.; HC **Mari Seli Ayan**.

4 **Lalane Jean-Robert** id.; HC **Lalàn Jan Wobè**.

Selection Sixteen

Kèk plant pou fè remèd†

Afyo: (non save l: Arracia Xanthorrysa). Li sèvi pou brili, plè, anflamasyon.

Amwaz: (artemisia vulgaris). Li bon pou fi ki gen vant mòde, kolik lè peryòd yo.

Asosi: (Momordica Charancia; yo di tou: sowosi, asowosi). Fèy li anmè kou fyèl. Li bon pou moun ki pa gen apeti. Yo sèvi ak li tou pou lafyèv palidis. Kosta Rika, Lagwadloup, yo rele li "sorosi" (daprè Arsène V. Pierre Noel, "Nomenclature polyglotte des plantes haitiennes et tropicales" 1971).

Aticho: (cynara scolymus). Li sèvi pou bese tansyon. Plant sa a, yo rele li[1] "bérigoule" nan kèk lòt peyi kote yo pale franse. Se enjenyè Saint-Romes ki premye plante aticho nan peyi nou, sou pwopriyete "La Chabonyè".

Ave: (petiveria alliacea) pèp la sèvi ak li pou lafyèv. Lagwadloup, yo rele li "danday". Odè ave fò anpil. Yo anplwaye l pou pinèz kabann. Li pa ta mal si nou ta di pandan nou la a: gen kèk komèsan sipèstisye ki sèvi ak ji fèy ave pou fè kòmès yo mache. Yo melanje ji fèy la ak diven wouj, lwil makristi pou monte yon lanp, nan lide sa kab atire kliyan.

Bayawonn: (prosopis juliflora). Rasin li bon pou lestonmak.

Berejenn[2]: (Pòto Riko, Sen Domeng: "berengena"; Kolonbi, Kiba, Meksik: "berenjena[3]"). Yo konn sèvi ak berejenn (Solanum Melongena) pou fè moun pise anpil.

Langchat: (osnon "langichat", "langlichat") ak fèy li yo fè remèd pou rim. Si w gen mal gòj, annik pile fèy langichat, pran ji a, gagari l. Ji fèy langichat ap ba w sa sou 2 chèz!

(† This article is one of a regular section in *Haïti Progrès*, "Lang Manman Nou[4]", by Mango Dyesifò, pseudonym for Raymond Philoctète.)

Vocabulary

plant	plant (n.)	anflamasyon	swelling, inflamation
remèd	remedy (n.)	amwaz	mugwort
afyo	arracacha	vant	stomach
non	name	mòde	bite (vb.)
save	scientific, scholarly	vant mòde	stomach ache
sèvi	serve	kolik	abdominal cramps
brili	burn (n.)	lè	during, at the time of
plè	wound (n.)	peryòd	period, menses

asosi	balsam apple	melanje	mix (vb.)
fèy	leaf	diven	wine
anmè	bitter	wouj	red
kou	like (prep.)	lwil	oil (n.)
fyèl	bile	makristi	castor oil plant, palma christi
apeti	appetite	lanp	lamp
lafyèv	fever	lide	idea
palidis	malaria	kliyan	client
Kosta Rica	Costa Rica (DOKA: Kostarica)	bayawonn	mesquite
Lagwadloup	Guadaloupe	rasin	root
aticho	artichoke	lestonmak	chest
bese	lower (vb.)	berejenn	eggplant
tansyon	bood pressure, tension	Pòto Riko	Puerto Rico (DOKA: Pòtoriko)
enjenyè	engineer	Sen Domeng	Dominican Republic
premye	first	Kolonbi	Columbia
plante	plant (vb.)	pise	pee, urinate
ave	garlic weed	langchat	cat tongue
odè	smell, odor	rim	cold (illness)
fò	strong	mal gòj	sore throat
anplwaye	use (vb.)	annik*	just (+ vb.)
pinèz	bug	pile	crush
kabann	bed	gagari	gargle
sipèstisye	superstitious	chèz	chair
ji	juice	ba w sa sou 2 chèz	solve your problems in a jiffy
mache	work, function (vb.)		

Notes

1 **plant sa a, yo rele li** left-dislocation with resumptive pronoun*.

2 **berejenn** the more common spelling is **berejèn**.

3 **berengena ... berenjena** the pronunication would be the same, according to the rules of Spanish orthography; however, **berenjena** is the correct version.

4 **Lang Manman Nou** *our mother tongue.*

Selection Seventeen

Avètisman tanpèt

Nou te lokalize[1] [youn tanpèt][2] jodi an ki dizuit novanm lanne diznèf san katreven uit, a katrè dimaten, a sèz pwen zewo degre latitid nò e swasant kenz pwen zewo degre lonjitid lwès, sètadi a de san swasant kenz kilomèt osid sidwès vil yo rele Tibiwon an. Li kontinye pran menm direksyon nò nòdwès lan, avek on vitès uit kilomèt a lè. Pi gwo van ke[3] nou anrejistre ladan n, nou evalwe l[4] a senkant senk kilomèt lè, men nou remake ke van sa yo gen on[5] tandans pou yo ogmante, pou yo vin pi gwo nèg[6]. Sant sistèm nan, li kapab pase a pli de san ven kilomèt a lwès ekstrèm pwent preskil sid peyi Dayiti, nan mitan lannwit lan. Li posib tou pou n obsève okou jounen an, gwo lapli ki kapab akonpaye avèk gwo van ki kapab monte jiska karant kilomèt lè nan Sid[7], avèk Grand Ans peyi Dayiti. Nou mande tout popilasyon rejyon zòn sid lan ki demere sou kote rivyè, sou kote kòt, sou kote k gen dlo pou yo pran anpil prekosyon an ka ke gen inondasyon. Nou mande tou, tanpri souple[8], a tout ti anbakasyon, ti bwa fouye, ti kannòt ki lan zòn kòt ki ale de lavil Okay a vil Jeremi pou yo rete nan pò yo, pou yo pa deplase, tanpri silvouplè[9].

Vocabulary

lokalize	locate
tanpèt	storm
dizuit	eighteen
lanne	year
katrè*	four o'clock
dimaten	in the morning (after time of day)
sèz	sixteen
pwen	point
zewo	zero
degre	degree
latitid	latitude
nò	north
lonjitid	longitude
lwès	west
sètadi	that is (to say)
kilomèt	kilometer
osid	to/in the south
sidwès	southwest
direksyon	direction
nòdwès	northwest
lan*	the
vitès	speed
a lè	per hour
van	wind
anrejistre	record, register (vb.)
evalwe	evaluate
tandans	tendency
ogmante	increase, augment
sistèm	system
pli de	more than
ekstrèm	furthest, extreme
preskil	peninsula
lannwit	night
posib	possible
okou	in the course of, during
lapli	rain (n.)
akonpaye	accompany
jiska	up to, until
karant	forty
popilasyon	population
demere	live, inhabit
sou kote	on the side of, next to
rivyè	river
kòt	coast
prekosyon	precaution
inondasyon	flood
tanpri	please

souple	please	bwa fouye	dugout (boat)
anbakasyon	craft, vessel	kannòt	rowboat
bwa	wood	deplase	move (vb.)
fouye	dig	silvouplè	please

Notes

1 **lokalize** this is a new borrowing in HC.

2 **youn tanpèt** the original reference to the storm is made earlier in the announcement.

3 **ke** use of **ke** in relative clause is becoming more common*.

4 **pi gwo van ... nou evalue l** **pi gwo van** and **l** are coreferential: the preposing of the direct object (left- dislocation*) serves to emphasize it.

5 **gen on** this is pronounced 'gon'; see note Selection 6.

6 **gwo nèg** functions here as an adjective.

7 **Sid** one of the departments of Haiti, taking up the western part of the southern peninsula.

8 **tanpri souple** the use of both words together is for emphasis, and is very common.

9 **tanpri silvouplè** see preceding note.

Selection Eighteen

Kominike - anplwaye aksidante

Direksyon OFATMA[1] te kontan anpil poutèt kolaborasyon li jwenn bò kot patwon yo, li pwofite di yo men wout pou yo swiv lè yo gen anplwaye yo aksidante.

Se pou patwon an vini ak aksidante a, ak tout kat idantifikasyon l, nan lopital la. Patwon an dwe mande nan sekretarya a fomil RI pou drese rapò aksidan an ansanm ak de foto aksidante a, e yo toude, dwe siyen fòm sa a.

Twa premye jou aksidante a fè nan lopital, se sou kont patwon an. Patwon an dwe ede aksidante a nan demach pou l jwenn[2] kòb li ak laswenyay jan lalwa mande l la[3].

Premyèman, fò l jwenn tout kalite swen ka l mande jouk li gaya. Dezyèmman, si aksidan ki rive l la ta fè l pa kapab travay, non sèlman yo dwe ba l swen medikal, depi sou katryèm jou yo dwe peye l jouskaske l ka repran travay li. Twazyèmman, kòb yo dwe peye l la, fèt pou l de tyè lan sa l te konn touche a, men fò kòb sa a pa pi plis pase mil goud ni pi piti pase swasant di goud pa mwa. Katryèmman, si pa malè aksidante a ta fè vwèl pou peyi san chapo[4], kòb yo ta dwe ba li a ap tou sèvi pou[5] antere l.

Vocabulary

direksyon	management
kolaborasyon	collaboration
bò kot	on the part of
pwofite	take the opportunity
wout	road
aksidante	injured in an accident
idantifikasyon	identification
dwe*	should, must
fomil	form (paper)
drese	draw up
rapò	report (n.)
aksidan	accident
toude	both
fòm	form (n.)
kont	account
demach	steps (to achieve sth.), attempt
kòb	100th of a **goud** (Haitian currency); money (in general)
laswenyay	treatment, care
jan	way
lalwa	law
swen	care (n.)
gaya	healthy
rive	happen
katryèm	fourth
peye	pay (vb.)
jouskaske	until (conj.)
repran	start again
tyè	third (fraction)
mil	thousand
ni	nor
pi piti	less
pase*	than (in comparative construction)
pa	per
pa mwa	per month
katryèmman	fourthly
pa	by
malè	misfortune
pa malè	by misfortune
vwèl	sail (n.)

fè vwèl pou peyi san chapo — die

antere — bury

Notes

1 **OFATMA Office d'Assurance du Travail, Maladie, Maternité**: *Office of Work, Illness, Maternity Insurance.*

2 **pou l jwenn ...** i.e. *for him to receive.*

3 **jan lalwa mande l la** note the use of the determiner at the end of the relative clause*. See also in the text: **aksidan ki rive l la, kòb yo dwe peye l la, sa l te konn touche a, kòb yo ta dwe ba li a.**

4 **fè vwèl pou peyi san chapo** *to set sail for the country without hats,* i.e. *to die,* because when you die, you no longer need a hat!

5 **ap tou sèvi pou ...** *will be used instead to ... .*

Selection Nineteen

Trafik bracewos

Men kounyeya n ap pale de peyizan; n ap vin lakay pa nou[1] kote ke[2] anbochaj la[3] kontinye ap fèt e jiska prezan pa gen ankenn kominike ofisyèl ki soti sou zafè sa a. Ministè Travo Sosyal[4] pa di ankenn anyen[5], ni gouvènman an jeneral, men, nou aprann patikilyèman nan zòn sidès la, se pa de peyizan[6] ke y ap anbake sou ti bato pou voye yo al koupe kann nan batèy nan peyi panyòl. Se konsa genyen KOJEREL ki se Komite Jèn pou Relèvman Marigo[7] ki pwoteste ak tout fòs li devan zak represyon ke oun sèjan Fòs Ame Dayiti yo rele Sentilè Jan Pyè ap fè manm li yo sibi. Ladan yo genyen Enso Kowachi, yo kraze msye[8] anba baton, kounyeya se lopital li ye nan vil Jakmèl[9].

Depi jou ki te twa novanm nan, sèjan Sentilè ap òganize trafik brasewos sou je tout moun[10] nan bouk nan, dapre sa nòt de près[11] la presize. Chak jou se senk, sis, sèt ti bato ki chaje avèk moun ki ap pati ale nan peyi panyòl de fason ilegal dapre sa ke jèn sa yo konnen. Sèjan an, dapre sa yo di, touche on afè de san senkant dola pou chak bato ki rive kite pò Marigo a.

Semèn pase a, devan sitirasyon grav sa a, gen Enso, li menm, ki se youn jèn ki ap milite nan mouvman sa a, te denonse[12] trafik sa a ki ap fèt nan Radyo Eksprès, nan vil Jakmèl. Sèjan twouve li vekse[13], li arete li, e li kase tèt msye, li mare l, li maspinen l anba kout baton e li lage li twa ka mò. Kou wèl ye la, li kouche sou kabann lopital, nan lopital Sen Michèl nan vil Jakmèl, toujou dapre sa nòt de près la presize.

Dapre dènye ransèyman nou genyen, dapre sa nòt la di, sèjan Sentilè fè konnen ke otorite yo voye l al pran youn ti repo nan youn lòt pòs, siman, dapre sa jèn yo panse, pou l kapab al jwi lajan ke l te fin pran an, paske yo pa pini l pou zak sa yo ke l te fè. Konsa yo mande tout òganizasyon nan peyi a pou tabli solidarite ansanm avèk yo pou yo kapab jwenn jistis pou jèn sa a ke yo maspinen.

Sa fè dezyèm jèn nan zòn sa a ke yo maspinen anba kou poutèt ke yo t ap denonse gen trafik ki ap fèt k ap voye Ayisyen al koupe kann de fason ilegal nan peyi Repiblik Dominikèn[14].

Vocabulary

anbochaj	recruiting (var. of **anbochay**)	koupe	cut (vb.)
prezan	present (time)	kann	sugarcane
pa ... ankenn*	no + n., not ... any	batèy	sugarcane workers' camp
kominike	statement	komite	committee
ofisyèl	official	relèvman	recovery
gouvènman	government	fòs	strength
anbake	embark	represyon	repression
bato	boat	sèjan	sergeant

ame	arm (vb.)	baton	stick
sibi	undergo, suffer	mò	dead
ladan	among	kou wèl ye la	right now
msye	man; 3s pronoun	kouche	lie (down)
baton	stick	dènye	last (adj.)
brasewos	braceros (Sp.) (sugarcane cutters)	ransèyman	information
		repo	rest
je	eye	siman	surely
bouk	small town	panse	think
presize	say, clarify	jwi	enjoy
sèt	seven	fin*	have just
pati	leave (vb.)	pini	punish
dola	dollar	tabli	establish
grav	serious	solidarite	solidarity
milite	militate	jistis	justice
mouvman	movement	dezyèm	second (adj.)
denonse	denounce, inform on	poutèt ke	because
twouve	find (vb.)	ilegal	illegal
vekse	annoy, upset	Repiblik Dominikèn	Dominican Republic
maspinen	to beat (someone) up		

Notes

1 **lakay pa nou** emphatic possessive*, as the previous news item dealt with another country.

2 **kote ke** the **ke** is not necessary, as **kote** is the locative relative pronoun*.

3 **anbochaj la** i.e. to work in sugarcane fields of the Dominican Republic. See also Selections 13, 26, 40.

4 **Ministè travo sosyal** should be **Ministè travay ak afè sosyal**, *Ministry of Labor and Social Affairs.*

5 **ankenn anyen** double negative for emphasis.

6 **se pa de peyizan** i.e. there are many more than two!

7 **Marigo Marigot** a town in southern Haiti, approximately 40 miles from the border with the Dominican Republic.

8 **msye** sometimes used as the equivalent of **li.**

9 **Jakmèl Jacmel** a town approximately 20 miles to the west of Marigot.

10 **sou je tout moun sou** does not mean *under* in HC; this is a careless translation from Fr. HC would be **anba** or **devan.**

11 **nòt de près** the **de** is a translation of the Fr. **note de presse**.

12 **te denonse** should be **ki te denonse**.

13 **sejan twouve li vekse** i.e. *the sergeant was vexed.* **li** is reflexive*, **vekse** has the passive reading*.

14 **Repiblik Dominikèn** adj. is in feminine as it is taken from French, **la République Dominicaine.**

Selection Twenty

Rapò Gouvènman an sou masak ventnèf novanm nan

Gen youn rapò ke gouvènman KNGP[1] a te kòmande dat sa a[2], e ki te sòti tout dènyèman -- ou te tande li -- ke jeneral Pwospè Avril[3] pibliye. Li menm, li pa jwenn koupab, oubyen si li jwenn koupab, li pa konnen yo, paske jeneralman, se tout moun ki gen lè akize nan zafè sa a, dapre sa rapò ankèt la fè konnen sou masak ventnèf novanm. Moun yo lonje dwèt plis sou li[4] oubyen enstitisyon se KEP[5] a li menm ki pat do[6] òganize eleksyon etan done[7] klima kraze brize ki te gen lan peyi a anvan eleksyon dapre sa ke rapò a di. Yo lonje youn ti dwèt tou sou Ministè Enfòmasyon ki li menm li pat bay bon jan enfòmasyon avèk tout zouti ke l gen lan men l pou te evite sa te rive e nan rapò sa a tou yo te lonje dwèt sou komisè gouvènman, madanm Mirèy Zamò Plivyòz, ansanm avèk lapolis ki pat fè travay yo byen.

Men, an jeneral, tout chay la te tonbe sou do KEP a pou jan ke li te kondwi zafè eleksyon, dapre sa rapò a te di. AFP[8] ki ap fè kòmantè sou sa, li di ke jiska prezan yo pa janm di ki ès moun nan rapò a[9] ki[10] te fè zak sa yo, oubyen ki te kòmande yo alòske nan laprès la yo te gentan bay non moun ki te kòmande pou te fè zak sa yo kò ansasinay[11] sou moun sa yo ki te de inosan ki ta pral vote.

Kidonk ventnèf novanm mil nèf san katreven uit ap fè youn anne depi ke masak lan te fèt. Gouvènman dekrete jounen sa a youn jounen dèy nasyonal kote[12] --. Plizyè òganizasyon, òganizasyon ki ap defann dwa moun yo, pa vle ke pèp la bliye dat sa a; ap gen seremoni k ap fèt nan tout peyi a.

Vocabulary

kòmande	order (vb.)	klima	climate
dat	date, day	jan	kind, type
dènyèman	recently, lately	zouti	tool
pibliye	publish	evite	avoid
koupab	guilty	komisè	prosecutor
oubyen	or	lapolis	police
jeneralman	generally	chay	weight, cargo
genlè*	seem	tonbe	fall (vb.)
akize	accuse	do	back (n.)
ankèt	inquiry	kondwi	lead (vb.)
masak	massacre (n.)	kòmantè	comment (n.)
ventnèf	twenty nine	gentan	already
lonje	hold out, stretch out	kò	corps
dwèt	finger	ansasinay	assassination
lonje dwèt sou	to point a finger at	de*	some
do*	should, must	inosan	innocent
etan done	given	vote	vote (vb.)

dekrete	declare, decree (vb.)	defann	defend
dèy	mourning	dwa moun	human rights
plizyè	several	seremoni	ceremony

Notes

1 **KNGP Konsèy Nasyonal Gouvènman Pwovizwa**, *National Council of Provisional Government* .

2 **dat sa a** i.e. 29 November; the 1987 elections, held on that date, were suspended after a massacre of the would-be voters. See Wilentz 323. See also Selections 14, 31, 38.

3 **Pwospè Avril** president of Haiti September 1988 - March 1990.

4 **moun ... sou li moun** and **li** are coreferential, **li** being the object of a preposition within a relative clause*.

5 **KEP Konsèy Elektoral Pwovizwa**, *Provisional Electoral Council.*

6 **do** var. of **dwe** *.

7 **etan done** Fr. **étant donné** *given.*

8 **AFP Agence France Presse**, the French newswire service.

9 **nan rapò a** would be better placed after **di.**

10 **ki ès moun ... ki** Fr. translation; should be **ki lès moun ... ki***.

11 **fè ... kò ansasinay** assassinate as a group (i.e. death squad assassinations).

12 **kote** this is a mistake on the part of the announcer.

Selection Twenty-One

Grafiti 1

Nou vle yon lidè ki pap van[1] peyi a. Nou vle Luc B. Innocent[2].

Vocabulary

lidè	**leader**	vann	**sell**

Notes

1 **van** IPN spelling is **vann** .

2 **Luc B. Innocent** French spelling of name. He was a presidential candidate in the elections of November 87, who was killed in October 88, accused of heading a guerrilla commando unit entering Haiti from the Dominican Republic.

Selection Twenty-Two

Timoun mandyan ak Lafanmi Selavi

Anpil timoun ap kite pwovens yo antre nan kapital la pou yo vin chèche lavi. Anpil timoun sot Okap vin mete sou sa k genyen k ap trimen nan kapital lan, ki ap mal viv, sa ki, chans pou yo, jwenn youn ti plas nan Lafanmi Selavi[1]. Timoun sa yo ap vin gwosi sa k la deja; anpil mizè an plis. Annou koute kolaboratè nou Jan Loran ki t al eseye pran kontak ak pil timoun sa yo k ap sot nan provens vin mete sou sa k la deja.

Youn makòn timoun, senk a set konsa, monte sou do youn bis Kap-Pòtoprens nan estasyon Okap pou antre Pòtoprens lan[2]. Rive nan Pilbowo[3], chofè a ki siprann ti mesye sa yo, fè yo desann, yo menm bò kote pa yo, pase pye yo sou[4] Twa Vyèj[5], youn lòt bis Okap-Pòtoprens, ki te an pàn sou wout lan. Ti mesye sa yo ki kap genyen sòti sèt pou rive nèf an konsa, pa gen ni de ni twa lwa danse[6] nan tèt yo[7], Pòtoprens, kapital peyi Dayiti an. Ki sa y ap vin fè? Twa ladan yo, Dyesen, Doudou, avèk lòt konpayèl yo, te aksepte reponn nou:

"Ki bò ou soti la?"

"Okap"

"Ki bò ou prale kounyeya?"

"Pòwoprens[8]."

"Ki sa ou pral fè Pòtoprens?"

"M pral mande."

"Ou pral mande? Eske manman ou oubyen papa ou konn kote ou prale, kote ou ale?"

"Non, yo te konnen se Okap mwen ye."

"Se moun ki bò ou ye?"

"Pò Mago[9]."

"Depi ki lè ou kite Pò Mago w al Okap?"

"Depi lòt jou, ane pase."

"Depi ane pase?"

"Wi."

"E se ki laj ou gen kounyeya?"

"M pa konn laj an m[10]."

"Ou pa konn laj ou. Poukisa w ap kite Okap pou ou antre Pòtoprens?"

"Anyen."

"Pou anyen? Men ou gen on bagay ki fè ou pa ka ret Okap? Sa k fè ou pa ret Okap?"

"Anyen."

"Se mande ou tap mande Okap tou?"

"Wi."

"Lè ou rive Pòtoprens w ap tou rete[11]?"

"Wi."
"Men si ou wè ou mande Pòtoprens, ou pa jwenn, sa w ap fè?"
"Anyen, n ap jwenn, n ap manje."
"En?"
"N ap jwenn."
"Se kòman yo rele w?"
"Dyesen."
"Dyesen?"
"Wi."
"Manman ou la[12], papa ou la?"
"Wi."
"Se konbyen pitit manman ou genyen?"
"Li genyen onz."
"Onz pitit. Se ou ki pi piti?"
"Wi."
"E ou menm, se kòman yo rele ou?"
"Doudou."
"Kòman?"
"Doudou"
"Se ki bò ou pral la, Doudou?"
"Pòtoprens."
"Se moun ki bò ou ye?"
"Moun Lenbe[13]."
"Moun Lenbe. Depi ki lè ou Okap?"
"Depi lòtre jou."
"Depi lòtre jou?"
"Wi."
"Sa ou pral fè Pòtoprens?"
"M pral mande."
"Ou pral mande. Eske manman ou ak papa ou konnen ou kite Okap ou pral Pòtoprens?"
"Wi, mwen te di sa anvan m ale." [...]
"Lè ou di yo sa, sa yo di ou?"
"Yo pa di m anyen."
"Men lè ou rive Pòtoprens si gen lòt ti moun ki kale ou, ou pa gen moun Pòtoprens[14], kisa w ap fè?"
"M a prale, m ap vini lakay an m."
"W ap vin lakay ou?"
"Wi"
"Men èske ou kwè lè ou rive Pòtoprens, ou mande, gen moun k ap ba w?"
"Wi."
"Wi, gen moun k ap ba w?"

"Wi."

Sou tout wout Pilbowo an, ou jwenn timoun sa yo ap kouri dèyè bis, mande senk kòb dis kòb -- sa yo rele ekzòd riral lan[15]: pati kite zòn kote w ap viv nan, tonbe nan fè eksprès sou kamyon[16] k ap antre nan vil Okap. Rive nan vil Okap, bagay la sanble pa mache kòm sa dwa, ousnon, lòt ta pote nouvèl bay yo kòman sa ye Pòtoprens, yo pa mande rete[17]. Eske timoun sa yo gen moun Pòtoprens? Non. Ki kote y ap desann?

Younn landan yo te reponn nou; lè moun ap dòmi anba galri Pòtoprens, yo pa fè w peye pou sa. Poukisa yo pa ret ak manman yo, chanje bèt[18], fè jaden ak papa yo?

Yo reponn nou, zòn lakay yo fin depafini, tout sa fanmi yo te genyen fin pase, alòs youn moun se met kò w deyò pou jwenn ak lavi an. Timoun sa yo vin gonfle nan kapital Pòtoprens -- bann ti moun ki te deja ap drive pil sou pil nan move kondisyon[19].

Vocabulary

timoun	child	an pàn	broken down
pwovens	province	kap*	be able, can
antre	go in, enter	rive	arrive
kapital	capital	sòti X (pou)	
chèche	seek, look for	rive X*	from X to X
sot*	leave, go out, come out	lwa	vodou spirit
mete sou	add to	danse	dance (vb.)
trimen	slave away	konpayèl	companion
chans	luck	aksepte	accept
plas	place, space	reponn	answer (vb.)
lafanmi	family	prale*	be going
gwosi	swell, grow larger	mande	beg
mizè	poverty, misery	èske*	question marker
an plis	more, in addition	manman	mother
annou*	let's (+ vb.)	papa	father
koute	listen	konn*	know
kolaboratè	colleague, workmate	non	no
kontak	contact (n.)	ye*	be
pran kontak	make contact	lè	time
makòn (always		ki lè*	when (interr.)
with **yon**)	many	wi	yes
konsa (following		m*	1s personal marker
number)	about, approximately	ret*	stay (vb.)
siprann	surprise (vb.)	manje	eat
desann	get down, go down	en	what (asking for repetition)
pàn	breakdown (vehicle, machine)	kòman	how

konbyen*	how much, how many	dòmi	sleep
pitit	child (offspring)	galri	veranda
onz	eleven	bèt	animal
kòman	what (asking for repetition)	jaden	garden, field
lòtre jou	the other day	fin*	have + vb. (perfective)
kale	beat, whip	depafini	ruin (vb.)
kwè	think, believe	alòs	so
kouri	run (vb.)	se + vb.*	have to + vb.
dèyè	behind	met*	put
dis	ten	kò	body
ekzòd	exodus	met kò + personal marker* deyò	leave, depart
riral	rural	gonfle	swell (vb.)
fè eksprès	jump, hitch a ride	bann	group
kamyon	truck	drive	drift (vb.)
ousnon	otherwise	move	bad
nouvèl	news		
desann	stay (overnight)		

Notes

1 **Lafanmi Selavi** boys' home run by Father Jean Bertrand Aristide, (nicknamed 'Titid') named after one of the boys, Selavi. For more on Aristide, see Selections 32, 38, 42.

2 **nan estasyon ...Pòtoprens lan** the definite determiner here refers to the whole noun phrase *the station [in] Cape Haitian to go to Port-au-Prince.*

3 **Pilbowo** Puilboreau, peak of a mountain in the Massif Central, between Cape Haitian and Gonaïves.

4 **pase pye yo sou** i.e. *get on.*

5 **Twa Vyèj** *Three Virgins;* buses and taptaps usually have names, often with religious connotations.

6 **lwa danse** should have **ki** before **danse.**

7 **nan tèt yo** i.e. they have only one idea in their heads, to go to Port-au-Prince. The image is of being possessed by one of the vodou **loa**, or spirits.

8 **Pòwoprens** alternative pronunciation for **Pòtoprens** (Port-au-Prince).

9 **Pò Mago** Port Margot, a town in northern Haiti.

10 **laj an m** *my age;* this form of the possessive is typical of the area of Cape Haitian in particular, and of northern Haiti in general.

11 **w ap tou rete** **tou** + verb = *take the opportunity to* + verb.

12 **manman ou la** **la** here means *alive.*

13 **Lenbe** Limbé, a town in northern Haiti approximately 15 miles from Cape Haitian.

14 **ou pa gen moun Pòtoprens** i.e. *you don't have relatives or friends in Port-au-Prince.*

15 **ekzòd riral lan** soil erosion and lack of gentle rainfall (the storms just remove even more topsoil) force peasants to try their luck in the city, where less and less work is to be found. (A recent informal estimate: 75% complete unemployment among working age males in Port-au-Prince, with not all the remaining 25% in full time employment.)

16 **fè eksprès sou kamyon** Haitian equivalent of riding a freight train.

17 **yo pa mande rete** i.e. *they don't want to stay.*

18 **chanje bèt** lit. *change the animals' [place]* i.e. to tether them in another grazing spot; also *to bring home*, or *to take out to the field*; can include e.g. watering or feeding the animals.

19 **nan move kondisyon** the desperate situation of these destitute children led many to prostitute themselves to foreign homosexuals. This is one theory of why AIDS was supposedly relatively prevalent in Haiti (though some recent statistics show that the per capita incidence is higher in, for example, the U.S.). These young boys are not themselves homosexual, and therefore later have sexual relations with women, contributing to the spread of the virus.

Selection Twenty-Three

Jal[1] Avril ap pale sou grèv la

Kouman mwen wè ... kouman m wè sa ... m ap gade ... mwen wè youn sendika ... mwen kwè se on sendika ki fè l, -- ki bay modòd la[2]. Mwen wè on sendika ki pami sendika k ap mande pou aplike konstitisyon. M gade mwen wè on sendika ki mande oun grèv jeneral pou tout peyi a nan youn afè konfli travay ki genyen lan youn ti antrepriz nan Pòtoprens. M gade, mwen wè on sendika k ap mande aplike konstitisyon, k ap mande respè dè lwa[3], k ap mande on grèv jeneral ki antre nan politik.

Men sepandan m obsève tou, ke pa gen pèsonn ki di ki sa oun sendika ye, sètadi ke -- ou konnen nou toujou gen konstitisyon an -- si ou pran konstitisyon an [...] nan zòn sendika, ki sa l di sou sendika? Li di:

"La liberté syndicale est garantie: tout travailleur des secteurs privés et publics peut adhérer au syndicat de ses activités professionnelles pour la défense exclusive de ses intérêts de travail[4] " (Article 35:3) de konstitisyon 87 tout moun renmen an[5]: answit, pi ba, li di ou : (Article 35:4) "Le syndicat est essentiellement apolitique, à but non-lucratif et non-confessionnel[6]".

Ki sa sa vle di? Sa vle di ke dapre konstitisyon an, li pat prevwa k on sendika te gen dwa ap defann lòt bagay ke "ses intérêts de travail[7]", donk nan sosyete n ap viv la, m ap pale ou de efritmen tisi sosyal la, yo panse ke se gouvènman an ki fèt pou rete dan lalwa[8], men deyò a yo pa bezwen respekte lwa, yo pa bezwen respekte konstitisyon, se la pwoblèm nan.

O, ki jan pou m apreyande[9], ki jan pou m sezi on bagay konsa; [...] bagay sa a se pou l ta konstitye on test[10] pou gade sosyete a; èske li rive lan stad pou ke, menm si youn moun ap vyole lalwa pou l obeyi l? Sa ankò pwal sèvi mwen de test, pou m wè lan ki degre de matirite[11] sosyete a rive kounyeya, e ki pral pèmèt mwen evalwe ki kantite travay gouvènman sa a gen pou l fè ...

Vocabulary

kouman	as, how	answit	next, afterwards
sendika	union (labour)	ba	low
modòd	watchword, call (to do something)	pi ba	below (in text)
pami	among	prevwa	foresee
aplike	apply	sosyete	society
konstitisyon	constitution	efritman	unravelling
konfli	conflict (n.)	tisi	fabric, material
antrepriz	company, business	fèt pou *	should
politik	politics	lwa	law
pa ... pèsonn*	not anybody, nobody	la	there (loc.)

ò	now, but, well	stad	stage, point
ki jan*	how	vyole	break (the law), violate
apreyande	apprehend	obeyi	obey
sezi	seize, grasp	matirite	maturity
konstitiye	constitute	kantite	quantity

Notes

1 **Jal** var. of **Jeneral**

2 **modòd la** i.e. for the strike. See also Selections 5, 9, 10, 11, 32, 33, 42.

3 **dè lwa** **dè** here is from Fr. **des lois**; Avril's speech is very French influenced!

4 **"La liberté ...de travail"** Fr.: *Union freedom is guaranteed: all workers of the public and private sectors can belong to the union of their professional activities for the exclusive defense of their work interests.*

5 **tout moun renmen** the 87 Constitution was approved by popular vote.

6 **"Le syndicat ...non-confessionnel"** Fr.: *Unions are essentially apolitical, not for profit and non-confessional.*

7 **"ses intérêts de travail"** Fr.: *their work interests.*

8 **dan lalwa** **dan** is Fr., **dans la loi**; see note above re. **dè lwa**.

9 **apreyande** this is taken directly from French.

10 **sèvi mwen de test** **de** is Fr., **me servir de test**.

11 **ki degre de matirite** **de** is from Fr., which requires it after expression of quantity.

Selection Twenty-Four

Lekòl Nasyonal Labacou[1] (St Jean du Sud[2]) an dekonfiti

Afè lekòl nan peyi Dayiti, se tèt fè mal! Se pa sa ki enterese gwo zouzoun yo. Sou kesyon alfabetizasyon an, ONAAC[3] pa t renmèt anyen serye. Se gwo van, tikras[4] lapli[5]. Lè Misyon Alfa[6] te vin pran mayèt la, te vin gen yon espwa, men nan 2 tan 3 mouvman, gwo chabrak legliz katolik yo depatya l.

Si nan vil yo sitirasyon an konsa, pou andeyò menm se pa pale! Gen de zòn ki pa gen lekòl ditou. Lè w resi jwenn yonn, se kay pare solèy. Leplisouvan, se anba tonèl[7] elèv yo travay.

Se konsa jèn nan blòk Labacou, yon lokalite ki chita nan komin St Jean du Sud, ap rele osekou pou lekòl nasyonal Labacou a. Depi 1980, kay ki te abrite lekòl la te kraze. Zotobre pa t janm repare l. Popilasyon an te sètoblije mete kanpe yon tonèl ak pwòp ti avwa li.

Nan mwa septanm ki sot pase a, syklòn Gilbert[8] debake, tonèl al bwa chat, li kraze an miyèt moso. Depi lè sa a, afè lekòl, se bliye sa! Nan pwen[9] moun nan otorite konstipe[10] yo ki janm parèt pou vin bay pèp la yon ti koutmen. Lekòl pèp kraze, afè k gade pèp!

Moun nan Labacou mande kouman fè se yo ti peyizan ke gwo palto yo toujou meprize pi mal pase defen chen. Eske yo pa pitit natif natal peyi a tou?
Se menmman parèyman pou lekòl nasyonal La Cahouane[11] ki chita nan zòn Port-à-Piment[12].

Kite lekòl kraze san pa janm gen reparasyon, se pwogwàm[13] depatman edikasyon nasyonal.

Vocabulary

dekonfiti	ruin (n.)
tèt fè mal	headache
gwo zouzoun	bigwig
kesyon	question
renmèt	deliver
serye	serious
ti kras	little, a bit
mayèt	power
espwa	hope (n.)
nan 2 tan 3 mouvman	in a jiffy
legliz	church
katolik	catholic
depatya	destroy (with rage)
andeyò	countryside (as opposed to town)
resi	manage (to do something), succeed (in doing something)
yonn	one (pron.)
pare	deflect
solèy	sun
leplisouvan	most often
tonèl	bower
blòk	neighborhood, block
lokalite	place (n.)
abrite	shelter (vb.)
repare	repair (vb.)

sètoblije + vb.*	have to + vb.	parèt	appear
kanpe	stand up	koutmen	hand (help)
mete kanpe	erect (vb.)	gade	concern (vb.), be (someone's) business
pwòp	own (adj.)		
avwa	savings, fortune	palto	jacket
septanm	September	gwo palto	big guy, powerful person
debake	arrive, disembark	meprize	despise
al(e) bwa chat	bite the dust, die	defen	dead
miyèt	crumb	chen	dog
moso	piece	natif natal	native
an miyèt moso	in tiny pieces	menmman	
nanpwen	there is/are no/ none ...	parèyman	exactly the same
konstipe	constipate	reparasyon	repairs

Notes

1 **Labacou** should be **Labakou**

2 **St Jean du Sud** this name is given in French.

3 **ONAAC** Fr. acronym: **Office Nationale d'Alphabétisation et d'Action Communautaire** *National Office of Literacy and Community Action.*

4 **tikras** DOKA has two words: **ti kras.**

5 **gwo van tikras lapli** i.e. 'all talk'.

6 **Misyon Alfa** Mission Alpha, the Catholic Church literacy program; see Ferguson, 136 and Wilentz, 120,177.

7 **anba tonèl** **tonèl** is a simple structure of poles supporting a thatched covering, and is a traditional place for talking in the countryside, church or school.

8 **syklòn Gilbert** should be **siklòn Jilbè**.

9 **Nan pwen** DOKA has one word.

10 **otorite konstipe** this is a pun on the Fr. expression **autorités constituées,** *established authorities.*

11 **La Cahouane** this name is given in French.

12 **Port-à- Piment** idem.

13 **pwogwàm** should be **pwogram**.

Selection Twenty-Five

Dwa moun nan Meksik

Nan peyi Meksik menm menm, se sitirasyon dwa moun ki ap bay anpil preokipasyon, kote gen plis ke mil moun ke yo asasinen depi mil nèf san katreventwa nan peyi sa a, dapre enfòmasyon òganizasyon ki ap defann dwa moun bay jodi a nan Jenèv nan peyi Laswis. Gen plis ke mil moun ke yo asasinen nan peyi Meksik pou rezon sosyal, oubyen pou rezon politik depi lanne mil nèf san katreven twa, se sa ke prezidan lig meksiken ki ap defann dwa moun nan, mesye Victor Delafuente deklare jodi a. Pami moun ki mouri yo, gen ladan yo uit san peyizan ke grandon touye yo[1] paske yo pa vle vann ti bout tè ke yo rete a; gen katreven sis pwofesè lekòl ki tap defann dwa yo; epi gen trant jounalis ladan yo. Se jounalis ki tap denonse afè kòripsyon ki ap fèt nan lapolis ansanm avèk fonksyonè gwo chabrak[2] ki ap pran kòb nan men moun ki ap vann poud dapre enfòmasyon ke li bay jodi a nan Jenèv.

Msye Delafuente fè konnen ke vyolans sa a, se pi patikilyèman ti peyizan yo ki viktim anba l paske yo menm yo pa dakò[3] pou gwo pwopriyetè grandon vin achte ti bout tè ke yo gen lan men yo. Prezidan lig meksiken ki ap defann dwa moun nan, kouwè l li ye a, ap fè youn vire nan peyi Ewòp yo pou l kapab rive fè opinyon piblik nan peyi sa yo pran konsyans ke y ap vyole dwa moun nan peyi Meksik. Li di ke li obsève la, depi ke yo te kreye asosyasyon sa a lan mwa mas mil nèf san katreven senk, kote ke y ap denonse de fason sistematik jan ke y ap vyole dwa moun nan peyi Meksik -- depi lè sa a, gen youn ti bès, dapre sa l di, nan afè kò asasinay[4] ke y ap fè sou moun k ap defann dwa yo nan peyi sa a, youn gwo peyi nan Amerik Latin nan. Konwè l ye la Delafuente fè konnen gen uit san dis peyizan ki disparèt e y ap chèche yo sou gouvènman Miguel de la Madrid la e pa janm gen ankenn anyen ki di sou sa. Li sitou fè tounen sa a nan okazyon premye desanm ki pral vin la kote genyen prezidan Salinas ki se on prezidan disèt janvye[5] ke Meksiken yo pa respekte ditou ki pral pran pouvwa a, ki pral ranplase Miguel de la Madrid ki t ap dirije peyi sa a pandan ane ki sòt pase la yo.

Vocabulary

preokipasyon	concern, worry (n.)	pwofesè	teacher
Jenèv	Geneva	kòripsyon	corruption
Laswis	Switzerland	fonksyonè	civil servant
politik	political	poud	powder, (by extension) drugs
prezidan	chairman, president	vyolans	violence
lig	league	viktim	victim
meksiken	Mexican	dakò	in agreement
deklare	declare	vire	tour (n.)
mouri	die	kouwè l li ye a	right now
touye	kill	Ewòp	Europe
rete	still have	opinyon	opinion

konsyans	awareness	Amerik Latin	Latin America
pran konsyans	become aware	konwè l ye la	right now
kreye	create	disparèt	disappear
de	in	tounen	trip (n.)
sistematik	systematic	okazyon	occasion
bès	decrease (n.)	pouvwa	power
asasinay	assassination	ranplase	replace

Notes

1 **yo** pronoun coreferential with **uit san peyizan .**

2 **fonksyonè gwo chabrak** **gwo chabrak** functions here as an adjective.

3 **yo pa dakò** i.e. *they don't want.*

4 **kò asasinay** i.e. death squads.

5 **prezidan disèt janvye** 17 January 1988 was the date of the elections won by Leslie Manigat; these elections were boycotted by a large percentage of the population, and were widely held to be fraudulent.

Selection Twenty-Six

Entèvyou ak Doktè Pol Etyèn

"Yè mwen wè on gwoup Ayisyen, ti sak yo nan tèt yo, k apral antre nan kazèn dominiken an. Anndan kazèn nan gen on gwo machin CEA[1] (oun sa yo rele patana) ki gen pou pote yo, men pandan m mande on gad dominiken, kote tout Ayisyen sa yo prale, li di m, 'An, yo pral koupe kann'. Mwen di 'Men, yo ilegal.' Li rete, li di m, 'Non non non non, lè ou tande se youn afè de kann, nou kite yo pase menm si yo ilegal.'"

"Yo pat gen moun avèk yo, yo te pou kont yo, Ayisyen yo?"

"Bon, te genyen, te genyen ... sèl Ayisyen yo ye, men gen younn mwen eseye abòde, genlè se li k te chèf twoup la, men li ... yo, yo pa vle pale."

"Men pat gen Dominiken avè yo?"

"Hen?"

"Pat gen Dominiken avèk yo, paske gen on ...?"

"Mwen pat wè Dominiken ditou, Ayisyen sèlman."

"Anhan, èske yo te pale[2] avèk yo?"

"Bon, mwen te eseye pale avè yo, men yo gen on jan pa vle pale e yo gen on jan kòm si m ta di ou, ou konnen yo vin sou teritwa dominiken an san papye, san anyen ditou, donk, yo pa vle pran chans ap pale, jis yo pase lan ti chemen krochi, yo antre lan kazèn nan."

"Dapre ou menm, doktè Etyèn, ou kwè moun sa yo, yo lage lan batèy deja?"

"Bon, e ... m pa konnen si vrèman yo lage yo lan batèy, paske l te fin apremidi[3] e tout tan kamyon patana k la pa plen, yo pap mennen yo lan batèy."

"Men èske sa ta vle di, gen anpil Ayisyen kouwèl ye la a, ki pran desizyon an pou kont kò pa yo oubyen avèk lòt moun ki ap antre sou fontyè a?"

"Bon, gen ... Ayisyen yo pa ekzanp, mwen te eseye poze younn oun kesyon, yo di m konsa ke se lavi yo pral chèche, sa vle di ke gen anpil Ayisyen ki vwayaje pou pwòp kò pa yo, paske yo pap fè anyen lòt bò a, yo bezwen chèche lavi; men gen oun bann lòt se mèsenè[4] ki sòt Sen Doming peye pa peyi a[5], ki al lan Jakmèl sitou, [...] donk yo peye youn seri de mèsenè[6] k al Jakmèl epi mèsenè yo di moun yo, swa yo pral lan otèl, swa yo pral lan kafe[7] swa yo pral koupe kann, men kondisyon yo pi bon epi moun yo menm se sa yo tap tann pou y ale."

"Bon, ki lè zafra a pral louvri la?"

"Bon, zafra pratikman ouvri, sòf kèlke santral ki ponko ouvri, men pratikman zafra ouvri. Yè menm, vis prezidan an te inogire ouvèti Osama[8]."

"Anhan"

"Well, dou[9], si ... si nou menm, kounyeya nou pa fè oun jan an Ayiti pou anpeche moun sa yo vini nan nenpòt kondisyon, ebyen se pèn pèdi, paske moun yo ap toujou bezwen vini."

"An wi, e doktè Etyèn, an menm tan ou tap pale nou talè a de youn seminè ki louvri tou e lan San Pedro de Makoris mwen kwè sou keksyon afè Ayisyen yo."

"An, bon, ekzakteman, nan San Pedro de Makoris genyen oun seminè ki rele El Batèy, se konsa yo batize tit seminè sa a. Seminè sa a ap reyalize dirèkteman nan Inivèsite Santral de Lès[10] nan lès peyi a. Achevèk Santo Domingo a, se li k te bay ouvèti a. Eben, msye fè on pakèt deklarasyon."

"Se ki sa msye di konsa?"

"Ebyen, msye di premyèman, li menm se on konesè pwoblèm Aysisyen yo ki vini nan batèy yo; msye fè konnen ke ebyen, li vrèman inakseptab, li inakseptab pou levanjil e egalman pou moral kretyèn[11], ke yo fè silans sou sitirasyon Aysisyen ap viv kounyeya nan batèy.

"Li di nou pa kab fèmen zye nou sou sitirasyon sa a, paske nan lès, gen pli de san batèy e gen pli de trant mil Ayisyen. Achevèk la kontinye pou l di, Ayisyen yo k rantre la yo rantre san papye, donk sa fasilite gouvènman dominiken an pou pa bay yo okenn posibilite[12], okenn posibilite pou yo reklame dwa yo."

Vocabulary

yè	yesterday	poze	put
sak	bag	poze oun kesyon	ask a question
apral*	be going	vwayaje	travel (vb.)
kazèn	barracks	pou pwòp kò pa yo	on their own
anndan	inside	bann (always with **yon**)	many
patana (Sp.)	flatbed truck		
gad	guard (n.)	mèsenè	mercenary
an	um (interj.)	swa ... swa ...	either ... or ...
pou kont yo	on their own	otèl	hotel
abòde	approach (vb.)	kafe	coffee; brothel
hen?	hmm?	zafra	sugar harvest
anhan	uhmm	louvri	open
teritwa	territory	pratikman	practically
papye	paper	ouvri	open
chans	chance	sòf	except
prans chans	take the/a chance	kèlke	some
jis	just, merely	santral	center
krochi	crooked, winding	ponko*	not yet
doktè	doctor	vis	vice, deputy (prefix)
lage	let out, release	inogire	inaugurate
e	uh	ouvèti	opening
apremidi	afternoon	well (Eng.)	well
mennen	take, lead	nenpòt	any, whatever
kouwèl ye la a	right now	ebyen	well (interj.)
desizyon	decision	pèn	effort
pou kont kò pa yo	on their own	pèdi	waste (vb.)

an menm tan	at the same time	konesè	connoisseur
keksyon	question	inakseptab	unacceptable
ekzakteman	exactly	levanjil	gospel
batize	baptize	egalman	equally
tit	title	moral	moral
reyalize	hold (event)	silans	silence (n.)
dirèkteman	directly	zye	eye
invèsite	university	rantre	go in
santral	central	fasilite	make easy, facilitate
lès	east	posibilite	possibility
achevèk	archbishop	reklame	demand
pakèt (after **yon**)	a lot, many		

Notes

1 **CEA Consejo Estatal del Azúcar** *State Sugar Council,* of the Dominican Republic. This organization signs contracts with the Haitian Government to hire Haitians on a seasonal basis to cut sugarcane in the Dominican plantations. See especially Lemoine 1985.

2 **èske yo te pale ...** **yo** should be **ou**.

3 **l te fin apremidi** **fin** is completive modal verb*: *completely afternoon.*

4 **mèsenè** i.e. mercenaries taking Haitians, or convincing them to go, to the Dominican Republic. See also Selections 13, 19, 40.

5 **peye pa peyi a** while a passive interpretation exists in HC, the agent (here, **peyi a**), cannot be expressed* in 'true' HC; this example is a direct translation of the Fr. equivalent.

6 **seri de mèsenè** **de** is due to Fr. influence.

7 **kafe** means *coffee,* but also *brothel,* so this could mean they will pick coffee, or work in a brothel. It is not clear, if the meaning is *brothel,* whether the Haitians do not understand the euphemism, or whether they know what awaits them.

8 **Osama** region of the Dominican Republic.

9 **well, dou ...** the speaker starts, stops, and starts again differently.

10 **Inivèsite Santral de Lès** **de** is a translation from the Fr. equivalent.

11 **moral kretyèn** the feminine form is used, as in Fr. **la morale chrétienne**.

12 **posibilite** a common form of this word is **posiblite**.

Selection Twenty-Seven

Grafiti 2

Radio Hayti intè[1] te kokobe. Sa pa di se mouri[2] li mouri pou sa. An nou mete tèt nou ansanm pou nou devlope peyi a. Twonpèt la kònen baboukèt la[3] tonbe. An nou[4] bouke fè anachi pou nou pa krible libète.

Vocabulary

kokobe	crippled	baboukèt	makeshift bridle, muzzle
devlope	develop	bouke	stop (vb.)
twonpèt	trumpet	anachi	anarchy
kònen	sound (vb.)	krible	riddle with holes

Notes

1 **Radio Hayti intè** IPN spelling is **Radyo Ayiti Entè**, a private radio station.

2 **se mouri li mouri** reduplication for emphasis*.

3 **baboukèt la** i.e. the muzzle on free speech.

4 **An nou** DOKA has **annou**.

Selection Twenty-Eight

Tire lannwit nan Kafou

Genyen youn nòt la ki sòti nan Kafou[1]. Eben, Kafou di depi kèk tan nan Pòtoprens espesyalman nan Kafou, chak jou lè nwit la pral koumanse, pandan tout lannwit nan ou tande zam otomatik k ap chante san rete. Kapital la devni youn vrè chand batay, ou ta di se nan peyi Vyetnam ou byen nan Teksas ou byen nan chan, kote pou ti krik ti krak ou tande tire.

Bon, ki moun ki ap tire konsa a? Dapre ankèt ke pati a[2] mennen, se lame Dayiti ak lapolis ki ap tire konsa, kòm kwa dire pou bay popilasyon an sekirite. An efè, si ankèt nou di laverite, lame ak lapolis demisyone de vrè misyon yo. Poukisa? Paske de enstitisyon sa yo ki ta dwe pi serye nan peyi a vin genyen ou ta di oun vrè konpòtman makout[3], paske se sèl makout Divalye yo ki te toujou ap tire pou yo te kapab kenbe pèp la lan laperèz, pou diktati Divalye a te kab pran plas li nètalkole nan peyi a. Si youn moun oubyen oun gwoup moun vle bay pèp la sekirite, se pa tire pou y ap tire tout lannwit, men se bon jan patwouy yo dwe mete sou pye, se efektif lame a ak lapolis yo dwe ogmante, se lajan militè yo ak lapolis yo dwe monte, ak mwayen lojman, ak lokomosyon, mwayen lamanjay tou yo dwe amelyore. Men kouman youn gouvènman, lame ak lapolis ta kapab bay youn pèp bon jan sekirite? Se sèlman lè y ap tire lannwit pou anpeche moun dòmi pou fè moun pantan lan dòmi, pou fè moun viv nan laperèz, nan kè sote? [...]

Bagay sa a pa gen lòt non, se endisiplin, se enkonpetans, se youn konpòtman makout. Jandam pa dwe pè nannwit; lè nèg yo ap tire konsa lannwit, se pè ke yo pè[4], se pa plis, se pa mwens, se gate bal pou granmèsi, se fè leta fè defisi alòske Ayiti se peyi ki pi pòv ki genyen lan lemonn[5].

Bagay sa a, afè ap tire tout lannwit lan, pa ka kontinye konsa; se poutèt sa Inyon Nasyonal pou Defans Demokrasi ak Dwa Moun (UNDDH[6]) nan tout peyi a mande gouvènman militè ak gran katye jeneral pou afè tire lannwit lan sispann nan kapital la, ke yo mete sou pye bon jan patwouy. Se pa tire lannwit ke pèp la vle kounyeya, men se sekirite, manje, sante ak lekòl pou l voye pitit li.

Aba tire (se nòt la k ap pale toujou) aba tire lannwit, viv bon jan patwouy lannwit! Se poutèt sa yo mande mesye militè yo nan kat kwen peyi a pou yo montre yo pi disipline, pi vijilan sou pwoblèm ensekirite a. Inyon Nasyonal pou Defans Demokrasi ak Dwa Moun (UNDDH) mande Gran Katye Jeneral Fòs Lame Dayiti pou bay mesye militè yo youn nouvo fòmasyon sou demokrasi, sou dwa moun, [...] pou pwosesis demokratik la kapab fèt pi byen nan peyi a, paske se chak moman ou tande youn militè ou byen on polis kominal ap maltrete pèp la. Militè yo dwe respekte dwa moun nan tout peyi a, se sèl garanti pou bon jan rekonsilyasyon rive fèt.

Pou pati a se Jisten Bocha, prezidan fondatè UNDDH ki siyen.

Vocabulary

nwit	night
koumanse	begin
zam	weapon, arm
otomatik	automatic
chante	sing
devni	become
vrè	real, true
chand batay	battle field
Vyetnam	Vietnam
Teksas	Texas
chan	field
krik	peep (utterance)
pou ti krik	
ti krak	for any reason at all
tire	shooting, shots; shoot
mennen	conduct (vb.)
lame	army
kòm kwa dire	supposedly
sekirite	security
efè	effect
an efè	indeed, in fact
laverite	truth
demisyone	resign
konpòtman	behavior
makout	macoute (n. and attr.)
kenbe	keep
laperèz	fear
diktati	dictatorship
bon jan	decent, adequate
patwouy	patrol (n.)
mete sou pye	set up (vb.)
efektif	size
lajan	wages
militè	soldier
mwayen	means (n.)
lojman	lodging
lokomosyon	transportation
lamanjay	food
amelyore	improve
endisiplin	lack of discipline
enkonpetans	incompetence
jandam	policeman
pè	be afraid, fear
nannwit	(at) night
mwens	less
gate	spoil, waste (vb.)
bal	bullet
pou granmèsi	for nothing, in vain
defisi	deficit
pòv	poor
lemonn	world
inyon	union
defans	defense
demokrasi	democracy
militè	military
katye jeneral	headquarters
gran katye	
jeneral	general headquarters
sispann	stop (vb.)
manje	food
aba	down with
kat	four
montre	show (vb.)
disipline	discipline (vb.)
vijilan	watchful, vigilant
ensekirite	lack of security
fòs	force
nouvo	new
pwosesis	process (n.)
demokratik	democratic
moman	moment
polis	policeman
maltrete	mistreat
garanti	guarantee (n.)
rekonsilyasyon	reconciliation
fondatè	founding, founder

Notes

1 **Kafou** Carrefour, a very populous, disadvantaged section of Port-au-Prince, known for its brothels and gambling activities.

2 **pati a** i.e. the party that sent the note.

3 **konpòtman makout** **makout** is used here as an adjective. The **tontons macoutes**, as they are known in Fr., were a militia created by François "Papa Doc" Duvalier. They terrorized the population (see Dupuy, 160,188-9,196, Wilentz, 159,171-2). The name means *bogeyman*, who supposedly comes to carry off naughty children in his **makout**, a kind of shoulder bag. See also Selections 38, 42.

4 **se pè ke yo pè** **ke*** is redundant.

5 **peyi ki pi pòv ki genyen lan lemonn** Haiti is the poorest country in the Western Hemisphere, not the world.

6 **UNDDH** French acronym: **Union Nationale pour la Défense de la Démocratie et des Droits Humains**, *National Union for the Defense of Democracy and Human Rights.*

Selection Twenty-Nine

Grafiti 3

Nou min'm[1] gène[2] la Saline[3] nou mande reconstrui[4]. Nou pa vle crase-a[5], pa pale de sa ancò[6]

O! mezanmi gade kijan yo bliye noumen'm[7] pèp la Saline. Poukisa?... Nou mande pou tout sitwayen onèt panse ak nou[8].

Vocabulary

rekonstwi	rebuild	sitwayen	citizen
mezanmi	goodness (interj.)	onèt	honest

Notes

1 **min'm** **menm** in DOKA.

2 **gène** **jèn** or **jenn** in DOKA.

3 **La Saline** Fr. spelling; one of Port-au-Prince's larger shanty towns.

4 **reconstrui** should be **rekonstwi.**

5 **crase-a** should be **kraze a.**

6 **ancò** should be **ankò.**

7 **noumen'm** note variation in spelling within text.

8 **panse ak nou** neologism; more 'creole' would be **gen yon panse pou nou** or **sonje nou.**

Selection Thirty

Grafiti 4

Nou min'm[1] gène[2] la Saline se nou yo pi maltrete min[3] nou con'n[4] valè nou.

Vocabulary

valè	value

Notes

1 **min'm** see note Selection 29.

2 **gène** see note Selection 29.

3 **min** **men** in DOKA.

4 **con'n** **konn(en)** in DOKA.

Selection Thirty-One

Ventnèf novanm nan se youn jounen dèy nasyonal

N ap retounen ankò nan dat ke pèp ayisyen an pa fèt pou yo bliye; ladan yo ventnèf novanm[1], byen antandi[2]. Gouvènman militè a dekrete ventnèf novanm youn jounen dèy nasyonal; se sa youn arete ki parèt venteyen novanm nan Pòtoprens fè konnen; arete sa a di ke drapo a jou sa a, sa vle di madi ekzakteman nan uit jou, li pap monte nèt, se nan mitan y ap monte l youn fason pou montre ke peyi a an dèy, epi tou, jou sa a pap gen travay, pap gen lekòl, kòmès pap louvri, ni faktori, tout bagay sa yo ap fèmen. Sa vle di youn jounen dèy nasyonal, youn jounen chomay tou.

Gouvènman militè a deklare ke li vle retire chapo l byen ba douvan pakèt moun sa yo ki kite lavi yo[3], alòske yo te genyen youn bout papye sèlman nan men yo pou yo te ale fè youn ak pou yo te kapab vote. Yo te fè kò ansasinay sou yo jou dimanch ventnèf novanm mil nèf san katreven sèt, alòske sèl zam yo te gen lan men yo se te youn bout papye sa yo rele bilten -- yo ta prale nan biwod vòt yo.

N ap fè ou sonje ke nan finisman semèn nan, pi presizeman samdi, nou te deja bay youn lèt ke jeneral Pwospè Avril te voye bay sektè politik nan peyi a kote l te envite yo pou yo ansanm avèk li mete pou yo kapab selebre jounen souvni sa a, pou yo pa bliye, kote l te mande, dat sa a, pou pa fè plenyen, plenyen pap bay anyen[4]; men tou pou pa tire revany. Men, li pa di ki lè ni ki bò ke y ap fè seremoni sa a, kote tou -- nan lèt sa a -- li tap poze tèt li kesyon[5]: eske yo kwè ke peyi sa a kondane pou l toujou viv menm bagay sa yo? E li menm li te reponn pwòp kesyon ke l te poze, li di manman pitit yo, timoun ki pèdi manman yo ak papa yo epi ansanm avèk lòt timoun nan peyi a ap reponn: Non. Peyi a fèt pou l jwenn youn wout pou l kapab sòti nan sa li ye. Se poutèt sa, li envite tout sektè, dapre sa l di, pou yo kapab selebre.

Nan menm lèt sa a tou li te di ke gen kesyon ki pou poze piske ventnèf novanm nan, se pa youn bagay brid sou kou[6] k te vin tonbe sou tèt pèp la, se youn seri de bagay ki fè yo te rive a[7] vent nèf novanm. La li te poze kesyon: ki ès moun ki pat fè sa pou yo te fè pou evite ke sa (pat) rive[8], ki ès moun tou ki te fè lachte, ki pat pran wòl yo pou yo te kapab defann sa, epi tou ki ès moun ki te fè erè. Se pou rezon sa yo, li te mande pou tout moun kapab ansanm selebre jounen sa a pou yo pa bliye jou ventnèf novanm nan, kote l te pale de Riyèl Vayan[9]. Men, lan lèt sa a - kouwè ke nou te fè remake l ke jeneral Pwospè Avril te voye bay sektè politik nan - pat janm gen ni mo jistis ni mo reparasyon ni rekonsilyasyon ki te ekri ladann, lèt sa a ke nou te jwenn youn kopi ke nou menm nou te li pou ou pa bò isit.

Men pandansetan sa a gen plizyè òganizasyon tankou senk òganizasyon ki ap defann dwa moun, yo menm, yo fè parèt youn kominike kote yo di kijan yo pral selebre jou ventnèf novanm sa a. Men sa l di:

Ventnèf novanm janmen janmen pa dwe janm[10] gen sa ki pou rive ankò. Nou menm òganizasyon ki ap goumen nan zafè dwa moun tankou lòt sektè ki ap lite pou chanjman nan peyi Dayiti, nou pa bliye kouman fòs tenèb yo te kraze brize nan youn larivyè san, dwa kretyen vivan ki tap fè devwa sitwayen yo nan eleksyon ventnèf novanm mil nèf san katreven sèt. Evenman sa a pral genyen youn anne depi ke l te fèt[11]; fòk tout sektè alawonnbadè ta selebre jou sa a kòmsadwatèt, dapre sa senk òganiszasyon sa yo presize. Se poutèt sa nou mande tout Ayisyen ki vle youn peyi kote lajistis avèk lalibète boujonnen, youn peyi kote ke yo respekte dwa tout kretyen vivan, pou yo pote kole nan selebrasyon jounen ventnèf novanm nan. Men pwogram jounen sila a, (sa se pwogram senk òganizasyon ki ap defann dwa moun yo):

Premyèman, pwosesyon pasifik avèk bouji limen epi siy dèy ki ap sòti nan tou kwen kapital la pou rive nan Riyèl Vayan nan maten gran bonè;

Dezyèmman, seremoni relijyèz nan non tout moun sa yo ki viktim mati yo;

Twazyèmman, mesaj pou jounen sa a: nou mande tout reprezantan an deyò yo epi nan pwovens yo pou yo bati youn pwogram konsa; nou mande pou tout lekòl konsakre jounen ventuit novanm nan kòm youn tan espesyal pou reflechi sou sa ki te pase jounen ventnèf novanm mil nèf san katreven sèt la; nou mande pou drapo tout lekòl avèk biwo leta yo monte demi ma jou sila a; nou mande radyo avèk televizyon pou yo pase mizik dèy avèk kozman sou jounen ventnèf novanm nan; apati dat sila a n ap rele ventnèf novanm nan kalandrye demokrat yo Jou Mati Demokrasi nan peyi Dayiti; nou dakò pou nou rele Riyèl Vayan Ri dè Mati[12], dapre sa senk òganizasyon sa yo presize. Nou pa gen dwa bliye mati ventnèf novanm yo. Youn pèp san memwa se youn pèp ki san demen.

Moun ki siyen se Rezo Nasyonal ki ap Defann Dwa Moun, madanm Simonn Kastra (RENADDWAM); Sant Ekimenik Dwa Moun, se Sorèl Yasent; Enstiti Mobil Ediksasyon Demokratik, IMED, se Rozalvo Blèz; Sant Pwomosyon Lafontan Jozèf ki ap Defann Dwa Moun, se Renan Pyè; epi avèk Lig Ayisyen ki ap Defann Dwa Moun, se mèt Jozèf Maksi ki siyen pwogram sa a nan okazyon premye anivèsè ventnèf novanm mil nèf san katreven sèt kote ke eleksyon sa a te fini nan san pèp la. Jiska prezan, moun pa konnen egzakteman konbyen moun ki mouri, yo estime a plis ke san moun ki te mouri jou sa a.

Vocabulary

retounen	return (vb.)	finisman	end (n.)
byen antandi	of course	presizeman	precisely
arete	decree (n.)	samdi	Saturday
parèt	be published, appear	envite	invite
drapo	flag	selebre	celebrate
madi	Tuesday	souvni	memory (of event)
chomay	unemployment, idleness	plenyen	complain
retire	take off, remove	revany	revenge
ak	act (n.)	tire revany	take revenge
bilten	ballot	kondane	condemn
vòt	vote (n.)	brid	bridle
biwod vòt	polling station	kou	neck
sonje	remember	lachte	cowardliness

fè lachte	behave like a coward	pasifik	peaceful
wòl	role	bouji	candle
pran wòl	play a role	limen	light (vb.)
defann	prevent	siy	sign (n.)
erè	mistake (n.)	bonè	early
kouwè	like, as	relijyèz	religious
kopi	copy (n.)	mati	martyrdom, martyr
li	read	mesaj	message
pa bò isit	here	reprezantan	representative (n.)
pandansetan	meanwhile	bati	build
janmen	never	konsakre	devote
lite	fight, struggle (vb.)	espesyal	special
chanjman	change (n.)	reflechi	reflect
tenèb	darkness, evil	ma	mast
larivyè	river	demi ma	half mast, half staff
kretyen vivan	person, human being	televizyon	television
devwa	duty	mizik	music
evenman	event	kozman	talk (n.)
fòk	it is necessary	apati	starting from
fòk (+ subj. + vb.)*	subj. + must/should + vb.	kalandrye	calendar
alawonnbadè	all together	demokrat	democrat
kòmsadwatèt	as is fitting, in the right way	memwa	memory
lajistis	justice	rezo	network
lalibète	liberty	ekimenik	ecumenical
pote kole	join together, stick together	pwomosyon	advancement, promotion
pwosesyon	procession	anivèsè	anniversary

Notes

1 **ventnèf novanm** the anniversary of the election massacre in 1987. See also Selections 14, 20, 38.

2 **byen antandi** this is a direct borrowing of the Fr. **bien entendu**, lit. *well understood.*

3 **kite lavi yo** better would be: **pèdi lavi yo** or **kite lavi a**.

4 **pap bay anyen** i.e. *will not do any good.*

5 **poze tèt li kesyon** **tèt li** is reflexive* *(himself).*

6 **brid sou kou** lit. *bridle on [the] neck [of the horse],* i.e. the horse is bolting; hence, something sudden or unexpected.

7 **rive a ...** the **a** is a translation from the French **arriver à** *to arrive at.*

8 **pou evite ke sa pat rive** **pat** is a mistake in the reading, and should be ignored.

9 **Riyèl Vayan** This is the street in Port-au-Prince (**Ruelle Vaillant**), the site of a school used as a polling station, where a large number of Haitians were massacred as they lined up to vote on the morning of the elections; shortly afterwards, Carlos Grullón, a Dominican journalist, was also killed there, and two US journalists were wounded. (See Wilentz, 323).

10 **janmen janmen pa dwe janm ...** i.e. *should never ever happen again.*

11 **pral genyen youn anne depi ke l te fèt** i.e. *it will be one year since it happened.*

12 **Ri dè Mati** in Fr. **Rue Des Martyrs** *Street of Martyrs.*

Selection Thirty-Two

Jan Ogis Mezye[1] ap pale sou grèv jeneral la

Onon tout travayè ayisyen, onon tout òganizasyon popilè, onon ouvriye, peyizan, etidian, chofè, onon tout moun k ap lite nan kan pèp la, kominike Minis Enteryè parèt pou l di grèv la ilegal. Kominike sa a pa gen okenn sans, li denye tou fondman[2].

Pawòl Jeneral Pwospè Avril di sou televizyon nasyonal, kom kwa dire, grèv la se on grèv ki ilegal, pawòl sa yo pa gen okenn sans. Jeneral la fè konnen ke li etone anpil lè l wè kèk òganizasyon ak asosyasyon lanse on modòd de grèv[3] pou paralize on peyi poutèt on ti antrepriz Aciérie d'Haïti[4], e nou mande si tout ouvriye pa ouvriye, si tout ouvriye pa gen menm dwa.

Eh, grèv la lanse pou sis pwen; sis pwen sa yo[5], nou mande pou gouvènman satisfè yo:

Premyè pwen an, se kont patwon k ap revoke ouvriye nan faktori e patikilyèman nou pale nan antrepriz Comme Il Faut[6] avèk Aciérie d'Haïti, dènye a kote yo jete sou pave ak fòs gwo ponyèt plis ke senkant uit ouvriye.

Dezyèm pwen an, se kont gwo chabrak nan legliz ki vle depòte pè Aristid[7], e tout moun konnen ke pè Aristid se senbòl pòv yo. Se on travay serye l ap fè nan mitan mas pèp la e li lye ansanm enterè materyèl avèk espirityèl. Eske dezyèm pwen an pa gen rezon, kote pè Aristid te fin viktim de makout, masak Sen Jan Bosko a[8], olye pou yo ta ba l pwoteksyon, olye pou yo ta mande pou jije Frank Wome[9], evèk nan legliz yo, kounyeya se pè Aristid y ap chèche depòte.

Twazyèm pwen an, se kont makout k ap ansasinen pèp la chak swa, ekstradisyon e jijman Frank Women[10]

e lè nou konsidere chak swa nan mitan pèp la nan Pòtoprens e tout kote nan pwovens klima ensekirite ki tabli sou tout peyi a,

lè n konsidere Frank Women, patisipasyon dirèk li nan masak Sen Jan Bosko a, lè li te fè deklarasyon, di l reskonsab, li rekonèt se li menm ki chèf de bann avèk tout lòt akolit li yo ki al lan peyi san chapo, nou kapab site Gwo Chilè, Gwo Lachat[11] eks.,

èske Frank Women - èske pwen sa a pa jis? E lè Jeneral Pwospè Avril pale nan televizyon, yo poze l keksyon sou Frank Women, li di ke Frank Women se on sitwayen ki solisite azil politik on anbasad[12] ba li e dapre youn seri de konvansyon Ayiti siyen avèk peyi etranje, yo dwe respekte dwa dazil.

Vocabulary

onon	in the name of	kan	camp
travayè	worker	sans	sense, meaning

denye	devoid of
fondman	foundation
pawòl	word
kòm kwa dire	that is to say
etone	surprise (vb.)
lanse	issue (vb.)
satisfè	satisfy
revoke	fire, dismiss
dènye a	the latter
jete	throw
pave	street, paving stone
ponyèt	wrist
depòte	deport
pè	priest, father (in church)
senbòl	symbol
lye	connect, join
enterè	interest (n.)
materyèl	material
espirityèl	spiritual
gen(yen) rezon	be right, be correct
olye	instead of
pwoteksyon	protection
jije	judge (vb.)
evèk	bishop
twazyèm	third
ansasinen	asassinate
swa	evening
ekstradisyon	extradition
jijman	trial
konsidere	consider
patisipasyon	participation
dirèk	direct
rekonèt	admit, recognize
chèf de bann	ringleader
akolit	acolyte
al(e) lan peyi san chapo	to die
site	cite
eks.	etc.
jis	just, fair
solisite	ask for
azil	asylum
anbasad	embassy
etranje	foreign
dwa dazil	right of asylum

Notes

1 **Jan Ogis Mezye** activist in the CATH. See note Selection 9.

2 **denye tou fondman** this is taken directly from the Fr. **denié de tout fondement**.

3 **modòd de grèv de** is a translation from the French. For the general strike, see also Selections 5, 9, 10, 11, 23, 32, 33, 42.

4 **Aciérie d'Haïti** (Fr.) Haitian steelworks.

5 **sis pwen sa yo** the news item, however, only gives us three.

6 **Comme Il Faut** (Fr.) national tobacco company.

7 **pè Aristid** Father Aristide, Salesian priest, champion of the poor, presidential candidate in December 1990 elections. The traditional Catholic Church hierarchy tried to have him deported after the attack on his church. See also Selections 22, 38, 42.

8 **masak Sen Jan Bosco** Aristide's church, St Jean Bosco, was attacked by macoutes during Sunday mass on 11 September 1988; members of the congregation were murdered in the church, and Aristide went into hiding for several weeks. See also Selections 38, 42.

9 **Frank Women** Franck Romain, duvalierist, mayor of Port-au-Prince at the time of the church massacre, allegedly admitted being the instigator of the massacre.

10 **se kont makout ... ekstradisyon e jijman ...** this is a mistake in the broadcast; presumably, the point is against the macoutes, but asking for Romain's extradition and trial.

11 **Gwo Chilè, Gwo Lachat** participants in the church massacre; they were later recognized by the crowd guarding the church, and received the "necklace" (burning tire around neck).

12 **on anbasad** the embassy of the Dominican Republic.

Selection Thirty-Three

Kominike Ministè Enfòmasyon sou grèv la

Genyen Ministè Enfòmasyon avèk Kowòdinasyon ki fè parèt yon kominike lendi venteyen novanm lan, kote yo di ke gouvènman repiblik la, li note avèk kè kontan ke tout aktivite yo te reprann nòmalman jodi lendi venteyen novanm nan, malgre plizyè apèl yo te lanse pou te kapab paralize lavi nasyonal la avèk youn grèv jeneral ilegal[1]. Devan kalte konfyans sila a ke tout yo akòde gouvènman an lan tout garanti ke l te pwomèt, gouvènman an, li felisite diferan sektè konsène yo pou temwayaj kote l wè moun yo vrèman sou - nan[2] zafè politik yo sanble yo granmoun, yo gen sans responsablite sivik tou. Li remèsye patikilyèman mond[3] ouvriye yo, ki, malgre difikilte nan transpò nan kòmansman matine an, pa te kite yo manipile. Men, yo te konprann nan konjonkti ekonomik ki difisil sila a, travay la se sèl vwa sali[4] pèp la.

Li remèsye tou endistriyèl avèk kòmèsan, chofè transpò an komen yo, reskonsab lekòl, paran avèk elèv e tout moun ki te kontinye aktivite yo lan lari jodi a, kote yo siyifye, yo montre klèman volonte yo pou yo pa riske - en - konpwomèt lapwosesis[5] dyalog avèk kowoperasyon ki kòmanse pou byen nasyon an. Se pou sa ke gouvènman an, li reyafime a tout moun[6] detèminasyon l pou l kapab pouswiv, kontinye nan chemen ke l adopte a, e kontinye pwopoze dyalog menm a moun sila yo ki jodi a ankò, yo kwè ke se youn devwa pou yo pou yo detounen yo de chemen dyalog sila a.

Se youn nòt ki pote siyati Minis Enfòmasyon avèk Kowòdinasyon, msye Antoni Vijini Sen Pyè.

Vocabulary

kowòdinasyon	coordination	kite*	let, allow
malgre	in spite of	manipile	manipulate
apèl	call, appeal (n.)	konjonkti	juncture
kalte	kind (n.)	ekonomik	economic
konfyans	confidence	vwa	way
akòde	grant (vb.)	sali	salvation
pwomèt	promise (vb.)	endistriyèl	industrialist
felisite	congratulate	komen	common
diferan	different	an komen	in common, public
temwayaj	evidence, proof	paran	parent
granmoun	adult	siyifye	signal (vb.)
responsablite	responsability	klèman	clearly
sivik	civic	volonte	willingness
remèsye	thank (vb.)	riske	risk (vb.)
difikilte	difficulty	konpwomèt	compromise (vb.)
kòmansman	beginning (n.)	lapwosesis	process
matine	morning	dyalog	dialogue

kowoperasyon	cooperation	adopte	adopt
byen	good (n.), wellbeing	pwopoze	propose
nasyon	nation	ankò	still (adv.)
detèminasyon	determination	detounen	turn away
pouswiv	follow		

Notes

1 **youn grèv jeneral ilegal** see also Selections 5, 9, 10, 11, 23, 32, 42.

2 **sou - nan** announcer is rephrasing.

3 **mond** **mond** is Fr. translation, *world* is usually **lemonn**.

4 **sèl vwa sali** both **vwa** and **sali** are direct French borrowings; a more truly 'creole' way of expressing this would be: **sèl chemen pou pèp la sove**.

5 **lapwosesis** should be **pwosesis.**

6 **li reyafime a tout moun** the **a** is not HC, and is due to French translation.

Selection Thirty-Four

Vaksinasyon: enpòtans li lan peyi a

Lafwa dènye mwen te pale konbyen prevansyon konte lan yon peyi tankou Ayiti, paske kouwè mwen te di Ayiti twò pòv pou l trete tout maladi ki genyen lan milye a. Donk li toujou pi bon pou nou chèche evite maladi anvan ke maladi frape lan pòt nou.

Men nou konnen lan peyi a moun ap mouri tankou mouch akòz de maladi: timoun tankou granmoun. Pou timoun yo menm se pa pale[1]. Koklich ap fè je yo sòti; tetanòs ap fè yo redi; difteri ap toufe yo; laroujòl ap ravaje yo. E leplisouvan malgre remèd fèy[2], remèd doktè, remèd ougan[3], timoun sa yo al lan peyi san chapo paske kouwè m ap di n ankò li toujou pi difisil pou trete vye maladi sa yo.

Se sa ki fè lasyans medikal anplwaye vaksinasyon pou li pran devan defason ke tout vye maladi sa yo ka rete lan kokiy yo. Se pa vaksinasyon sèlman ki kab elimine maladi lan peyi a. Gen anpil lòt bagay ki konte tou tèlke bon gouvènman ak bon pwogram sanitasyon, edikasyon, distribisyon sante toupatou lan peyi. Sepandan nou kab di ke vaksinasyon se yonn lan bagay ki kab anpeche vye jèm maladi fin touye[4] tout moun lan peyi an[5]. E lò n ap pale de vaksinasyon n ap pale de yon vaksinasyon total kapital[6] ki pa repoze sèlman sou charite ke lòt peyi ap fè nou; n ap pale de yon vaksinasyon sistematik ke pwòp gouvènman pa nou fèt pou li fè ak lajan peyi a k ap sòti lan pòch malere ak malerèz. Genyen yon pwovèb[7] ki di: lè ou pa gen manman, ou tete grann. Se yon fason pou nou di w ke nenpòt ki pwogram vaksinasyon ap toujou kab ride w sove yon pitit si ou gen chans jwenn li pou pitit sa a.

Sa k vaksinasyon an? Se yon piki oubyen yon remèd k ap fè yon kretyen vivan evite sèten maladi. Ann Ayiti[8], tetanòs, koklich, difteri, laroujòl, polyo, malmouton ap fè anpil dega kay timoun. Yon jan pou nou prevni pwoblèm sa yo se vaksine[9] timoun yo. Menm fanm ansent fèt pou vaksine kont tetanòs pou evite tetanòs kay tibebe a. Menm granmoun ta fèt pou li vaksine tou. Men lan peyi nou an toutotan pa gen yon pwogram solid, natif natal, nou fèt pou nou bay timoun yo yon tichans[10] dabò, paske kò yo pi ròròt[11] e yo plis san defans kont maladi.

Si nou voye je n sou foto[12] ki tou pre a, n a wè 2 timoun k ap soufri ak maladi polyo. Mis oubyen vyann do ak kou yo vin tou rèd. Yo pa menm kab chita byen. Nou mèt di si manman oubyen papa yo t al vaksine yo kont maladi a mizè sa a pa ta rive timoun sa yo.

Donk se konsa apati de de (2) mwa chak timoun fèt pou yo koumanse resevwa vaksen kont difteri, tetanòs, koklich ak polyo. A kat (4) mwa, yo dwe resevwa yon dezyèm dòz vaksen kont menm maladi sa yo e a sis (6) mwa y a resevwa yon twazyèm dòz kont difteri, koklich ak tetanòs. Ozanviron[13] kinz[14] (15) mwa se vaksen kont laroujòl, malmouton ak saranpyon yo ta fèt pou resevwa. Fòk mwen di w ke tout orè vaksen sa yo gen dwa chanje selon ijans sitiyasyon an e se sa ki fè fòk nou koute pawòl doktè lan zòn nou ye a pou nou konnen ki lè pou nou mennen timoun yo al pran vaksen. Paske lò nou sonje ke difteri sa nou rele ankò kroup la gen dwa toufe yon timoun an de tan twa mouvman, nou menm papa ak manman ta fèt pou pran oserye anpil afè vaksinasyon an pou nou pa di si m te konnen.

Men kounye a genyen yon maladi chabon k ap tonbe sou do malere anplis de tout lòt mizè yo genyen. Eske li pa ta bon si te gen yon pwogram sistematik pèmanan de vaksinasyon kont maladi chabon lan peyi a pou pwoteje tout moun k ap travay ak zannimo, sitou moun k ap travay lan chan ki kontamine ak jèm maladi chabon an, paske vaksen kont maladi sa a ekziste tou?

Fòk nou konnen gen de ti pwoblèm vaksinasyon gen dwa bay. Men pwoblèm sa yo ap toujou pi piti parapò a benefis vaksen yo bay lè yon kretyen vivan pran li. Doktè oubyen enfimyè ap toujou kab fè w konnen ti pwoblèm sa yo defason ke w kapab boule ak yo. Y a toujou kab di nou ki lè pwoblèm sa yo gen dwa rive. Sa ki pi enpòtan, se chache konnen ki lè pou mennen timoun yo al vaksine, paske se youn lan pi gwo kado ou ta kab fè yo.

Vocabulary

vaksinasyon	vaccination	distribisyon	distribution
enpòtans	importance	toupatou	everywhere
lafwa	time (instance)	jèm	germ
prevansyon	prevention	lò	when
konte	count (vb.)	totalkapital	first-rate
twò (+ adj. or adv.)	too (+ adj. or adv.)	repoze	rest (vb.)
		charite	charity
trete	treat (n.)	pòch	pocket
maladi	disease, illness	malere	poor man
milye	environment, surroundings	malerèz	poor woman
frape	knock (vb.)	pwovèb	proverb
akòz de	because of	grann	grandmother
koklich	whooping cough	ride	help (vb.)
tetanòs	tetanus	sove	save
redi	stiffen	piki	injection
difteri	diphtheria	sèten	certain
toufe	suffocate	polyo	polio
laroujòl	rubella, German measles	malmouton	mumps
ougan	vodou priest	dega	damage (n.)
vye	horrible, ugly	prevni	prevent
lasyans	science	vaksinen	vaccinate
devan	lead (position)	ansent	pregnant
defason	so that	tibebe	baby
kokiy	shell (n.)	toutotan	as long as
elimine	eliminate	solid	solid
tèlke	such as	dabò	at first
sanitasyon	sanitation	wòwòt	immature

voye je sou	glance at	oserye	seriously
pre	near	kounye a	now (var. of **kounyeya**)
soufri	suffer	chabon	coal, charcoal
mis	muscle	maladi chabon	anthrax
vyann	flesh, meat	anplis de	in addition to
rèd	stiff	pèmanan	permanent
mèt*	may	zannimo	animal
vaksen	vaccine	kontamine	contaminate
dòz	dose	ekziste	exist
ozanviwon	around, at about	parapò a	compared to
saranpyon	measles	benefis	benefit (n.)
orè	timetable	boule ak	deal with
selon	according to	chache	try (to do); seek
ijans	urgence	kado	present, gift
ankò	also, in addition	fè kado	give a gift
kroup	croup		

Notes

1 **se pa pale** i.e. *it does not bear mention.*

2 **remèd fèy** i.e. *herbal remedies.*

3 **remèd ougan** in addition to religious functions, the ougan is traditionally also the community doctor, possessing knowledge of both natural herbal and supernatural cures. While a Haitian might go to a medical doctor for treatment, if one is available (in 1967, there were 0.68 doctors for every 10,000 inhabitants -- see Dupuy, 165), they will go to the ougan first.

4 **fin touye fin** is completive modal*, referring to the future, i.e. *prevent that the horrible germs of disease will end up killing ....*

5 **lan peyi an** the nasalized form **an** is influenced by the preceding nasal in **lan.**

6 **total kapital** DOKA has one word.

7 **pwovèb** proverbs are widely used in Haiti, and are truly part of the linguistic culture.

8 **Ann Ayiti** should be **an Ayiti.**

9 **vaksine** DOKA has **vaksinen.**

10 **tichans** should be two words.

11 **ròròt** DOKA has **wòwòt.**

12 **foto** the article in *Haïti Progrès* was illustrated.

13 **ozanviron** should be **ozanviwon**; DOKA has **anviwon** only.

14 **kinz** should be **kenz.**

Selection Thirty-Five

Presizyon sou "gramè[1] kreyòl"

Si n'ap[2] ekri sou "Gramè Kreyòl", se pa paske nou pi fò pase tout mounn[3]. Nou menm tou, lè n'ap ekri kreyòl, nou kapab fè fot nan fraz-la[4], swa nan fason nou ekri youn mo. Nou menm, nou konsyan fot sa yo egziste nan kreyòl ayisyen an, epi nou veyatif bò kote pa nou. Men, nan tou kounye a[5], gen lòt mounn k'ap ekri kreyòl, sanble yo pa konsyan ditou si lanng-lan gen lwa pou yo respekte, osnon yo kareman fè esprè pou yo pa respekte lwa lanng-lan. Se poutèt sa nou wè li nesesè pou nou raple mesyedam-yo alòd detanzantan.

Depi kèk tan, nou remake "*Haiti Progrès*" chanje fason li te konn ekri kreyòl-la. Lè nou pran *Haiti Progrès* nan mwa Avril[6] 86, se pa menm jan-an kreyòl-la ekri nan Desanm 86. Enpi, nan fason nouvo sa a pou ekri kreyòl, nou wè genyen 2 gwo chanjman. Younn se sou "ti tirè", lòt la se sou "apostwòf". An nou[7] chita ansanm pou nou fè youn ti kozman[8] sou sa.

TI TIRE

Règ Kreyòl la di: "Nou kapab sèvi ak ti tirè, si nou vle, pou makònen youn mo ak kèk fòm gramè ki vini apre li, tankou:
- fòm atik defini yo: fi-a, nèg-la, pèlen-an.
- fòm adjektif posesif yo: papa-li, pitit-mwen.
- pwonon konpleman retresi yo: nèg-la di-m li te wè-m yè."

Kòm règ-la di "... si nou vle ...", nou dakò ak jounal-la lè li pa mete ti tirè-a. Pase, gen fraz menm, l'ap difisil pou makònen "detèminan"-an ak mo ki mache ak li a.

APOSTWOF:

Nan plizyè lanng tankou Franse, Angle[9], nou abitye vale youn pati son nan mo-yo lè n'ap pale. Nan Kreyòl-la tou, gen youn digdal ka kote nou vale youn pati son nan mo yo[10].

- Gen egzanp mo, nou vale youn bout epi lòt bout la rete.
    Jan ret (rete) lakay li.
    Mwen gen (genyen) dis kòb.

- Genyen lè menm, lè n'ap pale, nou vale youn pati son, men lè n'ap ekri, nou ekri tout mo a.
    Yo pal anpil. (lè n'ap ekri nou mete) Yo pale anpil.
    Tout al atè. (lè n'ap ekri nou mete) Tout ale atè[11].
    Li ganpil lajan. (lè n'ap ekri) Li gen anpil lajan.

- Men nan fòm gramè, tankou pwonon sijè, osnon lòt konpayèl vèb tankou "te", lè nou vale youn mòso son, nou mete youn apostwòf.
    M'gen dis kòb. (Mwen gen dis kòb).
    M'te vin lakay-ou, epi ou t'ap dòmi.
    Gèda pa la, l'al lekòl.

Dènye pati sa a, se youn règ ki sòti nan Lwa Otograf Ofisyèl la. Men sa Lwa-a di: "Nou kapab sèvi ak apostwòf pou pwonon sijè yo.

Egzp: M' vini rele ou, epi ou pa vini. M', n', l', se mo tankou lòt mo. Fò nou kite youn ti espas anvan nou kòmanse mo ki vini apre a".

P.B. (Pa Bliye)

Gen youn pakèt kote, menmsi se pa tout kote, nou kapab pa vle itilize apostwòf-la. Men lè sa a[12], fò nou swiv konsèy Pierre Vernet[13] ba nou an, pou nou mete tout mo-a an kè.

KI SA NOU MANDE

Bò kote pa nou, nou pa mande gwo. Menm jan nèg ayisyen fè mache sou pinnga-yo lè y'ap ekri franse, nou t'a renmen pou jounal-la respekte Lwa Septanm 79 la, espesyalman pati ki gen rapò ak keksyon "apostwòf" la.

Dezyèmman, youn nèg save gen dwa genyen pozisyon pa li sou ekritman[14] kreyòl la. Men jouk kounyeya, pi fò moun k'ap ekri kreyòl se Lwa Septanm 79 la yo swiv. Pa gen lòt otorite ankò. Si youn mounn save t'a gen youn pozisyon ki pa nan sans Lwa-a, epi li t'a vle vin fè nou lalwa, fòk t'a gen youn "Akademi Nasyonal Kreyòl" ki pou t'a kore-l. Antan sa poko rive[15], nou t'a mande pou tout ayisyen alawonnbadè respekte Lwa Ofisyèl Kreyòl la. Nou kwè sa va pèmèt nou estabilize ekritman kreyòl la pi byen pou kounyeya, epi lòt ti poblèm[16] piti yo, n'a regle yo pannan nou sou gran-chemen.

Sosyete Koukouy Seksyon Kanada
12650 68e Ave R.D.P.
Montréal, Québec HIC-IW3

Vocabulary

presizyon	clarification	enpi	and
gramè	grammar	tirè	hyphen
fot	mistake (n.)	apostwòf	apostrophe
fraz	sentence (n.)	makònen	tie together
egziste	exist	detèminan	determiner (grammatical)
veyatif	watchful, careful	mache	walk (vb.)
lang	language	mache ak	go with
kareman	openly	atik	article
esprè	purposely	defini	definite
nesesè	necessary	pèlen	trap (n.)
raple	recall	adjektif	adjective
raple alòd	call to order	posesif	possessive
mesyedam	people	pwonon	pronoun
detanzantan	from time to time		

konpleman	complement (n.) (grammatical)	konsèy	advice
retresi	postposed	kè	chorus
vale	swallow	an kè	together
son	sound (n.)	pinga*	emphatic negative for imperative form
digdal (always with **yon**)	many	mache sou pinga-yo	be very careful
egzanp	example	save	knowledgeable
atè	on the ground	pozisyon	position
ale atè	fall through, fail	ekritman	writing
sijè	subject (n.)	akademi	academy
vèb	verb	kore	secure, support (vb.)
mòso	bit, piece	antan	while
òtograf	spelling, orthography	va*	verb marker [+irrealis]
espas	space	estabilize	stabilize
menmsi	even if	pannan	while
itilize	use (vb.)	koukouy	firefly

Notes

1 **gramè** in fact, this article is about punctuation and spelling, not grammar.

2 **n'ap** the use of the apostrophe is explained in the article.

3 **mounn** spelling variation under debate: one argument is that if *n* after *a*, *e*, and *o* nasalizes the preceding vowel, but remains itself unpronounced (as in **tan** for example), to mark the pronounced *n* after a nasal vowel, a second must be added (see also **lanng** and **pinnga** in this article). DOKA has **moun, lang** and **pinga.** See chapter on HC spelling.

4 **fraz-la** the use of the hyphen is explained in the article.

5 **nan tou kounye a** should be **nan tan kounye a.**

6 **Avril** names of months are not normally written with initial capital letter.

7 **An nou** DOKA has **annou.**

8 **ti kozman** more usual is **ti koze.**

9 **Franse, Angle** names of languages are not normally written with initial capital letter.

10 **nan mo yo** note inconsistency of author in use of **ti tirè.**

11 **Tout al atè ... Tout ale atè** The form **al** is in fact seen written frequently.

12 **lè sa a** lit. *at that time*, here, *in that case.*

13 **Pierre Vernet** (Fr. spelling) director of the Center for Applied Linguistics, State University of Haiti.

14 **ekritman** this word is rare. More usual is **ekriti.**

15 **Antan sa poko rive** i.e. *until that happens.*

16 **poblèm** should be **pwoblèm.**

Selection Thirty-Six

Asanble Popilè = Pouvwa Popilè

Asanble Popilè se yon bagay ki nan tradisyon pèp ayisyen. Lè esklav yo te konn reyini pou yo diskite kijan pou yo òganize, kijan pou yo reziste e batay kont blan[1] yo, esklav yo te fòme Asanble Popilè.

Seremoni Bwa Kayiman[2] nan lannwit 14 Daou 1791, se te yon bèl ekzanp Asanble Popilè Revolisyonè pou te[3] dechouke[4] sistèm lesklavaj.

Asanble Pèp la se kote pèp la reyini pou l poze pwoblèm, pou li montre li pa dakò, pou li òganize lit li kont yon sistèm k ap toupizi l, kote li pwopoze solisyon pa l e li pran dispozisyon lite pou fè solisyon pa l pase.

Asanble Popilè revolisyonè se kote pèp la refize aksepte tout pisans yon ti ponyen moun k ap lay[i]te kò yo, taye banda sou tèt li.

Gwo chabrak yo pa janm vle pèp la pale, yo vle pou se yo sèl ki pou pale, pou yo aji sou non pèp la. Yo toujou vle fè kwè se yo k ap fè pou pèp la. Y ap viv sou do l e yo toujou pran pòz y ap fè l kado, y ap fè l lacharite, y ap fè l favè.

Asanble Popilè se pou pèp la rasanble fòs li, reklame dwa l. Tout Ayisyen nan peyi a gen dwa a tout bagay san mande favè. Dwa pou manje, sante, lekòl, deplase, travay, pran plezi, jistis, byen loje, dwa pou yo respekte l. Dwa sa yo, pèp la fèt pou l reklame yo.

Asanble Popilè se kote pèp la òganize l pou tèt pa l[5], pou l defann enterè pa l, san li pa sou lèzòd pèsonn[6]. Pèp la gen dwa nan sendika, pèp la gen dwa nan asosyasyon, pati politik. Pèp la dwe vize pou se reprezantan dirèk li ki nan kò leta: lajistis, lachanm, nan ministè, nan palè a. Menm lè se pèp la ki chwazi tout moun sa yo, yo pa gen dwa pran plas Asanble Popilè yo ki pou pèmèt pèp la gen je louvri sou tout aktivite dirijan yo.

Asanble Popilè a dwe rantre[7] nan mès politik peyi a, konstitisyon peyi a dwe rekonèt Asanble Popilè a kòm pouvwa popilè bòkote pouvwa ekzekitif la, pouvwa lejislatif la, pouvwa jidisyè[8].

Asanble Popilè se nanm demokrasi a. Anvan 7 fevriye[9], pèp la te konn fè Asanble Popilè pou te ranvèse Janklod[10], reyinyon jèn, ti legliz[11], fratènite, reyinyon katye, eksetera.

Apre 7 fevriye mouvman sa yo te dwe aprofondi[12] pou etann yo nan tout kwen peyi a, mouvman sa yo te dwe gen enfliyans sou chwa dirijan peyi a.

Vocabulary

tradisyon	tradition	diskite	discuss
esklav	slave	reziste	resist

batay	fight (vb.)	rasanble	gather
blan	white (person), foreigner	plezi	pleasure
fòme	form (vb.)	pran plezi	take pleasure, have fun
kayiman	cayman, alligator	loje	lodge (vb.), lodging (n.)
daou	of August	lèzòd	the orders
revolisyonè	revolutionary	vize	aim (vb.)
dechouke	uproot	lachanm	= House of Representatives
lesklavaj	slavery	palè	palace
toupizi	spin, run around	chwazi	choose
dispozisyon	preparation	dirijan	leader
pran dispozisyon	make preparations	mès	custom
refize	refuse	ekzekitif	executive
pisans	power	lejislatif	legislative
ponyen	handful	jidisyè	judiciary
layite	display, show off	nanm	substance, soul
taye	cut, trim (vb.)	ranvèse	overthrow (vb.)
taye banda	show off	reyinyon	meeting
aji	act (vb.)	fratènite	fraternity
pòz	pose (n.)	apwofondi	get deeper
lacharite	charity	etann	spread
favè	favor	enfliyans	influence (n.)

Notes

1 **blan** lit. *white*, but now means any foreigner (including e.g., black Americans).

2 **seremoni Bwa Kayiman** this is a reference to the vodou ceremony that was held by the slaves at which Boukman, the vodou leader, called for armed revolution against the French. (See Wilentz, 186, Ferguson, 6, and Carpentier (1969).)

3 **pou te dechouke** construction not normal; better would be **pou dechouke**.

4 **dechouke** originally, a term used for pulling up a tree by its roots to clear a field, etc. The noun, **dechoukaj**, was used for the popular movement, after Jean-Claude Duvalier's departure, to rid the country of duvalierist sympathizers and macoutes; this involved emptying houses or offices of everything moveable, and destroying it, but looting was not tolerated by the **dechoukè** themselves. This grassroots, spontaneous movement revived after Namphy's departure in September 1988, and Avril's departure in March 1990. (Note that the action is not new in Haiti, just the use of this word to designate it.)

5 **pou tèt pa l** lit. *for its own self*, i.e. just for themselves.

6 **san li pa ... pèsonn** note double negative after **san.**

7 **rantre** i.e. *become part of.*

8 **pouvwa jidisyè** should be followed by the determiner **a**.

9 **7 fevriye** date of Baby Doc's departure from Haiti.

10 **Janklòd** Jean-Claude "Baby Doc" Duvalier.

11 **ti legliz** the people's church (See Wilentz, 186).

12 **aprofondi** should be **apwofondi.**

Selection Thirty-Seven

Lèt sou alfabetizasyon

Zanmi nou yo

Nou tande ak gwo lapenn kijan tout bagay pase. Nou pap janm bliye bon jan travay KENA[1] ak DEA[2] te fè pandan egzistans yo. Nou pap janm bliye travay lekti ak ekriti ki te marye ak konsyantizasyon nou te konn simaye nan mitan pèp la.

Se granmèsi travay louvri je sa a ki fè anpil nan nou, ti peyizan, kapab reklame dwa nou, kapab soti nan fè nwa pou janbe nan gwo limye[3]. Nou di nou gwo mèsi pou sa. Nou pwofite fè nou konnen gwo tristès ki neye kè nou lè antèt Legliz Katolik yo deside kraze KENA ak DEA.

Nou espere travay nou fè a pap pase nan gagòt ni tounen yon senp lekòl diswa ak bèl diskou anba tonèl[4]. Se nou menm ti peyizan ki konnen kouman je klere ak pran konsyans la te bon pou nou.

Mezanmi, nou pa gen chans vre[5]. Jan mesye gwo chèf yo ak nèg lajan yo pa vle wè *Radyo Solèy*[6] ak jounal *Bòn Nouvèl*[7]. Bri kòmanse kouri y ap gen menm avni ak[8] *Misyon Alfa*[9], paske monseyè yo gen lide fè yon pase men nan yo[10]. Kounye a, gwo zotobre yo ansanm ak lenmi pèp la ap banbile, yo nan lajwa paske yon pòsyon nan volonte yo deja satisfè.

Nou menm ti peyizan, nou pa pèdi espwa paske nou kwè nan òganizasyon pèp la. Pèp la pèdi yon batay, men li pa pèdi lagè a. N ap toujou kontinye òganize nou pou revandikasyon nou yo kapab satisfè.

Misyon Alfa, Radyo Solèy ak jounal *Bòn Nouvèl,* bon kouray.

Pèp la avèk nou!

Gen 36 moun ki siyen

Vocabulary

me	May (month)	janbe	cross (vb.)
lapenn	pain, sorrow	mèsi	thanks, thank you
egzistans	existence	tristès	sadness
lekti	reading	neye	drown
ekriti	writing	antèt	head, leader
marye	go with, match	deside	decide
simaye	sow, scatter	gagòt	mess, disorder
granmèsi	thanks to	tounen	turn (into), become
nwa	black	senp	simple, mere
fè nwa	darkness	diswa	evening (attr.)

diskou	speech	lajwa	joy
klere	light up, clear	pòsyon	portion
bri	noise, rumour	volonte	will, desire
kouri	spread (vb.) (of rumour)	batay	battle (n.)
avni	future	lagè	war
monseyè	bishop	revandikasyon	demand (n.)
lenmi	enemy	kouray	courage
banbile	rejoice		

Notes

1 **KENA Konsèy Episkopal Nasyonal Alfabetizasyon** *National Episcopal Council for Literacy.*

2 **DEA Direksyon Entèdyosezèn Alfabetizasyon** *Interdiocesan Board for Literacy.*

3 **limye** should be **limyè.**

4 **anba tonèl** the expression is almost a cliché (President Manigat was known for his **ti koze anba tonèl**, 'little chats' with the people). See Selection 24.

5 **nou pa gen chans vre** the use of **vre** at the end of a phrase is emphatic, i.e. *you really are not lucky.*

6 **Radyo Solèy** Catholic radio station in Port-au-Prince.

7 **Bòn Nouvèl** Catholic magazine, in HC, published in Port-au-Prince.

8 **menm avni ak ...** *the same future as ....* Better would be **ap pase menm jan**.

9 **Misyon Alfa** See note Selection 24.

10 **fè yon pase men nan yo** i.e. *make changes in.*

Selection Thirty-Eight

Deklarasyon RDC[1] sou masak ventnèf novanm nan

Ventnèf novanm k ap vin la[2] a fè l youn anne jou pou jou denpi ke bandi kriminèl yo te fè gwo zak sasina sou patriyòt demokrat ki tap vote nan Riyèl Vayan[3]. Pou memwa san moun sa yo, ke bal ak manchèt ansasen makout te dechèpiye pou diktati Nanfi[4] an te ka kontinye, pou n montre respè n pou san inosan ventnèf novanm katrevensèt yo e pou tout lòt viktim inosan, RDC ap antreprann yon mach ki rele Mach pou Liberasyon. Mach sila a ap derape nan legliz Sen Jan Bosko[5] ke bandi yo te boule onz sektanm[6] ki sòt pase an, pou rive Riyèl Vayan an pasan pa Bèlè e Lali[7]. Sa se oun fason pou nou pwoteste kont metòd kraze zo ke diktatè ak talon kikit[8] ap fè pèp la sibi, pèp sa a ki san zam e [...] ki ap chèche demokrasi ak liberasyon n[9].

N ap pwofite fè mach pou liberasyon sila a pou n mande kèk lòt bagay enpòtan:

Premyèman, pou Riyèl Vayan rele Riyèl Mati; liberasyon sòlda patriyòt disèt sektanm yo[10] e tout prizonye politik; pou netwayaj[11] nasyonal la reprann kounye an[12]; dezame e revoke tout makout atache[13] ak chèf seksyon[14] k ap matirize peyizan yo; pou Konferans Episkopal la pwononse l sou depòtasyon pè Jan Bètran Aristid[15]; pou yo reprann[16] nan travay yo[17] tout travayè ke yo revoke[18] abitrèman paske y ap reklame dwa yo[19]; pou bandi ak eksplwatè respekte dwa tout sendika ak dwa sivil e politik tout sitwayen demokrat.

Tout moun ki sonje votan patriyòt sa yo k te mouri rache nan Riyèl Vayan, tout moun ki vle ke rejim k ap founi kriminèl depi senkantsèt[20] disparèt de peyi a[21], tout moun ki vle ke jistis, demokrasi ak pwogrè tabli nan peyi Dayiti, nou mande yo pou yo vini nan mach sila a. Sa se pozisyon RDC.

RDC ke Edi Volel, ki frè mèt[22] Iv Volel[23], ap dirije kouwèl ye la.

N ap fè ou sonje jou sa a yon ekip sanmanman te debake pi patikilyèman nan Riyèl Vayan avèk gwo zam fann fwa ansanm avèk manchèt, kote ke yo te rache tout moun ki tap vote e gen anpil moun ki te blese. Bilan[24] jou sa a, li te lou anpil; ven kat moun te mouri dapre premyè enfòmasyon ki te sòti, swasant katòz lezòt te blese grav, kote yo te pote yo[25] ale lopital. Yo te fè sa plizyè kote nan kapital la, epi tou nan peyi a. Dapre dènye enfòmasyon ki te rive ranmase[26] kèk tan apre masak sa a, ta gen pou pi piti san moun ki te pèdi lavi yo jou sa a avèk kòm sèl zam yo te gen lan men yo, youn bout bilten yo ta pral[27] jete pou yo te vote pou youn moun ke yo te vle pou te chita sou chèz boure a[28].

Vocabulary

bandi	bandit	patriyòt	patriot
kriminèl	criminal	manchèt	machete
sasina	assassination	ansasen	assassin

dechèpiye	tear to pieces	abitrèman	arbitrarily
antreprann	undertake	eksplwatè	exploiter
mach	march, walk (n.)	votan	voter
derape	leave, depart	rache	cut to pieces, kill with machete or axe
an pasan pa	passing by, via	rejim	regime
metòd	method	founi	supply (vb.)
zo	bone	senkantsèt	fifty seven
diktatè	dictator	pwogrè	progress
talon	heel	frè	brother
talon kikit	high heels (of shoes)	fann	split, crack (vb.)
sòlda	soldier	zam fann fwa	sophisticated weapon
prizonye	prisonner	blese	wound, injure
netwayaj	cleaning, clean-up	bilan	balance sheet, score
kounye an	now (var. of **kounyeya**)	lou	heavy
dezame	disarm	swasant katòz	seventy four
atache	attaché	lezòt (pl. only)	others
matirize	torture, make a martyr of	grav	seriously
konferans	conference	ranmase	gather
episkopal	episcopal	pou pi piti	at least
pwononse	make a pronouncement	boure	stuff (vb.)
depòtasyon	deportation		

Notes

1 **RDC** Fr. acronym: **Rassemblement des Démocrates Chrétiens,** *Assembly of Christian Democrats.*

2 **kap vin la** this **la** cannot be translated into English.

3 **Riyèl Vayan** See Selection 31, and also 14, 20.

4 **diktati Nanfi** Henri Namphy was head of the government up to, and after, the aborted November elections.

5 **legliz Sen Jan Bosko** Aristide's church. See also Selections 32, 42.

6 **sektanm** variation on **septanm**, cf. **responsab/reskonsab.**

7 **Bèlè e Lali** Bel Air and Lalue are neighborhoods in Port-au-Prince.

8 **talon kikit** lit. *high heels;* here used to refer to provincial macoutes who affected high heels to make themselves appear taller, and thus more important. See also Selections 28, 42.

9 **ak liberasyon n** **n** is the short form of **nl***, i.e. of the people.

10 **solda patriyòt disèt sektanm yo** the date of the coup that brought Prosper Avril to power; a group of sergeants brought down Namphy ("Namphy II", as he ousted the "elected" president Manigat in June 1988, to take power for the second time) who was seen as responsible for the massacre at Aristide's church the previous week.

11 **netwayaj** i.e. the 'cleaning up' (removing macoutes and duvalierists) of the government, administration, etc.

12 **kounye an** var. of **kounye a**; the nasalized **an** is affected by the **n** of **kounye.**

13 **atache** since Avril's government, this term refers to former VSN members (i.e. macoutes), who has been 'attached' in a special capacity to the FAd'H (**Forces Armées d'Haïti,** *Haitian Armed Forces*).

14 **chèf seksyon** the **seksyon** is an administrative district. The **chèf seksyon** are rural police chiefs, who often exploit the peasants.

15 **depòtasyon Jan Bètran Aristid** A reference to the attempt to remove Aristide from Haiti. See also Selections 22, 32, 42.

16 **pou yo reprann** impersonal **yo**.

17 **travay yo** this **yo** refers to the following **tout travayè**

18 **yo revoke** impersonal **yo.**

19 **y ap reklame dwa yo** i.e. the workers.

20 **depi senkant sèt** the year of François "Papa Doc" Duvalier's election.

21 **disparèt de peyi a** it would be better to use the preposition **nan.**

22 **mèt** form of address for lawyers.

23 **Iv Volel** Yves Volel, presidential candidate for November 87; gunned down outside police headquarters with a copy of the constitution in his hands, by a member of the police force. His killer goes unpunished.

24 **bilan** i.e. total casualties.

25 **kote yo te pote yo** misuse of **kote**; it seems it is changing function, and moving from being a locative relative pronoun to an object relative pronoun. The first **yo** is impersonal, the second refers to the wounded.

26 **ki te rive ranmase** passive construction* not normal for this kind of verb in HC.

27 **ta pral** the anterior of **prale*** is irregular.

28 **chèz boure a** i.e. the presidential throne.

Selection Thirty-Nine

Peyizan Jeremi ap reklame dwa yo

Malgre wòl peyizan ap jwe nan ekonomi peyi a, anpil moun pa gen yon zing respè pou yo. Yo pase yo nan betiz, yo rele yo "gwo zotèy", "moun nan mòn", "nèg fèy ..."

Peyizan nan Jeremi[1] fè tande vwa yo sou *Radyo Antiy* sou keksyon sa a. Si ta gen yon diferans ant yo menm ak moun lavil, se paske richès peyi a mal separe. E lè n ap pale moun lavil, fòk nou di ki kalite moun lavil. Anpil nan yo ap trimen, ap penpennen, menm jan ak yon dal peyizan.

Fòk nou di touswit tout peyizan pa menm: gen peyizan pòv, gen kèk peyizan tou ki rich. Lè zòt ap pale de gwo zòtèy, se ti peyizan afèpabon y ap pale. Epoutan, ekonomi peyi a, se sou do yo li chita. Se yo ki travay tè. Taks yo peye a sèvi pou fè lekòl lavil, peye anplwaye leta, etsetera era. Men yo pa jwi anyen. Chak jou, se bat dlo pou fè bè.

Kounye a, peyizan pa mache tètanba ankò. Yo wè nesesite pou òganize yo pou kraze tout vye prejije, pou dechouke yon vye sistèm mafreze k ap depafini yo depi dikdantan. Se pou sa ou jwenn *Mouvman Peyizan Milo*[2] *(MPM), Mouvman Peyizan Obòy*[3] *(MPB), Mouvman Peyizan Jan Rabèl*[4] ...

Li klè peyizan pa wè nan boutèy nwa ankò.

Vocabulary

jwe	play (vb.)
zing	tiny bit
betiz	prank, absurdity
pase youn moun nan betiz	make fun of someone
zòtèy	toe
mòn	hill, mountain
Antiy	Antilles
diferans	difference
richès	wealth
separe	divide, separate
penpennen	struggle (vb.)
dal (with **yon**)	many
touswit	right away
rich	rich
zòt	others
afèpabon	with problems, in trouble (financial)
epoutan	and yet
taks	tax
bat	churn, beat
bè	butter
tètanba	with head down, upside down
nesesite	need, necessity
prejije	prejudice (n.)
mafreze	wretched, rotten
dikdantan	a long time
klè	clear (adj.)
boutèy	bottle
wè nan boutèy nwa	be deceived, taken in

Notes

1 **Jeremi** Jérémie, a town on the southern peninsula.

2 **Milo** Millot, a town in northern Haiti, site of Henry Christophe's Sans Souci Palace, and at the foot of the mountain where his famous Citadelle Laferrière still stands (see Ferguson, 12).

3 **Obòy** Le Borgne, a town in northern Haiti.

4 **Jan Rabèl** Jean Rabel, a town in northwestern Haiti, which was the site of a massacre in July 1987, in which as many as 500 people were killed (see Ferguson, 158 ff). See also note, Selection 42.

Selection Forty

Les petits paysans persistent[1]: "Bannou kochon kreyòl nou yo[2]!"

6 me 1988

Depi lè gouvènman makout Divalye a te mete ak gouvènman blan meriken[3] pou derasinen mezi kochon[4] ti malere peyizan nan tout rakwen peyi a, lavi ti peyizan vin chak jou pi mangonmen. Ti peyizan pa kapab voye pitit yo lekòl, ti peyizan pa kapab bay pitit yo laswenyay. Yo pèdi sèl mwayen yo te genyen pou mennen tout ti aktivite yo. Devan sitiyasyon malouk sa a, peyizan blije pran kanntè[5] al brave danje kay vwazen[6], oubyen al pase tray nan lanfè chan kann Sen Domeng[7].

Nou menm nan KOTPA (*Komite pou Oganizasyon Ti Peyizan Ayisyen),* nou di li lè li tan[8] pou leta ayisyen remèt ti peyizan yo kochon kreyòl yo[9]. Ti peyizan ayisyen bouke ak bèl pwomès malatchong zotobre ayisyen toujou ap fè nan radyo. Pandan tan sa a, gouvènman meriken an ak grannèg ayisyen ap mare gwo mago nan komès kochon grimèl ak manje pou kochon bwòdè sa yo[10]. Fòk zotobre ayisyen sispann konsidere ti peyizan malere pou bèkèkè. Se san grate tèt yo te asasinen kochon kreyòl nou ak 40 pou gwo[11], 20 pou mwayèn, 5 pou pitit. Se menm jan an tou pou yo remèt nou mezi kochon nou yo.

Poutèt sa, KOTPA ap mande pou tout ti peyizan kontinye mete tèt yo ansanm nan tout rakwen peyi a, paske se sèl nan bon jan òganizasyon, ti peyizan ap kapab rive pare tout move kou lènmi an ka pote. Bon jan òganizasyon, se sèl garanti ti peyizan ak malere genyen pou dechouke esplwatè ak move je, pou derasinen lamizè.
Pou fini, n ap di tout ti peyizan kenbe fèm, pa lage. Batay la pa fasil, se vre, men laviktwa ap pou nou kanmenm.

Pou KOTPA

Andrelis Chal, Jidit Pyè-Lwi, Jozèf Batis, Mak-Anri Silven, Jòj Mondezi

Vocabulary

mete ak	join, put together	danje	danger
meriken	(North) American	vwazen	neighbor
derasinen	uproot	tray	suffering
mezi + n.	every single + n.	lanfè	hell
rakwen	corner	remèt	give back
mangonmen	complicate	bouke	fed up, tired
malouk	awful	pwomès	promise (n.)
blije*	be obliged (to do something)	malatchong	false
kanntè	small sea craft, "boat-people" boat	grannèg	bigshot
brave	face, brave	mare gwo mago	make big money

grimèl	woman of light complexion	move je	scoundrel
kochon grimèl	pink pig (as opposed to creole pig)	lamizè	poverty
bwòdò	fancy, elegant	kenbe	stand (vb.)
bèkèkè	idiot	fèm	firm
grate	scratch (vb.)	fasil	easy
mwayèn	average (n.)	laviktwa	victory
kou	blow (n.)	kanmenm	all the same
esplwatè	exploiter		

Notes

1 **Les petits paysans persistent** French: *The small-holding peasants persist*

2 **kochon kreyòl nou yo** the "creole" pigs are small, hardy, and have black markings.

3 **gouvènman blan meriken** **blan**, meaning *foreigner*, emphasizes **meriken**. **Meriken** is the pejoritive variant of **ameriken.**

4 **derasinen mezi kochon** The native creole pigs were killed in an attempt to eradicate swine fever (see also Selections 8, 13).

5 **pran kanntè** a reference to the many Haitians who risk their lives as "boat people" in an attempt to escape to a better, safer life.

6 **kay vwazen** lit. *neighbor homes, next door,* i.e. *neighboring countries.*

7 **chan kann Sen Domeng** many Haitians go to work in the sugarcane plantations of the Dominican Republic. See also Selections 13, 19, 26.

8 **li lè li tan** lit. *it [is the] hour, it [is] time,* i.e. *it is high time.*

9 **remèt ... kochon kreyòl yo** one of the few Haitian verbs that takes an unmarked beneficiary* argument, i.e. not a serial verb construction*.

10 **kochon bwodè sa yo** the **grimèl** pigs, not as hardy as the creole pigs, require pigsties and fancy food, rather than being allowed to run free to forage for themselves.

11 **40 pou gwo ...** i.e. $40 US for the large, ...

Selection Forty-One

Ochan pou Ti Manno!

13 me 85 - 13 me 88, sa fè 3 rekòt[1] depi gwo atis popilè sa a te fè vwal pou peyi san chapo. Se te yon gason kanson[2], yon gason kouraj, pitit fyèl Ayiti Toma[3] ki t ap chante pwoblèm peyi a, pwoblèm moun, denonse tout sa k pa bon andidan sosyete nou an; ki lakòz jouskaprezan nou restavèk[4] kilti lòt pèp. Antoine Rossini Jean Baptiste, kidonk Ti Manno, te soti nan zantray tè Gonayiv; youn nan pi gwo vil istorik[5] peyi Ayiti. Ala nou ta engra, si jodi a nou pa ta retire chapo yon lòt fwa ankò douvan vanyan atis popilè sa a ki pa t janm dakò pou chante sa yo dikte l, men ki te vle chante sa ki soti nan fon kè l, nan kalbas tèt li[6].

Avèk Ti Manno, anpil moun te vin renmen tande konpa dirèk[7], yo te vin renmen danse l tou.

Kisa "Konpa Dirèk" la te ye? E kisa li ye jouk jodi a?

"Konpa Dirèk" la se yon kalite mizik ki trè cho, ki fè moun danse anpil. Ak "Konpa Dirèk", ou toujou sou konpa. Pi gwo pwoblèm lan, se mizisyen k ap jwe rit sa a. W ap mande sa k nan tèt mizisyen sa yo, sitou sa k ap konpoze chante yo. Tout moun sonje òkès ak minidyaz lontan. Genyen ladan yo ki sou sèn nan jouskaprezan. Anpil nan atis sa yo te konn chante bèlte lanati; ekri mizik (chante) sou fanm kaprina, mazora bèt lèd. Gen ladan yo ki te konn voye bèl nòt mizik pou "Chèf leta ak madanm li". Soufrans pèp la menm pa t janm enterese yo.

Se la a Ti Manno fè pwen sou yo. Ti Manno pa t sèlman konn fè moun danse, li te pwofite sèvi ak mizik konpa a pou fè yon lòt travay: louvri je pèp la, konsyantize l. Anpil lennmi laverite te rayi "Ti Manno" paske l te konn mete twòp kakachat deyò, e li te fè k koumanse. Men se domaj! Ala yon gwo atis nou pèdi! Jouskaprezan ayisyen konsekan ap kriye lanmò[8] Ti Manno.

Atis popilè sa a pa t vle rete yon konsèvatè. Li te vle mache pazapa ak reyalite a. Se sa k fè li te angaje mizik li yo, paske l pa t dakò pou kontinye ap chante bèlte lanati ak lanmou pandan peyizan ki nan grangou, ki lage de bwa pandye[9], blije koupe pye bwa[10], vann yo, pou yo ka pa mouri grangou ak pitit yo. Ti Manno pa t pè denonse eksplwatasyon ouvriye ap sibi anba men patwon, pwoblèm kanntè, maryaj enterè, rasis e latriye. Atis la mouri, men zèv li yo toujou vivan. Atis ayisyen yo k ap jwe mizik konpa, gen anpil travay pou yo ta fè, sitou nan pawòl k ap akonpaye chak mizik. Fòk atis konpa yo bay mizik la yon lòt direksyon, kontinye sou menm travay Ti Manno t ap fè lè l te vivan. Anyen pa chanje, se toujou vach anraje ayisyen ap manje nan peyi Etazini, Baamas, Giyàn, Sen Domeng ak nan pwòp peyi nou. Pouki sa pwoblèm sa yo pa chante[11]?

Ti Manno, nou sonje w, paske si w te la apre 7 fevriye[12], ou ta gen anpil pawòl pou di.

Ti Manno pa t yon konsèvatè, se te yon atis popilè pwogresis ki t ap chante pou chanje. Nou espere ke radyo, televizyon va voye moute kèk emisyon espesyal sou "Ti Manno" jou ki va 13 me 88 lan. Atis la mouri, men zèv li yo rete vivan. Se kòmsi li te fèk chante yo. "Operasyon men kontre" se sa nou bezwen, pawòl konsekan sa yo te soti nan fon kè "Ti Manno" anvan lanmò te trennen l al kay bawon[13]. Mèsi Ti Manno, kabare lonè respè[14] pou ou.

Vocabulary

ochan	hymn, anthem
rekòt	harvest
atis	artist
vwal	sail (n.)
kanson	pants
fyèl	stamina, bile
andidan	in
lakòz	cause (n.)
jouskaprezan	up to the present
restavèk	unpaid servant (child)
kilti	culture
kidonk	alias
zantray	womb
istorik	historic
ala*	emphatic marker
engra	ungrateful
fwa	time, occasion
vanyan	courageous
dikte	dictate
fon	bottom, depths
kalbas	gourd
konpa	rythm
cho	hot
mizisyen	musician
rit	rythm
konpoze	compose
chante	song
òkès	orchestra
minidyaz	group (of musicians)
lontan	before
sèn	stage (theater)
bèlte	beauty
lanati	nature
kaprina	old spinster
mazora	toothless person
lèd	ugly
soufrans	suffering (n.)
konsyantize	raise (someone's) consciousness
lennmi	enemy
rayi	hate (vb.)
twòp + n.	too much + n.
kakachat	catshit
mete kakachat deyò	expose the truth
domaj	pity, shame
konsekan	thoughtful, aware
kriye	weep
lanmò	death
konsèvatè	conservative
pazapa	apace
reyalite	reality
angaje	pledge, involve
lanmou	love (n.)
grangou	hunger, hungry
lage	leave, go away
bwa	arm (of body) (var. of **bra**)
pandye	hang down
pye bwa	tree
eksplwatasyon	exploitation
maryaj	marriage
maryaj enterè	marriage of convenience
rasis	racism
zèv	works
vivan	alive
pawòl	lyrics
mizik	song
vach	cow
anraje	madden, enrage
manje vach anraje	not be able to make ends meet
Baamas	Bahamas
Giyàn	French Guiana
pwogresis	progressive
moute	raise (vb.)

voye moute	present (vb.) (on radio and television)	kontre	meet
emisyon	program, broadcast	trennen	take, lead
kòmsi	as if	bawon	baron
operasyon	operation	kabare	tray

Notes

1 **3 rekòt** rural Haitians often count years by harvests, especially coffee harvests, **rekòt kafe.**

2 **gason kanson** i.e. *a real man.*

3 **Ayiti Toma** Haitians often call their country by this familiar name, cf. 'Uncle Sam' for the USA.

4 **restavèk** from Fr. **rester avec,** *stay with*: this term is applied to children who work as servants in exhange for somewhere to sleep, and food.

5 **vil istorik** Gonaïves was the site of the declaration of independence. Gonaïves is traditionally a center of important political events. It was the killing there of three protesting high school students in the fall of 1985 which sparked the national demonstrations that led to Baby Doc's removal from the country.

6 **kalbas tèt li** the image is similar to the 'vessel' (as a gourd is often used); cf. etymology of Fr. **tête** from Latin **testa** 'pot' or 'jug'.

7 **konpa dirèk** typical Haitian dance music.

8 **ap kriye lanmò** better would be **ap kriye pou lanmò.**

9 **de bwa pandye** i.e. with nothing to occupy them; out of work.

10 **koupe pye bwa** a reference to the problem of deforestation; the peasants cut trees to make and sell charcoal, the most commonly used fuel in Haiti. See also Selections 7, 8.

11 **pwoblèm sa yo pa chante** passive reading of **chante***; passivization of this type of verb is probably through French influence.

12 **7 fevriye** date of Baby Doc's leaving Haiti.

13 **kay bawon** i.e. Bawon Samdi, the vodou spirit of death and cemetaries; it is he who gives permission for a death brought about by vodou.

14 **lonè respè** see note Selection 11.

Selection Forty-Two

Mesaj[1] Jan-Bètran Aristid, 22 novanm 1988

Sè m yo, frè m yo, tout frè m Bondye sakre pè ki leve vwa yo ansanm ak nou menm, jenès vanyan peyi Dayiti a, peyizan katolik, pwotestan, vodouyizan, Ayisyen vanyan lòt bò dlo[2], Ayisyen vanyan bò isit, nou tout ki sot reyalize youn grèv jeneral[3] e legal, malgre deklarasyon youn jeneral ilegal[4], chapo ba pou nou! Chapo ba pou kouraj nou!

Ak kouraj, nou leve, nou pale. Mwen tande. Ak kouraj, nou leve, nou kanpe. Mwen wè. Mwen wè nou pale pou Bondye. Mwen tande vwa Bondye nan vwa nou. Mwen wè nou kanpe isit kòm lòt bò dlo, pou mwen kanpe avè nou isite non lòt bò dlo[5].

Bèl enspirasyon Lespri Sen! Bèl deklarasyon damou fratènèl ki envite m gade w nan zye, sè m, frè m, e di w sa Jezi ta di w nan lang pa l: *ani ohev oth, ani ohev otakh* [6] *je t'aime*[7], mwen renmen w.

Ou menm tou ki mare konplo sou do m[8], sou do pèp la, Monseyè Paolo Romeo, Monseyè Gayo, Monseyè Ligonde, Monseyè Kebwo e latriye[9], ban m chans gade w nan zye, de gras, pa jennen, gade mwen nan zye, mwen vin di ou: mwen renmen w.

Paske mwen renmen w, mwen oblije di w laverite: Verite ak lanmou se 50 kòb ak 2 gouden kole. Verite ak lanmou se Jezi nan Pòv yo.

Ala chans pou legliz Dayiti ki rich gras a pòv, nan youn peyi ki pòv[10] akòz rich.

Legliz la rich gras a nou menm pòv ki egzije verite san rete, verite tout kote.

Ala chans pou legliz Dayiti ki rich gras a pòv, nan youn peyi ki pòv akòz rich.

Legliz la rich gras a nou menm pòv ki anpeche Monseyè kache nan peche yo fè, lè yo fè manti pou fè konplo e fè silans.

Ala chans pou legliz Dayiti ki rich gras a pòv, nan youn peyi ki pòv akòz rich.

Legliz la rich gras a nou menm pòv ki dakò fè youn sèl kò pou evite inite tèt san kò[11].

Youn sèl nou fèb, ansanm nou fò. Ansanm, ansanm, nou se lavalas[12].

Kou lavalas pòv yo desann bradsou bradsa ak peyizan pòv, militè pòv, chomè pòv, militè pòv, ouvriye pòv, militè pòv, zanmi pòv, militè pòv, legliz pòv nou rele *Anashim Yavhe* yo; kou lavalas sa a desann, Bondye ap desann chabrak yo met atè pou l leve piti yo met anlè[13].

Konsilte Lik 1, 52[14]

Men pou anpeche lavalas *anashim Yavhe* yo desann enperyalis an soutàn[15] fè konplo pou vann nou bay enperyalis meriken. Se pou sa, fòk nou younn di lòt sa Jezi deklare nan Mak 2, 11[16], kidonk : leve, mache.

Wi, leve mache. Leve mache pou makout[17] sispann mache bwè san nan. Leve mache pou kriminèl bouke mache sou moun. Leve mache pou asasen sispann leve n nan kabann ak rafal bal[18].

Twòp san koule! Twòp inosan tonbe! Non! Sa se twòp!

Jeneral Avril, ou te di: Ayiti avili. Epi? Epi anyen! Nou di n ap bay Fòdimanch[19] nou chanje non Rechèch Kriminèl[20]. Epi? Epi anyen!

Pèp la grangou. Mizè nan kò l. Zam sou li. Tann! Ouvriye nan ka. Lekòl an ranyon. Inivèsite an releng. Tann! Peyizan antrave. Chèf seksyon andemon. Ret tann! Sa w cho konsa! Sen Jan Bosko[21] boule. Frank Women[22] sou moun. Mesye Avril[23] apiye l. Tann! Ti chèf ret ak gwo chèf[24]. Gwo chèf ret ak meriken. A! A! A!! Tann! M ap fè w labab[25], w ap pase men, w a blese! M pote w sou do[26], ou di mwen ou pile pwason! Chita tann! Esklavaj nan lame. Esklavaj nan Panyòl[27]. O! O! Tann toujou! Koudeta fèt. Koudeta refèt[28]. Jeneral ale. Jeneral tounen. Epi? Epi anyen. Tann pou tounen pwatann[29]!

Tribinal pèp la[30], anba tab la, gen rezon rekonèt gouvènman an kòm koupab e enkapab:

Nou koupab paske nou kite makout sovaj ap galope san kòd jistis nan tèt yo. Nou koupab paske nou refize mete Frank Women ak kriminèl masak yo[31] anba kòd. Nou koupab paske nou trayi sòlda 17 septanm[32], revoke militè patriyòt, pwoteje militè patripòch[33]. Nou koupab paske nou voye pèp la al mouri nan eleksyon sida seda[34] pou satisfè meriken anvan netwayaj la fèt. Nou koupab paske nou jwe menm jan ak Franswa Divalye[35].

Nou enkapab paske gouvènman an merite pou
Jistis 0
Sekirite 0
Netwayaj 1

Jeneral Avril, eske ou pa wè tren deraye Nanfi a[36] ap degrenngole desann pi vit avè w si anvan 29 novanm 88, ou pa lage sòlda, kenbe makout, mare Frank Women, fè netwayaj, bloke ensekirite[37]?

Kesyon an nan men w. Kreyon pèp la[38] nan men l. Benediksyon Bondye sou tèt li pou lagras la kontinye desann jis lavalas la desann tout divalyeris, tout makout, tout kriminèl pou tout tan k ap gen tan.

Amèn.

Vocabulary

sè	sister
Bondye	God
sakre	holy
leve	raise
jenès	youth, young people
pwotestan	protestant
vodouyizan	vodou practicing
enspirasyon	inspiration
lespri	spirit
sen	holy
damou	of love
fratènèl	brotherly
Jezi	Jesus
konplo	plot (n.)
gras	pardon, grace
de gras	please
jennen	embarrass
verite	truth
gouden	one quarter of a gourde
kole	stick (vb.)
50 kòb ak 2 gouden kole	one and the same thing
gras a	thanks to
egzije	demand (vb.)
kache	hide (vb.)
peche	sin
manti	lie (n.)
fè manti	lie, tell untruths
inite	unit
fèb	weak
lavalas	torrent
kou	when
bradsou bradsa	arm in arm
chomè	unemployed person
anlè	in the air
konsilte	consult
Lik	Luke
enperyalis	imperialist
soutàn	cassock
Mak	Mark
kidonk	to wit
bwè	drink (vb.)
bwè san	exploit to death
asasen	assassin
rafal	burst (n.)
avili	degrade
rechèch	investigation
nan ka	in trouble
ranyon	ruin, rag
an ranyon	in ruins
an releng	penniless
antrave	in a tight spot
andemon	on edge (person)
cho	in a hurry, worked up (person)
labab	beard
fè labab	shave
pile	step on
pwason	fish (n.)
esklavaj	slavery
Panyòl	Dominican Republic
koudeta	coup d'etat
refèt	done again
tounen	return
pwatann	green bean (lit. 'tender bean')
tribinal	court, tribunal
tab	table
enkapab	incompetent, incapable
sovaj	wild
galope	gallop, run around
kòd	rope
trayi	betray
patripòch	pun on **patriyòt** and **pòch**, *pocket*
sida	AIDS
tren	train (n.)
deraye	derail
degrenngole	rush down
vit	quickly
kenbe	capture
mare	arrest, tie up
kreyon	pencil
benediksyon	blessing
lagras	grace
divalyeris	duvalierist

Notes

1 **mesaj** Aristide recorded this speech and sent it to the different radio stations for broadcast on the day after the general strike of 21 November 1988. He was still in hiding at the time, after the massacre at his church on 11 September 1988, and communicated with the outside world via such taped messages.

2 **Aysisyen ... lòt bò dlo** i.e. the Haitian diaspora.

3 **yon grèv jeneral** i.e. the general strike of 21 November 1988. See also Selections 5, 9, 10, 11, 23, 32, 33.

4 **jeneral ilegal** i.e. Prosper Avril; Aristide considered him illegal because he took power in a coup.

5 **Mwen wè ... e non lòt bò dlo** a reference to the demonstration in Haiti and the diaspora to protest the attempt to deport Aristide.

6 **ani ohev oth, ani ohev otakh** Hebrew *I love you (fem.), I love you (masc.).* Note that Jesus' native spoken language was Aramaic, not Hebrew.

7 **je t'aime** Fr. *I love you.*

8 **sou do m** i.e. *against me.*

9 **Monseyè Paolo ... elatriye** the duvalierist Bishops, who were pushing for Aristide's removal from Haiti.

10 **youn peyi ki pòv ...** for the economic history and reasons for Haiti's poverty, see Dupuy (1989).

11 **inite tèt san kò** this is a reference to a passage in a message released by the Haitian Episcopal Conference earlier the same year: "The Church is a body of which Christ is the head and we are the members. Thus, as in all bodies, there must be a relation between the head and the members. Now, if the so-called "People's Church" is going to say "We have no need for the head of this church," that is as much as to say that it is severing itself not only from the body of the Church, but, similarly, from the head, which is Christ." (Quoted in Wilentz, 231).

12 **nou se lavalas** a reference to, and the title of, a record made by peasants in Jean Rabel, after the massacre there of hundreds of peasants in July 1987. See also Selection 39.

13 **desann chabrak yo ... met anlè** note the serial verb construction*.

14 **Lik 1, 52** "He has put down the mighty from their thrones, and exalted those of low degree".

15 **enperyalis an soutàn** i.e. the bishops.

16 **Mak 2, 11** this is the episode in the temple when the friends of the paralyzed man make a hole in the roof and let him down on his stretcher.

17 **makout** see also Selections 28, 38.

18 **rafal bal** a reference to the nightly shooting and killing in Port-au-Prince.

19 **Fòdimanch** Fort Dimanche, a notorious prison in Port-au-Prince, now a museum.

20 **Rechèch Kriminèl** a police unit in Port-au-Prince, renamed **Service Anti-gang** under Avril.

21 **San Jan Bosco** Aristide's church of St. John Bosco (see note on Frank Women ... below).

22 **Frank Women** see below.

23 **Mesye Avril** i.e. Prosper Avril.

24 **Ti chèf ret ak ...** cf. note on **restavèk**, Selection 41.

25 **M ap fè w labab ...** Haitian proverb: i.e. *I'm telling you the truth, trust me.*

26 **M pote w sou do ...** Haitian proverb: i.e. *Don't argue with me. Take it from me.*

27 **Esklavaj nan Panyòl** a reference to the continuing sale of Haitians to cut cane in the Dominican Republic (see Lemoine (1981)). See also Selections 13, 19, 26, 40.

28 **Koudeta refèt** a reference to the frequent coups in Haiti since the fall of the Duvalier regime.

29 **Tann pou tounen pwatann** lit. *wait (for) to turn into green beans;* the pun (for the rhyme) is on **tann**, both *wait* and *tender* (beans).

30 **Tribinal pèp la** i.e. popular opinion.

31 **Frank Women ak kriminèl masak yo** Romain, then mayor of Port-au-Prince, and the assassins who attacked Aristide's church on 11 September 1988. See also Selections 32, 38.

32 **sòlda 17 septanm** the sergeants who made the 17 September 1988 coup, ousting Namphy II (see note Selection 38).

33 **patripòch** as in *in someone's pocket.*

34 **eleksyon sida seda** i.e. the elections of 29 November 1987 which ended with the massacre of voters; the pun is on CEDHA (**Collège Electoral d'Haïti**, *Electoral College of Haiti*) and the deadly AIDS virus. See also Selections 14, 20, 31, 38.

35 **Franswa Divalye** François Duvalier, dictator of Haiti from 1957 to his death in 1971.

36 **tren deraye Nanfi a** the press made much of Namphy's reference to the **tren demokrasi a** that would bring political change to Haiti. But the train went off the rails ... .

37 **ensekirite** a reference to the shooting, looting, and general unrest that has become routine in Haiti, particularly in Port-au-Prince.

38 **Kreyon pèp la** i.e. the people are taking notes.

Translations of the Selections

Note on Translations

The translations of the Haitian Creole texts have been kept as close as possible to the original Creole meaning and word order wherever this does not interfere with comprehension and clarity. However, there are some common points where I have not kept strictly to the Creole structure, most saliently:

The definite determiner:

Haitian Creole and English diverge considerably in their use of the definite determiner, as a result, this aspect of the translations often does not directly correspond to the HC source text.

The copula (= *to be*):

Realization of the copula in Haitian Creole is often zero; I have supplied the verb in English.

Pou complementizer:

English has many different ways of introducing sentential complements; Haitian Creole has a much more reduced inventory, of which **pou** is very common. I have translated these occurrences using the most natural form in English.

Prepositions:

The meaning of prepositions often does not transfer between languages; also, in some contexts one language will use a preposition where another has none at all; for example, Haitian Creole does not always use a preposition in locative phrases, especially with names of towns. I have given the most natural form in English.

Verb markers:

Sometimes Haitian Creole will have, for example, a marked verb where in English a simple present is more appropriate. It is expected that the student will be aware of marked or unmarked verbs, and will not be confused by occasional non-one-to-one translations.

Relative Clauses and Cleft Sentences:

Haitian Creole makes use of relative clauses where English uses a simple adjective, prepositional phrase, etc., e.g.: Ayisyen **ki** nan lòt peyi ... *Haitians* ***Ø*** *in other countries.*

Structures of the form ***se/genyen*** **NP** ***ki*** **VP** are usually rendered more naturally in English by **NP** + **VP.**

Selection One

Baccalaureate Examination

Attention, attention, you who did not pass the baccalaureate examination this year, go now to the Christian Training Center of Haiti, ask for a half scholarship. The Christian Training Center of Haiti is located in Riyèl Kretyen, Enpas Fransik, number fourteen. For (all) information, telephone 5-6633, 5-6633, the Christian Training Center of Haiti.

Selection Two

Thanks

KOLFA (Association for the Liberation of Haitian Women) sends a big "hats off" in thanks to all friends, organizations, spoken and written press who helped us to make a success of the women's evening on Sunday 13 March 88 in Clara Barton [school]. Together, together, we will be able (to manage) to end injustice.

For KOLFA
Ketlin Moyiz

Selection Three

Louverture Bookstore

You will find all kinds of books on Haiti in Creole, French, Spanish, English. Books for bilingual education and literacy. You will find also records, tapes and all Haitian newspapers.

1502 Nostrand Avenue
Between Church & Snyder Ave
Tel: (718) 469-2295

Open every day from 10 o'clock to 9 o'clock

Selection Four

Medical training courses

Young women, young men, listen. Learn a profession to earn your living [lit: for your living], register starting today in the general nurse['s] assistant training course, which has its head office in the hospital Sen Jilbè de Nefontèn, Chemen de Dal eighty two (82). Whatever your age, you can become a good medical assistant with a valuable diploma which has the signature of many qualified technicians who have proved themselves in many important institutions in the country; also, it is the only private school where students also find a hospital [in which] to practice. The more the student practices, the more he will become good in the area. If you want to stay a long time in a job because of your proficiency, go to register without fear in the course for training as a medical assistant in the hospital Sen Jilbè, Chemen de Dal eighty two (82).

Selection Five

Notice from ESP

ESP reaffirms [its] notice of a short time ago -- ESP which is on the premises of Radio Caraib. The Higher Professional Institute asks everyone who is enrolled -- all pupils who usually come to school, to secretarial, typing, receptionist courses, [and] courses of accounting -- to come to class as usual today. (For) you will find taxis outside [for you] to come, and those who do not want to take taxis can come on foot as usual, because we are aware that the pupil makes sacrifices to find the money to give [i.e. 'pay'] each month. We would not like to lose a class because it is not advantageous for the pupil. So, we ask all the pupils to come to the classes in typing, secretarial, accounting, receptionist, etc., [and] journalism.

They are expecting all the students today; the school will function normally all day.

It is the Institute that signs.

Selection Six

Matter of Trash

What is happening in the streets of Port-au-Prince? Well, the matter of trash is still making [people] talk about it. Almost everywhere you go in [all] corners of the country you find a pile of trash with dirty water in it.

All the week before last everyone was calling for help for the matter of trash, and really it had diminished a little. Now we see it begins to get bigger again, so the citizens call on the people at the townhall, the people who are responsible for the matter of trash, to solve the problem for them, because health is already not what it should be in the country, so you can imagine what it's like if there is trash with water, flies, maggots, all around where there are people.

Selection Seven

Natural Fir Trees

The Association for the Fight against Erosion and for the Total Rehabilitation of the Environment sends [a note] to say that in the Christmas period there usually are families who want to make little decorations at home, to put up little Christmas trees which are made with natural fir trees. Well, ALERTE says this kind of fir you find only here in Haiti and Cuba, so it deserves our protection. ALERTE suggests to the merchants and all concerned in the matter of the Christmas trees, that the merchants put on the market synthetic Christmas trees with a price that everyone can afford for the week of December. ALERTE must make this choice for the people so that they can put up synthetic Christmas trees at home, and it says also that the synthetic Christmas tree keeps all its freshness, it does not become yellow, it does not dirty the house and you can use it each year, you will no longer need to spend [money] all the time.

Selection Eight

Statement from ANDAH

The National Association of Haitian Agronomists put out a statement which says:

- "Faced with the violent quarrels that there have been in Damien for more than a month and especially

- Faced with the rows which broke out on 17 November between the Minister of Agriculture and the bigshots in the Ministry

- While there is still not anything which has ever been said about the big profound problems that are ravaging the country's agriculture such as the problem of pigs, the problem of land, the problems of reforestation, water, [and] contraband which are ruining the condition of the nation, [and] the conditions of work of the technicians in the fields

- Faced with this situation, we in ANDAH (the National Association of Haitian Agroprofessionals) want to make everyone know:

Firstly, what is happening now has nothing to do with the problems of the country's agriculture.

Secondly, the majority of agronomists and other people who are working in the Ministry of Agriculture, are not with either one or the other group of those bigshots who are fighting for positions and money.

Thirdly, the attitude of these bigshots is sullying [the reputation of] all Haitian professionals before the country and other countries that are looking at it.

For the honor of the profession and all the Haitian professionals, for respect for the country, we, members of ANDAH, ask that the Minister, the Director General, and the Assistant Director General tender their resignation without wasting time (as quickly as possible), and we ask also the authorities which are responsible to take measures as quickly as possible, not only to replace people, but especially to reorganize the Ministry.

ANDAH asks all agronomists, all professionals who work in agriculture, all students in the faculty of agronomy, all groups and organizations of peasants, to mobilize (themselves) until we find a definitive solution to make the Ministry of Agriculture start to serve truly the country's agriculture."

For the national leadership of ANDAH, it is Maks Astre, Jeral Matiren, Jan Klod Amede, Pol Dirè, Antoni Dabe and Ari Laprich who put their signature.

Selection Nine

Strike in Port-au-Prince

The CATH is striking to protest against all that is not good that is happening in the country. So this Monday, activities in different sectors of the country [and] in Port-au-Prince were functioning at a slow pace. In the centre of the town there were some stores which were open; however, the majority of the (small) vendors did not come to sit on the side of the street; they stayed at home. School didn't operate at all as all the students stayed at home too.

As for the transportation, we can say it was one quarter [of the vehicles] that operated on all the routes. We noticed a few taxis which were driving around in the streets too.

In the factories, mainly in the industrial park, many workers were absent. There were a few factories which were not open, too. According to the workers, it is the drivers who worked who would have been the reason workers came to work; that allows the bosses to see whether it was bad faith or whether it was because they supported the strike (if) they didn't come. They were obliged to come also so as not to lose the day's money, but that does not mean they didn't support the strike.

[Note: the original of this last passage is rather garbled. The idea is: the fact that transportation was available means that workers could get to work if they wanted to. On the other hand, a worker who agreed in principle with the strike might have gone to work nonetheless, as she or he could not do without the money.]

Selection Ten

Strike in Cape Haitian

Our correspondent in Cape Haitian informs us that the strike was observed in that town; the schools were not functioning, trade and public transportation were almost paralyzed. Kiris Maksino for details:

"In Cape Haitian the observers estimated the success of the strike at about ninety five per cent. Almost all stores remained with their doors closed, public transportation was paralyzed. Whether it was taptaps which make [the trip to] Site Chovèl or other little trucks that connect the town of Cape Haitian with the surrounding areas including big Cape Haitian - Port-au-Prince busses, all these vehicles remained standing still. Just a few (single) taxis and private cars were driving around in the town.

Today, schools were not functioning in Cape Haitian, all pupils stayed (sitting) at home. The public markets did not (manage to) meet as they should, especially the Third Street Market which is always full -- today the vendors did not put their feet [inside]. Almost all activities in the town of Cape Haitian were paralyzed today, Monday, 21 November. This is Kiris Maksino from Cape Haitian."

Selection Eleven

Strike in Northeast department

In the Northeast department, we find the strike was ninety per cent successful, especially in Fort Liberty and many other towns in the Northeast. The public traffic was totally blocked, all the public vehicles remained standing in the station or in front of the door of their owners' houses.

As for the schools, the secondary schools, primary schools, public and private schools had to close their doors because the students did not go to school. In Fort Liberty, only the convent school operated today with a few students.

As for the state offices, all their doors were open. So, they were operating timidly with a few employees who went to the office, (to go) to give those offices some importance.

Selection Twelve

Letter from the Haitian Journalists Association

There is a letter which comes from the Association of Haitian Journalists addressed to the General Consul of Holland in Haiti, Mr Robert G. Patberg. The Association of Haitian Journalists wrote to him (to be able) to draw the attention of the General Consul to the case of their colleague, a journalist for *Haiti Observateur,* Rene Anjelo, (whom they) arrested in Saint Martin, in the Dutch part, on 8 November that just passed. He had with him his press card, and his passport also was in order. The journalist wanted to make a little report, during one week, on the Haitian community in Saint Martin. The arrest of Rene Anjelo, and also the fact that they put him in prison on Saint Martin island, is a violation of the San Jose of Costa Rica Convention on freedom of the press and also on the international agreement on the subject of travel rights. They did not give the journalist for *Haiti Observateur* any reason for the attitude of the authorities in Saint Martin. AJH therefore asks the General Consul to bring clarification to this matter. They ask too that he intervene with the persons responsible for foreign affairs in his country so that they respect the right to travel of Haitians and particularly the journalists who are on a mission in that region in the Caribbean. As we told you, this is a note which comes from the Association of Haitian Journalists.

Selection Thirteen

Events in the Southeast

The clandestine recruiting still is continuing in the Southeast zone in the country and our correspondent in the Tyòt zone is going to give us more details on that along with other information on that zone:

"The business of recruiting is continuing more intensively in all the southeast of the country, where people are coming from everywhere in order to go to Anse à Pitre where they have a rendezvous with the ferrymen who will take them across the border line to (go) get into Dominican vehicles. According to what they tell us, these ferrymen can earn fifty Haitian gourdes for every Haitian they can give to the Dominicans. When we contacted these peasants, they told us what makes them leave the country (to go) to cross into the Spanish country: it is because after Hurricane Gilbert, (they had) no-one (who) brought them any help. The little creole pig which was the source of their livelihood, the men from PEPADEP took (it) from them.

In another place in the commune of Belle Anse, blood was flowing between two groups, Bèl Anfòm and Pati Pèp. Why? It is because Bèl Anfòm (which) supports Jan Erol Kazimi as mayor, and Pati Pèp, which seems to have more members, (which) supports Master Bo as commune mayor, who was elected in the elections of 17 January; the people of Belle Anse say it is Master Bo they want to continue leading them in the commune. The matter is in the hands of the Department of the Interior (so that it can go) to prevent blood flowing in the commune of Belle Anse.

Still in the ward of Belle Anse, in Dipi, which is a commune subdivision in the commune of Tyòt, the section chief Kanòl Loti seems to be abusing the peasants a lot, as (lit. 'where') he lets the big landowners use him to settle their personal affairs.

The peasants living in Dipi ask the section chief Kanòl Loti to nip this business in the bud because he must not forget that when things get difficult, he will not even see the big guys.

This is Jan Ejèn, Radio Solèy, Tyòt."

Selection Fourteen

Anniversaries

Today is exactly one year since a team of outlaws set fire to a big facility that Radio Lumière has in the plain in (a place they call) Menelas. That meant that the radio was silent during a good length of time. It was not able to give information and it was not able to broadcast its programs all over the country.

Tomorrow it will be a year since they burned Salomon Market, [and] they tried to burn the Port-au-Prince BEK, and also the rectory in the town of Saint Marc. They turned upside down the office of the National Fund for Unity in the town of Petit Goâve.

Tomorrow also will make one year since the former general Claude Raymond denied in the press that he himself participated in or had anything to do with those smash and break acts which were done in the country before the elections of 29 November ended in the blood[shed] of the people.

Selection Fifteen

Letter from APN

Port-au-Prince, 4 April 1988

The National Popular Assembly (APN) sends a big "hats off" to all its sympathizers in Montreal who organized a supper to help us continue to do the work of consciousness-raising among the people. It was with a lot of happy hearts that we received $400.00 which will permit us to realize some small projects, for example: seminars, trips, etc.

It is a good example the compatriots in Canada give other Haitians in other countries like the United States, France, Mexico who, we believe, will follow that example. It is one of the ways we can make a contribution to the struggle of the Haitian people.

A big "hats off" to the group *Watch Them* and all the other people who participated in that supper. We say to Marie Celie Agnant: stay firm, don't give up.

For APN: Lalane Jean-Robert

Selection Sixteen

Some plants for making remedies

Arracacha: (its scientific name: Arracia Xanthorrysa). It is used for burns, wounds, swelling.

Mugwort: (artemisia vulgaris). It is good for women who have stomach ache [or] cramps during their periods.

Balsam apple: (Momordica Charancia; they say also: sowosi, asowosi). Its leaves are bitter like bile. It is good for people who don't have an appetite. They use it too for malaria fever. In Costa Rica, and in Guadeloupe, they call it "sorosi" (according to Arsène V. Pierre Noël, *Polyglot Nomenclature of Haitian and Tropical Plants* 1971).

Artichoke: (cynara scolymus). It is used for lowering blood pressure. This plant they call "bérigoule" in some other countries where they speak French. It was the engineer Saint-Romes who first planted artichokes in our country, on the property "La Charbonnière".

Garlic weed: (petiveria alliacea) The people use it for fever. In Guadeloupe, they call it "danday". The smell of garlic weed is very strong. They use it for bed bugs. It would not be bad if we said while we are there [i.e. 'on this topic']: there are some superstitious shopkeepers who use the juice of garlic weed to make their business work. They mix the juice of garlic weed with red wine [and] palma christi oil to set up a lamp, with the idea that that can attract clients.

Mesquite: (prosopis juliflora). Its roots are good for the chest.

Eggplant: (In Puerto Rico, Dominican Republic: "berengena"; in Columbia, Cuba, Mexico: "berenjena"). They often use eggplant (Solanum Melongena) to make people pee a lot.

Cat tongue (or else "langichat", "langlichat"): With its leaves they make a remedy for colds. If you have a sore throat, just crush leaves of cat tongue, take the juice, [and] gargle with it. The juice of cat tongue leaves will solve your problems in a jiffy.

Selection Seventeen

Storm warning

We located a storm today, 18 November 1988, at four o'clock in the morning, at 16.0 degrees latitude north and 75.0 degrees longitude west, that is to say at 275 kilometers to the south southwest of (the town they call) Tiburon. It continues to take the same north northwest direction, with a speed of 8 kilometers per hour. The strongest wind that we record in it, we estimate at 55 kilometers per hour, but we notice that these winds have a tendency to increase, to become stronger. The center of the system may pass at more than 120 kilometers to the west of the extreme tip of the south peninsula of Haiti, in the middle of the night. It is possible also that we will see in the course of the day, heavy rains which may be accompanied by strong winds which may go as high as 40 kilometers per hour in the South, and in Grand Anse in Haiti. We ask all the population in the region of the south zone who live next to rivers, next to the coast, next to places where there is [lit. 'that have'] water, to take many precautions in case there are floods. We ask also please all small crafts, little dugouts, little rowboats which are in the zone of the coast which goes from the town of Les Cayes to the town of Jeremie to stay in their ports, not to move, please.

Selection Eighteen

Press release - employees injured in accidents

The management of OFATMA was very pleased because of the collaboration it found on the part of the bosses; it takes the opportunity to say to them: here is the course they should follow when they have their employees injured in an accident.

The boss should come with the injured person, with all his identification cards, to the hospital. The boss should ask in the secretary's office for the RI form to draw up a report of the accident together with two photos of the injured person, and they both should sign this form.

The first three days the injured person spends in the hospital are on the account of the boss. The boss should help the injured person in the [various] steps [necessary] for him to receive his money and treatment the way the law requires.

Firstly, he must receive all the kinds of care his case requires until he is healthy. Secondly, if the accident which happened to him should make him not able to work, not only must they give him medical treatment from the fourth day, they must pay him until he can start his work again. Thirdly, the money they have to pay him must be two thirds of what he usually earned, but that money must not be more than a thousand gourdes nor less than seventy gourdes per month. Fourthly, if by misfortune the injured [person] should die, the money they should have given him will be used instead to bury him.

Selection Nineteen

Dealing in 'Braceros'

But now we will talk about peasants; we will come to our own home where the recruiting is still being done and until the present time there has been no official statement published about this matter. The Ministry of Labor and Social Affairs has not said anything at all, nor has the government in general, but we learn that, particularly in the southeast area, many [lit. 'not two'] peasants are being put in little boats and sent to go cut sugar cane in bateys in the Spanish country. So there is KOJEREL, the Committee of Young people for the Recovery of Marigot, which protests with all its strength in the face of the acts of repression that a sergeant of the Armed Forces of Haiti called Sentilѐ Jan Pyѐ is making its members undergo. Among them is Enso Kowachi, they smashed him with sticks, [and] now he is in hospital in the town of Jacmel.

Since 3 November, Sergeant Sentilѐ has been organizing the traffic of braceros under the eyes of everyone in the town, according to what the press release says. Each day five, six, seven little boats are loaded with people who are leaving to go to the Spanish country illegally, according to (what) these young people (know). The sergeant, according to what they say, gets a hundred and fifty dollars for each boat which manages to leave the port of Marigot.

Last week, faced with this serious situation, Enso himself, a young man working in this movement, denounced this traffic (which is being done) on Radio Express, in the town of Jacmel. The sergeant was annoyed; he arrested him [i.e., Enso], and he broke his head, tied him up, beat him up with blows of a stick and let him go three quarters dead. Right now, he is lying on a bed in the hospital, in St Michel hospital in the town of Jacmel, still according to what the press release specifies.

According to the last information we have, according to what the release says, Sergeant Sentilѐ made known that the authorities sent him to go take a little rest in another post. Surely, according to what the young people think, this was so that he could enjoy the money that he had just taken, because they have not punished him for these acts that he has done. Thus they [i.e members of KOJEREL] ask all organizations in the country to establish solidarity together with them, (in order to be able) to find justice for this young man that they [i.e. traffickers] beat up.

That makes the second young person in that area beaten up for denouncing this traffic, which is sending Haitians to go and cut sugarcane illegally in (the country of) the Dominican Republic.

Selection Twenty

Government report on the 29 November massacre

There is a report that the KNGP government ordered on that date, and which came out just recently, -- you have heard about it -- [and] which General Prosper Avril published. He himself didn't find any guilty people, or if he found guilty people, he doesn't know them, because generally, *everyone* seems to be accused in this affair, according to what the report on the inquiry makes known on the massacre of 29 November. The people that they are pointing their finger at most, or rather the institution, is the KEP itself; it should not have organized elections, given the climate of crush and break in the country before the elections, according to what the report says. They point a little finger also at the Minister of Information who himself did not give the right kind of information, considering all the tools that he had at hand to avoid what happened. In this report they also pointed fingers at the government commissioner, Madame Mirèy Zamò Plivyòz, together with the police, who did not do their job well.

But, in general, all the weight fell on the back of the KEP for the way that it ran the elections, according to what the report said. AFP, commenting on that, said that up to the present they never said in the report who are the people who committed those acts or who ordered them, while in the press they had already given the names of the people who ordered those acts of death squads against those (people who were some) innocent people who were going to vote.

So 29 November 1988 will make a year since the massacre was done. The government has decreed that day a day of national mourning. Several organizations, human rights defense organizations, do not want the people to forget that date; there will be ceremonies held all over the country.

Selection Twenty-One

Graffiti 1

We want a leader who will not sell the country. We want Luc B. Innocent.

Selection Twenty-Two

Beggar children and Lafanmi Selavi

Many children are leaving the provinces to go to the capital to seek a living. Many children leave Cape Haitian to come to add to those who are slaving away in the capital, who are living badly, those who, lucky for them, find a little place in Lafanmi Selavi. These children are coming to swell [the numbers of] those who are there already -- much more poverty. Let's listen to our colleague Jan Loran who went to try to make contact with these hordes of children who are coming out of the provinces to add to those who are there already:

Many children, about five to seven, got up on the back of a Cape Haitian - Port-au-Prince bus in the station in Cape Haitian to go to Port-au-Prince. [When they] arrived in Puilboreau, the driver, who surprised these little guys, made them get down; they, for their part, moved over to [lit. 'passed their feet to'] Twa Vyèj, another Cape-Haitian - Port-au-Prince bus, which was broken down on the road. These boys, who could be from about seven to nine years old, do not have two or three ideas [lit. 'spirits'] [which] dance in their heads, [it's only] Port-au-Prince, the capital of Haiti. What are they coming to do? Three of them, Dyesen, Doudou, and another companion [of] theirs, consented to answer us:

"Where have you come from?"
"Cape Haitian."
"Where are you going now?"
"Port-au-Prince."
"What are you going to do in Port-au-Prince?"
"I am going to beg."
"You're going to beg? Does your mother or your father know where you are going, where you go?"
"No, they knew I was in Cape Haitian ."
"Where are you from?" [lit. "It is [a] person [from] where you are?"]
"Port Margot."
"When did you leave Port Margot [and] go to Cape Haitian?"
"The other day, last year."
"Last year?"
"Yes."
"And what age are you now?"
"I don't know my age."
"You don't know your age. Why are you leaving Cape Haitian to go to Port-au-Prince?"
"Nothing."
"For nothing? But you have something that makes you not able to stay in Cape Haitian? What makes you not stay in Cape Haitian?"
"Nothing."
"Were you begging in Cape Haitian too?"
"Yes."
"When you arrive in Port-au-Prince, will you take the occasion to stay?"
"Yes."

"But if you see you beg in Port-au-Prince, [and] you don't find anything, what will you do?"
"Nothing, we will find something, we will eat."
"Eh?"
"We will find something."
"What is your name?" [lit. "It is how [that] they call you?"]
"Dyesen."
"Dyesen?"
"Yes."
"Is your mother alive, is your father alive?"
"Yes."
"How many children has your mother?"
"She has eleven."
"Eleven children. It is you who is the youngest?"
"Yes."
"And you, what is your name?"
"Doudou."
"What?"
"Doudou."
"Where are you going, Doudou?"
"Port-au-Prince."
"Where are you from?"
"From Limbé."
"From Limbé. How long have you been in Cape Haitian?"
"Since the other day."
"Since the other day?"
"Yes."
"What are you going to do in Port-au-Prince?"
"I'm going to beg."
"You're going to beg. Do your mother and your father know you left Cape Haitian [and] you are going to Port-au-Prince?"
"Yes, I said that before I went."
"When you told them that, what did they say to you?"
"They did not say anything to me ."
"But when you arrive in Port-au-Prince if there are other children who beat you, you don't have people [i.e. 'relatives'] in Port-au-Prince, what will you do?"
"I will leave, I will come home."
"You will come home?"
"Yes."
"But do you think when you arrive in Port-au-Prince, you beg, there will be people who will give to you?"
"Yes."
"Yes, there will be people who will give to you?"
"Yes."

On all the Puilboreau road, you find these children running behind buses, begging five cents or ten cents -- what they call the rural exodus: go off and leave the area where you are living, start jumping on moving trucks going in to the town of Cape Haitian. Having arrived in the town of Cape Haitian, either things seems not to work as they should, or else, others bring news to them how things are in Port-au-

Prince, [and] they don't want to stay. Do these children have people in Port-au-Prince? No. Where do they stay?

One of them answered us: when people (are) sleep(ing) under porches in Port-au-Prince, they don't make you pay for that. Why don't they stay with their mothers, looking after animals, doing the garden with their fathers?

They answered us: the area of their homes has been ruined, all that their families had is gone, so a person must leave to find a living. These little children come to swell [the numbers] in the capital Port-au-Prince -- groups of children who were already drifting one on top of the other in bad conditions.

Selection Twenty-Three

General Avril speaks on the strike

As I see ... as I see that ... I am looking ... I see a union ... I think it's a union that did it -- that gave the call. I see a union which is among the unions asking that [the government] apply the constitution. I look [and] I see a union which asks for a general strike for the whole country in a matter of work conflict in a small company in Port-au-Prince. I look, [and] I see a union which is asking to apply [the] constitution, which is asking for respect for the laws, which is asking for a general strike which enters into politics.

But however I observe also, that there is nobody who says what a union is, that is to say that -- you know we still have the constitution -- if you take the constitution in the area of unions, what does it say on unions? It says:

> "Union freedom is guaranteed: every worker of the private and public sectors can belong to the union of his professional activities for the exclusive defense of his work interests" (Article 35:3) of the '87 constitution which everyone likes. Next, further down, it says to you: (Article 35:4) "The union is essentially apolitical, non-profit and secular".

What does that mean? That means that according to the constitution ... it did not foresee that a union had the right to defend things other than "his work interests", therefore in the society we are living in -- I am talking to you about the unravelling of the social fabric -- they think that it's the government that should stay within the law, but outside they don't need to respect the law, they don't need to respect the constitution; here is the problem.

Now, how should I apprehend, how should I grasp a thing like this: this thing should constitute a test to examine society. Has it arrived at the stage that even if a person is breaking the law, it [i.e. society] has to obey him? That again is going to serve (me) as a test, for me to see what degree of maturity the society has reached now, and which is going to allow me to evaluate how much work this government has to do.

Selection Twenty-Four

National School at Labacou (St Jean du Sud) in ruins

The matter of schools in Haiti is a headache! It is not that which interests the bigwigs. On the question of literacy, ONAAC has not delivered anything serious. It is a lot of smoke, no fire [lit. 'a big wind, little rain']. When Misyon Alfa came to take over, there arose a hope, but in a jiffy, the bigshots in the Catholic church destroyed it.

If in the towns the situation is like this, for the *countryside*, it doesn't bear mention [lit. 'it's not to be talked of']! There are some areas which do not have schools at all. When you manage to find one, it is [just] a hut to deflect the sun. Most often, the students work under a *bower*.

So the young people in the Labacou neighborhood, a place which is situated in the St Jean du Sud commune, are calling "help" for the national school of Labacou. Since 1980, the house that sheltered the school has been demolished. The bigshots never repaired it. The population had to erect a bower with its own small savings.

Last September, hurricane Gilbert arrived, the bower bit the dust, it was smashed in tiny pieces. Since that time, the matter of the school, forget it! *No*-one among the constipated authorities ever appeared to give the people a little hand. The people's school is smashed, it is a matter which concerns the people!

The people in Labacou ask how it happens it is they, the small-holding peasants, that the big guys always despise worse than dead dogs. Are they not native children of the country too?

It is exactly the same for the national school in La Cahouane which is situated in the area of Port-à-Piment.

To allow schools to be demolished without there ever being repairs, that is the program of the Department of National Education.

Selection Twenty-Five

Human Rights in Mexico

In the country of Mexico, the human rights situation is causing much concern: more than a thousand people have been assassinated since 1983 in that country, according to information the human rights defense organization gave today in Geneva, Switzerland. More than one thousand people have been assassinated in Mexico for social reasons or for political reasons since the year 1983; that is what the president of the Mexican human rights defense league, Mr Victor Delafuente, declared today. Among the people who died, there are (among them) eight hundred peasants that the big landowners killed because they did not want to sell the little plots of land that they still have; there are eighty six school teachers who were defending their rights; and there are thirty journalists (among them). It is the journalists who were denouncing the corruption practiced in the police force and [by] important civil servants who take money from the hands [of] drugsellers, according to the information he gave today in Geneva.

Mr Delafuente makes known that it is most particularly the small-holding peasants who are the victims of this violence, because they (themselves) do not want bigshot bigtime landowners to come and buy the little plots of land that they have in their hands. The president of the Mexican human rights defense league, right now, is making a tour in the countries of Europe (to be able to manage) to make public opinion in those countries become aware that they are violating human rights in Mexico. He said that he observed there, that since they created this association in March 1985, in which they are denouncing in a systematic manner the way that human rights are violated in Mexico -- since that time, there has been a little decrease (according to what he said) in the matter of what death squads are doing to people who are defending their rights in that country, a big country in Latin America. Right now Delafuente makes known that there are eight hundred and ten peasants who have disappeared and who they are looking for under the government of Miguel de la Madrid; there has never been anything at all said about that. He especially makes this trip on the occasion of the first of December next, when President Salinas, who is a 17 January president that the Mexicans do not respect at all, is going to take power, and is going to replace Miguel de la Madrid who has been leading that country in recent years.

Selection Twenty-Six

Interview with Dr Paul Etienne

"Yesterday I saw a group of Haitians, their little bags on their heads, who were going to go in to the Dominican barracks. Inside the barracks [area] there was a big CEA truck -- one of those they call "patana" -- which was to transport them, but when I asked a Dominican guard where all these Haitians were going, he told me, 'Um, they are going to cut sugarcane'. I said, 'But, they are illegal.' He stopped, [and] he

told me, 'No, no, no, no, when it's a matter of of sugarcane, we let them pass even if they are illegal.'"
"They didn't have people with them, they were on their own, the Haitians?"
"Well, there were, there were ... only Haitians (they were); but there was one I tried to approach, it seemed it was he who was the head of the group, but he ... they, they did not want to talk."
"But there were not any Dominicans with them?"
"Hmm?"
"There were not any Dominicans with them, because there was a ...?"
"I didn't see any Dominicans at all, Haitians only."
"Uhmm, did you ['they' in text is error] speak with them?"
"Well, I tried to speak with them, but they had a way of not wanting to speak and they had a way as if I would say to you, you know they come on Dominican territory without papers, without anything at all, so, they don't want to take the chance of talking, they just go onto the little crooked path, they go into the barracks."
"In your opinion, Dr Etienne, do you believe that those people have been let out in the bateys already?"
"Well, uh, I don't know if really they have let them out in the bateys, because it was the middle of the afternoon and as long as the patana truck that is there is not full, they will not take them to the bateys."
"But would that mean that there are lots of Haitians right now, who have taken the decision either on their own or else with other people, who are going in across the border?"
"Well, there are ... the Haitians, for example, I tried to ask one a question, they told me that they are going to seek a living. That means that there are many Haitians who travel on their own, because they are not doing anything on the other side, they want to seek a living. But there is a group of other people who are mercenaries from Santo Domingo, paid by the country, who go to Jacmel especially [...]. So they pay a group of mercenaries who go to Jacmel, and the mercenaries tell the people either that they are going to hotels, or they are going to coffee, or they are going to cut cane, but the conditions are better; and that is what the people themselves were waiting [to hear] before going."
"Well, when is the sugar harvest going to open?"
"Well, the sugar harvest is practically open, except for some centers which are not yet open, but practically [speaking] the sugar harvest is open. Just yesterday the vice-president inaugurated the Osama opening."
"Uhum."
"Well, thus, if ... if we, now we do not do anything in Haiti to prevent these people coming under any conditions, well it's wasted effort, because the people will always want to come."
"Uh yes, uh, Dr Etienne, at the same time you were speaking to us just now about a seminar which opened too, in San Pedro de Macoris I think, on the question of the Haitian business."
"Ah, well, exactly, in San Pedro de Macoris there is a seminar which is called El Batey, that is what they called [lit. 'baptized the title of'] this seminar. This seminar is being held right in the Central University of the East, in the east of the country. The Archbishop of Santo Domingo gave the opening [speech]. Well, he made many statements."
"So what did he say?"
"Well, he said, firstly, that he is well acquainted with the problem of the Haitians who come to the bateys; he said that, well, it is really unacceptable, it is unacceptable

according to the Gospel and equally according to Christian morals, that they are silent on the conditions Haitians are living under now in the bateys.
"He said we cannot close our eyes on this situation because in the east, there are more than a hundred bateys and there are more than thirty thousand Haitians. The archbishop went on to say that the Haitians who go in, go in without papers, so that makes it easy for the Dominican government not to give them any possibility, any possibility to demand their rights."

Selection Twenty-Seven

Graffiti 2

Radio Haïti Inter was crippled. That does not say it *died* because of that. Let's put our heads together to develop the country. The trumpet has sounded, the muzzle has fallen. Let's stop making anarchy so we do not riddle freedom with holes.

Selection Twenty-Eight

Shooting at night in Carrefour

There is a note here which came from Carrefour. Well, Carrefour says that for some time in Port-au-Prince, especially in Carrefour, every day when the night is going to fall, [and] all night you hear automatic weapons, which are singing without stopping. The capital has become a real battle ground, you would say it is in Vietnam or else in Texas or else in the fields, where for any reason at all you hear shooting.

Well, who is shooting like that? According to an enquiry that the party conducted, it is the army of Haiti and the police who are shooting like that, supposedly to give the population security. Indeed, if our enquiry tells the truth, the army and the police have resigned from their true mission. Why? Because these two institutions, which should be the most serious in the country, have come to have, you would say, a true macoute behavior because it is only Duvalier's macoutes who were always shooting so that they could keep the people in fear, so that Duvalier's dictatorship could establish itself definitively in the country. If a person or a group of people want to give the people security, they should not be *shooting* all night, but they should set up adequate patrols, they should increase the size of the army and the police force, they should raise the wages of the soldiers and the police, and they should improve means for lodging, and transportation, means for food too. But how could a government, army and police give a people decent security? Is it only when they are shooting at night to prevent people sleeping, to make people jump in their sleep, to make people live in fear, in shock?

This thing does not have another name, it's lack of discipline, it's incompetence, it's macoute behavior. Policemen should not be afraid at night; when the guys are shooting like that at night, they are *afraid,* it's no more, it's no less, it's wasting bullets for nothing, it's making the state build up a deficit while Haiti is the country which is the poorest in the world.

This thing, the matter of shooting all night, cannot continue like this. It is for this reason that the National Union for the Defense of Democracy and Human Rights (UNDDH), throughout the country, asks the military government and the general headquarters that the shooting at night stop in the capital, [and] that they put adequate patrols in the country. It's not shooting at night that people want now, but it's security, food, health and schools where they can send their children.

Down with shooting (it is the note which is still talking), down with shooting at night, up with decent patrols at night! It's for this reason they ask the military gentlemen in the four corners of the country to show themselves to be more disciplined, more watchful over the problem of the lack of security. The National Union for the Defense of Democracy and Human Rights, UNDDH, asks the General Headquarters of the Armed Forces of Haiti to give the soldiers new training in democracy, in human rights, so that the process of democracy can be done better in the country, because every moment you hear a soldier or else a commune policeman is mistreating the people. The military must respect human rights in all the country, it's the only guarantee for good reconciliation (to manage to be done).

For the party it's Jistin Bocha, the founding chairman of UNDDH, who signs.

Selection Twenty-Nine

Graffiti 3

We, the youth of la Saline, we ask for rebuilding. We do not want the smashing, do not talk of that any more.

Oh! goodness, look how they forget us, the people of la Saline. Why? ... We ask that every honest citizen think of us.

Selection Thirty

Graffiti 4

We the youth of la Saline, it is us they treat worst but we know our value.

Selection Thirty-One

29 November 1988 as a day of national mourning

We are coming back again to dates that the Haitian people should not forget; among them 29 November, of course. The military government declared 29 November a day of national mourning; this is what a decree that was published on 21 November establishes; this decree says that the flag on that day -- that means Tuesday exactly in one week -- will not go up completely, they will fly it at half staff [lit. 'it is in the middle they will put it up'], a way to show that the country is in mourning, and also, that day there will not be work, there will not be school, businesses will not open, nor factories, all those (things) will close. That means a day of national mourning, a day of idleness too.

The military government declared that it wants to take off its hat very low before those many people who lost their lives, while they had only a piece of paper in their hands to enable them to vote [lit. 'to go to do an act to be able to vote']. They attacked them on Sunday, 29 November 1987, while the only weapon they had in their hand was a piece of paper, what they call ballots -- they were going to the polling station.

We are reminding you that at the weekend, more precisely Saturday, we already presented a letter that General Prosper Avril sent to the political sector in the country in which he invited them to get together with him, to commemorate that day of remembrance, so that they do not forget. He also asked that on that date, people not make complaints -- complaining will not accomplish anything; but also that they not take revenge. But, he does not say when nor where they will have that ceremony. Also -- in this letter -- he was asking himself the question: do they think that this country is condemned always to go through these same things? And he himself answered his own question, he said the mothers of children, children who lost their mothers and their fathers together with other children in the country, will reply: No. The country must find a way (to be able) to get out of what it is in. Because of that, he invites all sectors (according to what he says) to commemorate [the day].

In this same letter also he said that there are questions which should be asked because 29 November was not an unexpected thing that came to fall on the heads of the people, it was a series of things that brought them to 29 November. There [i.e. in the letter] he asked the question: Who did not do what they should have done to avoid this happening? Who also behaved like cowards? Who did not play their part so they could prevent that? And also, who made mistakes? It is for these reasons, he asked that everyone commemorate together that day so they do not forget 29 November -- here he spoke of Ruelle Vaillant. But, in this letter -- which, as we pointed out, general Prosper Avril sent to the political sector -- there was never either the word justice or the word reparation or reconciliation written in this letter of which we found a copy that we read for you here.

But meanwhile there are several organizations, such as five organizations for the defense of human rights, which published a statement where they say how they are going to commemorate this 29 November. Here is what it says:

The [events of] 29 November never ever should [lit. there ever be that [thing] that might] happen again. We, the organizations that are struggling in matters of human rights, like other sectors which are fighting for change in Haiti, we do not forget how the forces of evil smashed up in a river of blood the rights of people who were doing their duty as citizens in the elections of 29 November 1987. It is going to be one year since that deed was done; all sectors, all together, should commemorate that day as is fitting (according to what these five organizations state). Therefore we ask all Haitians who want a country where justice and liberty blossom, a country where they respect the rights of all people, to join together in commemoration of 29 November. Here is the program for that day (this is the program of the five organizations for the defense of human rights):

Firstly, a peaceful procession with lighted candles and signs of mourning, which will come out of all corners of the capital to arrive in Ruelle Vaillant in the morning very early;

Secondly, religious ceremonies dedicated to all those people who were the victims of martyrdom;

Thirdly, message for that day: we ask all the representatives in the countryside and in the provinces to set up a program like this; we ask that all schools devote the day of 29 November as a special time to reflect on what happened on 29 November 1987; we ask that the flags of all schools and state offices be flown at half mast that day; we ask radio and television to put on music of mourning and talks on 29 November; starting from that date we will call 29 November in the calender of the democrats, the Day of the Martyrdom of Democracy in Haiti; we agree to call Ruelle Vaillant 'Rue des Martyrs', according to what these five organizations state. We must not forget the martyrs of 29 November. A people without memory is a people without a tomorrow.

The people who sign are the National Network which Defends Human Rights, Mrs Simone Kastra (RENADDWAM); the Ecumenical Center for Human Rights, Sorèl Yasent; the Mobil Institute for Democratic Education, IMED, Rozalvo Blèz; the Lafontan Jozèf Center for Advancement which Defends Human Rights, Renan Pyè; and with the Haitian League which Defends Human Rights, it is Master Jozèf Maksi who signed this program on the occasion of the first anniversary of 29 November 1987 when that election ended in the blood of the people. Up to the present, people do not know exactly how many people died; they estimate that more than one hundred people died that day.

Selection Thirty-Two

Jean Auguste Mesyeux speaks about the general strike

In the name of all Haitian workers, in the name of all popular organizations, in the name of workers, peasants, students, drivers, in the name of everyone who is struggling in the camp of the people, the statement of the Minister of the Interior was published to say the strike was illegal. This statement makes no sense, it is devoid of all foundation.

The words General Prosper Avril said on national television, that is to say that the strike is a strike which is illegal, those words do not have any meaning. The General made known that he was very surprised when he saw that some organizations and associations issued a call for a strike to paralyze a country because of a little company called Steelworks of Haiti, and we ask if all workers are not workers, if all workers do not have the same rights.

Eh, the strike was called for six points: these six points we ask the government to satisfy: the first point is against bosses who are firing workers in factories, and particularly we talk about the companies Comme Il Faut and Steelworks of Haiti, the latter (where they) threw on the street with strong arm tactics more than fifty eight workers.

The second point is against the bigshots in the church who want to deport Father Aristide, and everyone knows that Father Aristide is the symbol of the poor. It is a serious job he is doing among [lit. in the midst of the mass of] the people and he connects together material and spiritual interests. Is the second point not correct, that Father Aristide had just been a victim of the macoutes, at the massacre at St Jean Bosco, instead of giving him protection, instead of asking for the trial of Franck Romain [lit. to judge F.R.], the bishops in the church are now trying to deport Father Aristide.

The third point is against macoutes who are assassinating the people every evening [and] the extradition and trial of Franck Romain.

When we consider each evening among the people in Port-au-Prince and everywhere in the provinces the climate of insecurity that has been established over all the country;

When we consider Franck Romain, his direct participation in the St Jean Bosco massacre, when he made a statement, said he was responsible, he admitted it was he who was the ringleader with all the other acolytes of his who went to their deaths -- we can cite Gwo Chilè, Gwo Lachat, etc., -- isn't Franck Romain -- isn't this point fair? And when General Prosper Avril spoke on television, [and] they asked him questions about Franck Romain, he said that Franck Romain is a citizen who asked for political asylum which an embassy gave him, and in accordance with a series of conventions Haiti signed with foreign countries, they must respect the right of asylum.

Selection Thirty-Three

Statement from Ministry of Information regarding the strike

The Ministry of Information and Coordination published a statement Monday 21 November, in which they say that the government of the republic notes with happy heart that all activities started again normally today, Monday, 21 November, in spite of several calls issued in order to paralyze national life with an illegal general strike. In the light of this unanimous show of confidence in the government -- in all the guarantees that it promised -- the government congratulates the different sectors concerned for the evidence in which it sees the people are really on ... in political matters they seem to be adults, they have a sense of civic responsibility too. It thanks particularly the world of the workers, who, in spite of difficulties in transportation in the beginning of the morning, did not let themselves be manipulated. But, they understood that at this difficult economic juncture, work is the only way to salvation for the people.

It thanks also industrialists and merchants, the public transportation drivers, those in charge of schools, parents and students and everyone who continued their activities in the street today, by means of which they signalled ... they showed clearly their willingness not to risk ... um ... compromise the process of dialogue and cooperation which has started for the good of the nation. Therefore the government reaffirms to everyone its determination to follow, to continue on the road it has adopted, and to continue to propose dialogue even to those people who today still think that it is their duty to turn (themselves) away from this road to dialogue.

It is a note which carries the signature of the Minister of Information and Coordination, Mr Anthony Virginie St Pierre.

Selection Thirty-Four

Vaccination: Its importance in the country

The last time I talked about how much prevention counts in a country like Haiti, because, as I said, Haiti is too poor to treat all the diseases that there are in the environment. So it is always better for us to seek to avoid disease before disease knocks on our door.

But we know that in the country people are dying like flies because of illness: children as well as adults. For the children, it does not bear mention [lit. 'is not to be talked of']. Whooping cough is making their eyes pop; tetanus is making them stiffen; diphtheria is suffocating them; rubella is ravaging them. And usually in spite of remedies of leaves, remedies of the doctor, remedies of the ougan, these children die because, as I am telling you again, it is always more difficult to treat these horrible diseases.

That is why medical science uses vaccination to get ahead, so that all these horrible diseases can stay in their shells. It's not vaccination only which can eliminate disease in the country. There are lots of other things which count too, such as good government and a good program of sanitation, education, [and] distribution of health services everywhere in the country. Nevertheless we can say that vaccination is one of the things which can prevent the horrible germs of disease ending up killing everyone in the country. And when we speak of a vaccination program we are speaking of a first-rate vaccination program which doesn't rest only on charity that other countries give us; we are talking of a systematic vaccination program which our own government should conduct with the money of the country which comes out of the pockets of the poor men and poor women. There is a proverb which says: when you don't have a mother, you suckle grandmother. It is a way for us to tell you that any program of vaccination will always be able to help you save a child if you have the luck to find it for that child.

What is vaccination? It is an injection or a remedy that will make a person avoid a certain illness. In Haiti, tetanus, whooping cough, diphtheria, rubella, polio, mumps are doing a lot of damage to children. One way for us to prevent these problems is to vaccinate the children. Even pregnant women should be vaccinated against tetanus to avoid tetanus in the baby. Even an adult should be vaccinated too. But in this country of ours as long as there is not a solid program, native [to the country], we must give the children a little chance at first, because their bodies are more immature and they are more without defense against illness.

If we glance at the photograph which is right near, we will see 2 children who are suffering from (the disease) polio. The muscles or the flesh of their back and neck become all stiff. They can't even sit well. We may say if their mother or father had gone to get them vaccinated against the disease this misery would not have happened to these children.

So from two (2) months each child must start to receive vaccine against diphtheria, tetanus, whooping cough and polio. At four (4) months, they must receive a second dose of vaccine against these diseases and at six (6) months they will receive a third dose against diphtheria, whooping cough and tetanus. Around fifteen (15) months it is vaccine against rubella, mumps and measles they should receive. I must tell you that all these vaccine timetables can change according to the urgency of the situation, and it is that which makes it necessary that you listen to the words of the doctor in your area so that you know when you should take the children to (go to) get vaccine. Because when you remember that diphtheria, which we call also 'croup', can suffocate a child in no time at all, you yourselves, fathers and mothers, should take very seriously the business of vaccination so that you do not say: if only I had known.

But now there is anthrax which is falling on the backs of the poor in addition to all the other miseries they have. Wouldn't it be good if there were a permanent systematic program of vaccination against anthrax in the country to protect everyone who is working with animals, especially the people who are working in fields that are contaminated with the germ of anthrax, because the vaccine against that disease exists too?

You should know there are some little problems vaccination can give. But these problems will always be smaller compared to the benefits the vaccines give when a person takes it. The doctor or the nurse will always be able to tell you about these little problems so that you can deal with them. They will always be able to tell you when these problems can happen. What is more important, is to try to know when to take the children to (go to) be vaccinated, because it is one of the biggest presents you could give them.

Selection Thirty-Five

Clarifications on "Creole Grammar"

If we are writing about "Creole Grammar", it is not because we are better than everyone [else]. Ourselves, also, when we are writing Creole, we can make mistakes in the sentence, or in the way we write a word. We ourselves are aware these mistakes exist in Haitian Creole, and we are watchful on our part. But, nowadays, there are other people who are writing Creole, it seems they are not aware at all if the language has rules they should respect, or they openly [and] purposely do not respect the rules of the language. It is because of this we see it is necessary for us to call the people to order from time to time.

For some time, we have noticed "*Haiti Progrès*" has changed the way it used to write Creole. When we take *Haiti Progrès* in the month of April 86, it is not the same kind of Creole written in December 86. And, in this new way of writing Creole, we see there are 2 big changes. One is about the "hyphen", the other is about the "apostrophe". Let's sit down together to have a little chat about that.

THE HYPHEN

The Creole Rule says: "You can use the hyphen, if you want, to tie together a word with some grammatical form which comes after it, like:
- forms of the definite articles: the girl, the guy, the trap.
- forms of the possessive adjective: his father, my child.
- the postposed complement pronoun: the guy told me he had seen me yesterday."

As the rule says " ... if you want ... ", we agree with the newspaper when it does not put the hyphen, because, there are even sentences, in which it is difficult to tie together the "determiner" with the word that goes with it.

THE APOSTROPHE

In several languages like French [and] English we are used to swallowing a part of the sound in the words when we are speaking. In Creole too, there are a lot of cases where we swallow a part of the sound in the words.

- There are examples of words [in which] we swallow one bit and the other bit stays.

John stays at home.
I have ten cents.

There are even times, when we are speaking, that we swallow a part of the sound, but when we are writing, we write all the word.

They talk a lot. (When we are writing we put) They talk a lot.

Everything fell through. (When we are writing we put) Everything fell through.

He's got a lot of money. (When we are writing) He has got a lot of money.

- But in the forms of grammar, like subject pronoun, or other markers of verbs like "te", when we swallow a bit of the sound, we put an apostrophe.

I've got ten cents. (I have got ten cents.)
I came to your house, and you were sleeping.
Gèda is not there, she went to school.

This last part is a rule which comes from the Official Spelling Rule. Here is what the Rule says: "You can use the apostrophe for the subject pronouns.
Ex.: I came to call you, and you didn't come. *M', n' l',* are words like other words. We must leave a little space before we start the word that comes after."

D.F. (Don't forget)
There are a lot of places, even if it is not all places, [where] we may not want to use the apostrophe. But in that case, we must follow the advice that Pierre Vernet gave us, [that is] that we should run [lit. 'put all'] the word together.

WHAT WE ASK

For our part, we do not ask a big thing. The same way Haitian guys are very careful when they are writing French, we would like for the newspaper to respect the Rule of September 79, especially the part which has to do with the question of the apostrophe.

Secondly, a knowledgeable guy has a right to have his own opinion about the writing of Creole. But up until now, most people who write Creole follow the Law of September 79. There is no other authority yet. If a knowledgeable person were to have an opinion which is not in the sense of the Rule, and he would like to come and dictate the law to us, there should be a "National Creole Academy" which would support him. Until that happens [lit. while that still has not happened] we would ask all Haitians everywhere to respect the Official Creole Law. We believe that will allow us to stabilize the writing of Creole better for now, and [as for] the other little problems, we'll solve them as we go along [lit. 'while we are on the main road'].

Sosyete Koukouy Seksyon Kanada
12650 68e Ave R.D.P.
Montréal, Québec, HIC-IW3

Selection Thirty-Six

People's Assembly = People's Power

The People's Assembly is [a thing which is] in the tradition of the Haitian people. When the slaves used to meet to discuss how they should organize (themselves), how they should resist and fight against the whites, the slaves formed People's Assemblies.

The ceremony at Cayman Woods on the night of the 14 August 1791, was a good example of a Revolutionary People's Assembly uprooting the system of slavery.

The People's Assembly is where the people meet to set forth problems, to show they are not in agreement, to organise their struggle against a system which is making them spin, where they propose their own solutions and make preparations to fight to make their own solutions pass.

Revolutionary People's Assemblies are where the people refuse to accept all the power of a small handful of people who are posturing, showing off.

The big guys never want the people to talk, they want to be the only ones who should talk, [they want] to act in the name of the people. They always want to make everyone believe it is they who are acting for the people. They are living off their [i.e. the people's] backs and they always take the pose that they are making them a gift, they are giving them charity, they are doing them a favor.

People's Assemblies are for the people to gather their strength, to demand their rights. All Haitians in the country have the right to all things without asking favors. The right to food, health, school, transportation, work, having fun, justice, decent lodgings, the right to have people respect them. The people must demand these rights.

People's Assemblies are where the people organize themselves for their own selves, to defend their own interests, without being under the orders of anyone. The people have the right to be in unions, the people have the right to be in associations, political parties. The people must aim to have their direct representatives in the state body: Justice, the House of Representatives, in the Ministries, in the Palace. Even when it is the people who choose all these representatives, they [i.e. the representatives] do not have the right to take the place of the People's Assemblies which should allow the people to be aware of [lit. have open eyes on] all the activities of the leaders.

The People's Assembly must become part of the political customs of the country, the country's constitution must recognize the People's Assembly as popular power next to the executive power, the legislative power, the judicial power.

People's Assemblies are the substance of democracy. Before 7 February, the people used to form People's Assemblies to overthrow Jean Claude [Duvalier], [and form] youth meetings, "little churches", fraternities, neighborhood meetings, etc.

After 7 February these movements should have gotten deeper to spread themselves in all corners of the country, these movements should have had influence on the choice of leaders of the country.

Selection Thirty-Seven

Letter on literacy

Port-au-Prince, 7 May 88

Our friends,

We heard with great pain how everything happened. We will never forget the good work KENA and DEA did during their existence. We will never forget the work of reading and writing which went with the consciousness-raising you used to sow in the midst of the people.

It is thanks to that work of enlightenment that many of us, small-holding peasants, are able to demand our rights, able to come out of the darkness to cross to the great light. We say to you a big thank you for that. We take the opportunity to let you know the great sadness which drowned our hearts when the heads of the Catholic Church decided to crush KENA and DEA.

We hope the work you have done will not turn into a mess nor turn into a simple evening school with fine speeches under the bower. It is we, the small-holding peasants, who know how the eye-opening and the awakening were good for us.

Goodness, you really are not lucky. The way the boss men and the guys with money don't want to see *Radyo Solèy* and the newspaper *Bòn Nouvèl*! The rumor is beginning to spread that they will have the same future as *Misyon Alpha,* because the bishops have the idea of making changes in them. Now, the bigshots and the enemies of the people are rejoicing; they are joyful because a portion of their desire is already satisfied.

Ourselves, small-holding peasants, we don't lose hope because we believe in the organization of the people. The people have lost a battle, but they have not lost the war. We will still continue to organize ourselves so that our demands can be satisfied.

Misyon Alpha, Radyo Solèy and newspaper *Bòn Nouvèl,* keep your chin up.
The people are with you!

There are 36 persons who signed.

Selection Thirty-Eight

Statement from RDC regarding the 29 November massacre

The 29th of November which is coming makes it one year exactly since the criminal bandits committed the big acts of assassination on the democratic patriots who were voting in Ruelle Vaillant. For the memory of the blood of these people that the bullets and machetes of the macoute assassins tore to pieces so that the dictatorship of Namphy could continue, to show our respect for the blood of the innocent people of 29 November 87 and for all the other innocent victims, RDC is undertaking a march which is called "March for Liberation". This march is leaving from St John Bosco church, which the bandits burned last 11 September, to arrive at Ruelle Vaillant, passing through Bel Air and Lalue. This is a way for us to protest against the breaking-bones methods that the dictator with high heels is making the people undergo, those people who are unarmed and who are seeking democracy and liberation.

We are taking advantage of (making) this march for liberation to ask for some other important things:

Firstly, for Ruelle Vaillant to be called Ruelle Martyrs; [for] the liberation of the patriotic soldiers of the seventeenth of September and all political prisoners; for the national cleaning to start again now; [for the] disarming and dismissing of all macoute attachés and country sheriffs who are torturing the peasants; for the Episcopal Conference to make a pronouncement on the deportation of Father Jean Bertrand Aristide; for them to take back (at their jobs) all workers dismissed arbitrarily because they were claiming their rights; for the bandits and exploiters to respect the rights of all unions and the civil and political rights of all democratic citizens.

Everyone who remembers those patriotic voters who died cut to pieces in Ruelle Vaillant, everyone who wants the regime that has been supplying criminals since '57 to disappear from the country, everyone who wants justice, democracy and progress to be established in Haiti, we ask them to come on this march. That is the position of RDC, RDC which Edi Volel, the brother of Master Iv Volel, is leading right now.

We remind you that on that day a team of outlaws arrived, especially in Ruelle Vaillant, with big sophisticated weapons together with machetes, where they tore to pieces everyone who was voting and a lot of people were wounded. The balance sheet for that day was very heavy; twenty four people died according to the first information that came out, seventy four others were seriously wounded, and taken to the hospital. They did that in several places in the capital, and also in the [rest of the] country. According to the last information that could be gathered some time after that massacre, there were at least a hundred people who lost their life that day with, as the only weapon they had in their hand, (a piece of) a ballot which they were going to cast, to vote for a person that they wanted to sit on the padded chair.

Selection Thirty-Nine

The peasants in Jeremie demand their rights

In spite of the role peasants play in the economy of the country, a lot of people do not have a tiny bit of respect for them. They make fun of them, they call them "fat toes", "hillbillies", "leaf men ..."

The peasants in Jeremie made their voices heard on *Radio Antilles* on this question. If there is a difference between themselves and the town people, it is because the wealth of the country is badly divided. And when we speak of town people, we must say which kind of town people. A lot of them are slaving away, are struggling, the same way as a lot of peasants.

We must say right away all peasants are not the same: there are poor peasants, there are some peasants, too, who are rich. When the others speak of big toes, it is the small-holding peasants with problems they are talking about. And yet, the economy of the country sits on *their* backs. It is they who work the land. The taxes they pay are used to build schools in the towns, to pay the state employees, etc. But they do not enjoy anything. Every day, they are churning water to make butter.

Now, the peasants do not walk with their heads down any more. They see the need to organize themselves to smash all ugly prejudices, to uproot an old wretched system which has been ruining them for a long time.

That is why you find *Mouvman Peyizan Milo (MPM), Mouvman Peyizan Obòy (MPB), Mouvman Peyizan Jan Rabèl ...*

It is clear the peasants are no longer taken in.

Selection Forty

The small-holding peasants persist: "Give us back our creole pigs!"

6 May 1988

Since the time the macoute Duvalier government joined with the American government to uproot every single pig of the poor peasants in all corners of the country, the life of the small-holding peasants has become every day more complicated. The small-holding peasants cannot send their children to school, the small-holding peasants cannot give their children good care. They have lost the only means they had to conduct all their humble activities. Faced with this awful situation, the peasants are obliged to take "boat-people boats" to go to face the dangers in neighboring countries or else to (go) undergo suffering in the hell of the sugarcane fields in the Dominican Republic.

We in KOTPA (Committee for the Organisation of Small-holding Haitian Peasants), we say it is high time for the Haitian state to give back to the peasants their creole pigs. The Haitian peasants are fed up with the false promises the Haitian bigshots are always making on the radio. In the meantime, the American government and the Haitian bigshots are making big money in the business of "pink" pigs and food for these fancy pigs. The Haitian bigshots must stop thinking of the poor peasants as idiots. It was without a second thought [lit. 'scratching their heads'] that they killed your creole pigs paying 40 [dollars] for the big ones, 20 for the medium, 5 for the piglets. They should in the same way give back to you every single one of your pigs.

Because of this, KOTPA is asking that all small-holding peasants continue to put their heads together in all corners of the country, because it is only with good organisation that the peasants will be able (to manage) to deflect all the bad blows the enemy can give. Good organization is the only guarantee the peasants and the poor have to uproot the exploiters and scoundrels, to uproot poverty.

Finally, we say to all peasants, stand firm, don't let go. The battle is not easy, it's true, but victory will be yours all the same.

For KOTPA
Andrelis Chal, Jidit Pyè-Lwi, Jozèf Batis, Mak-Anri Silven, Jòj Mondezi

Selection Forty-One

Requiem for Ti Manno!

13 May 85 - 13 May 88, that makes three harvests since that great popular artist died. He was a real man, a man of courage, a gutsy child of Haiti who sang the problems of the country, the problems of people, and denounced all that was not good in our society; things which were the cause of the fact that up to the present we are still unpaid servants of the culture of another people. Antoine Rossini Jean Baptiste, alias Ti Manno, came from the womb of the land of Gonaives, one of the greatest historic towns of Haiti. How ungrateful we would be, if today we did not take off our hats one more time before this courageous popular artist who never agreed to sing what they dictated to him, but who wanted to sing what came from the bottom of his heart, from his head.

With Ti Manno, a lot of people grew to like to hear "direct rhythm", they grew to like to dance to it too.

What was the "Direct Rhythm"? And what is it (up till) today?

The "Direct Rhythm" is a kind of music which is very hot, which makes people dance a lot. With "Direct Rhythm" you are always on the beat. The biggest problem is the musicians who are playing that rhythm. You will ask what is in the heads of these musicians, especially those who are composing the songs. Everyone remembers the orchestras and small groups of before. There were amongst them some which are still on the stage now. A lot of these artists used to sing of the beauty of nature, write music (songs) of old spinsters, toothless ugly hags. There were among them some who used to dedicate beautiful notes of music to "the chief of state and his wife". The suffering of the people themselves never interested them.

It's there that Ti Manno scored points over them. Ti Manno not only used to make people dance, he took the opportunity to use the beat music to do another job: to open the eyes of the people, to raise their consciousness. A lot of enemies of truth hated "Ti Manno" because he used to expose the ugly truth [lit. 'put too much catshit outside'], and he had only just started. But it's a pity! What a great artist we lost! Thoughtful Haitians are still weeping for the death of Ti Manno.

This popular artist did not want to stay a conservative. He wanted to walk apace with reality. That is why he made his songs take a stand -- because he did not agree to continue singing about the beauty of nature and love while peasants who were hungry, who went away with their two arms hanging [i.e. with no work], were obliged to cut down trees, [and] to sell them, so as not to die of hunger with their children. Ti Manno was not afraid to denounce the exploitation the workers were undergoing at the hands of the bosses, the problem of the boat-people boats, marriages of convenience, racism, et cetera. The artist died, but his works are still alive. The Haitian artists who are playing 'beat' music have a lot of work to do, especially in the lyrics that accompany each song. The 'beat' artists must give the music another direction, continue with the same work Ti Manno was doing when he was alive. Nothing has changed, Haitians are still unable to make ends meet in the United States, Bahamas, French Guiana, Dominican Republic and in our own country. Why are these problems not sung?

Ti Manno, we remember you, because if you had been there after 7 February, you would have had a lot of words to say. Ti Manno was not a conservative, he was a progressive, popular artist who sang to change. We hope that the radio and television will present some special programs about "Ti Manno" on 13 May 88. The artist died, but his works stay alive. It is as if he had just sung them. "Operation hands meet" is what we need. These thoughful words came from the bottom of Ti Manno's heart before death took him (to go) to the baron's house. Thank you, Ti Manno, a tray of honor and respect for you.

Selection Forty-Two

Message from Jean Bertrand Aristide, 22 November 1988

My sisters, my brothers, all my brothers in God the Holy Father who raised their voices together with you, courageous youth of Haiti, Catholic, Protestant, [and] vodou-practicing peasants, courageous Haitians abroad, courageous Haitians here, you all who have just held a general and legal strike, in spite of the statement of an illegal general, hats off to you! Hats off to your courage!

With courage, you got up, you spoke. I heard. With courage, you got up, you stood up. I saw. I saw you speak for God. I heard God's voice in your voices. I saw you stand up here and abroad, in order for me to stand with you here, and not abroad.

Beautiful inspiration of the Holy Spirit! Beautiful declaration of brotherly love which invites me to look you in the eyes, my sisters, my brothers, and say to you what Jesus would say to you in his own language: *ani ohev oth, ani ohev otakh, je t'aime,* I love you.
You, too, who plotted against me, against the people, Bishop Paolo Romeo, Bishop Gayot, Bishop Ligondé, Bishop Kébreau and the rest, give me the chance to look you in the eye, please, don't be embarrassed, look me in the eye, I come to say to you: I love you.

Because I love you, I have to tell you the truth: Truth and love are one and the same. Truth and love are Jesus among the poor.

What luck for the church of Haiti, which is rich thanks to the poor, in a country which is poor because of the rich.

The church is rich thanks to you, the poor, who demand the truth without ceasing, truth everywhere.

What luck for the church of Haiti, which is rich thanks to the poor, in a country which is poor because of the rich.

The church is rich thanks to you, the poor, who prevent the bishops from hiding in the sins they commit, when they lie in order to plot and keep their silence.

What luck for the church of Haiti, which is rich thanks to the poor, in a country which is poor because of the rich.

The church is rich thanks to you, the poor, who agree to make one single body, to avoid (the unit of) a head without a body.

One alone, we are weak, together, we are strong. Together, together we are a torrent.

When the torrent of the poor descends arm in arm with the poor peasants, the poor soldiers, the poor unemployed, the poor soldiers, the poor workers, the poor soldiers, the poor friends, the poor soldiers, the church of the poor we call the *anashim Yavhe,* when that torrent descends, God will bring down the bigshots to the ground, so he can lift the humble up in the air.

Consult Luke 1, 52

But to stop the torrent of *anashim Yavhe* descending, the imperialists in cassocks plot to sell us to the American imperialists. It is for this reason, we must say one to the other what Jesus declared in Mark 2, 11, to wit: Get up and walk.

Yes, get up and walk. Get up and walk so that macoutes stop going around exploiting you to death. Get up and walk so that criminals stop walking among the people. Get up and walk so that assassins stop getting you out of your bed with bursts of bullets.

Too much blood has flowed! Too many innocent people have fallen! No! That is too much!

General Avril, you said: Haiti is degraded. And? And, nothing! You say you are giving up Fort Dimanche, you change the name of Criminal Investigation. And? And, nothing!

The people are hungry. Poverty is in their bodies. Weapons are fired at them. Wait! The workers are in trouble. The schools are in ruins. The University is penniless. Wait! The peasants are in a tight spot. The section chiefs are on edge. Stop and wait! Why are you in a hurry like that? St Jean Bosco burned. Franck Romain is among the people [i.e. free]. Mr. Avril supports him. Wait! The little leaders are servants of the big leaders. The big leaders are servants of the Americans. A! A! A! Wait!!! I'll shave your beard, you'll pass your hand over it, [to see if] you're wounded! I carry you on my back, [how can] you tell me you are stepping on fish! Sit and wait! Slavery in the army. Slavery in the Dominican Republic. O! O! Wait, still! Coups are made. Coups are made again. Generals go. Generals return. And? And, nothing. Wait for Godot!

The people's underground court is right to recognize the government as guilty and incompetent:

You are guilty because you let wild macoutes run around without the rope of justice around their necks. You are guilty because you refuse to put Franck Romain and the criminels of the massacre under the rope. You are guilty because you betray the soldiers of the 17 September, fire patriotic soldiers, and protect the patripocket soldiers. You are guilty because you send the people to go die in the "AIDS-CEDHA" elections to satisfy the Americans before the clean up was done. You are guilty because you play the same way as François Duvalier.

You are incompetent because the government has scored
Justice 0
Security 0
Cleanup 1

General Avril, don't you see Namphy's derailed train will rush down more quickly with you if before 29 November 88, you don't release the soldiers, capture the macoutes, arrest Franck Romain, do the cleanup, stop insecurity?

The question is in your hands. The people's pencil is in their hands. May God's blessing be on their heads so that grace will continue to come down until the torrent brings down all duvalierists, all macoutes, all criminals
Forever and ever
Amen.

Bibliography

Grammars

Targète, Jean. *Advanced Grammar of Haitian Creole.* Port-au-Prince: Ateliers Fardin, 1979.

Valdman, Albert. *Ann Pale Kreyòl: an introductory course in Haitian Creole.* Bloomington: Indiana University, Creole Institute, 1988.

Dictionaries

Freeman, Bryant C. *Survival Creole.* Port-au-Prince: La Presse Evangélique, 1990.

---. *Haitian Creole - English English - Haitian Creole Medical Dictionary, with Glossary of Food and Drink..* Port-au-Prince: La Presse Evangélique, 1990.

--- , with Jowel Laguerre. *Haitian - English English - Haitian Dictionary.* To appear.

Jeanty, Edner A. *Diksyonè Kréyòl/Dictionary. Creole - English Anglé - Kréyòl.* Port-au-Prince: La Presse Evangélique, 1985.

Targète, Jean. *A New Haitian Creole - English Dictionary* [manuscript].

Valdman, Albert. *Haitian Creole - English - French Dictionary.* Bloomington: Indiana University, Creole Institute, 1981.

Vernet, Pierre and Bryant C. Freeman. *Diksyonè Otograf Kreyòl Ayisyen.* Port-au-Prince: Sant Lengwistik Aplike, Inivèsite Leta Ayiti, 1988.

General

Dejean, Yves. *Comment écrire le créole d'Haïti.* Quebec: Collectif Paroles, 1980.

Gilbert, Glen G. *Pidgin and Creole Languages: Essays in memory of John E. Reinecke.* University of Hawaii Press, 1987.

Hall, Robert A. Jr. *Pidgin and Creole Languages.* Cornell University Press, 1966.

Hymes, Dell. *Pidginization and Creolization of Languages.* Cambridge University Press, 1971.

Joseph, John E. "Model-rejection as an impediment to creole standardization" in Frances Ingemann, ed. *1982 Mid-America Linguistics Conference Papers.* Lawrence: The University of Kansas Linguistics Department, 1983.

Kotey, P. and H. Der Houssikian, eds. *Language and Linguistic Problems in Africa.* Hornbeam Press, 1977.

LePage, R. B., ed. *Proceedings of the Conference on Creole Language Studies.* Creole Language Studies No. 11. Macmillan, 1961.

Li, C., ed. *Word Order and Word Order Change.* University of Texas Press, 1975.

Mühlhäusler, Peter. *Pidgin and Creole Linguistics.* Basil Blackwell, 1986.

Muysken, Pieter, ed. *Generative Studies on Creole Languages*. Foris Publications, 1981.

Nida, Eugene A. "Translating the New Testament into Haitian Creole". *The Bible Translator*, Vol 18, No. 1, Jan 67.

Pompilus, Pradel. *Contribution à l'étude comparée du créole et du français à partir du créole haïtien: Phonologie et lexicologie*. Port-au-Prince: Editions Caraïbes, 1973.

------. *Manuel d'initiation à l'étude du créole*. n.d.

------. *Le Problème Linguistique Haïtien*. Port-au-Prince: Editions Fardin, 1985.

Romaine, Suzanne. *Pidgin and Creole Languages*. Longman, 1988.

Valdman, Albert. *Le créole: structure, statut et origine*. Paris: Editions Klincksieck, 1978.

------, ed. *Pidgin and Creole Linguistics*. Bloomington: Indiana University Press, 1977.

Vernet, Pierre. *Techniques d'écriture du créole haïtien: Aspects phonético-phonologique, morpho-syntaxique et sémantique*. Port-au-Prince: Imprimerie Le Natal, 1980.

Genesis

Bickerton, Derek. "Beginnings", in Hill, 1979.

---. *Roots of Language*. Ann Arbor: Karoma, 1981.

Carrington, Lawrence D. "The Substance of Creole Studies: A Reappraisal", in Gilbert, 1987.

Gilbert, Glen G. "Language and the Bioprogram Hypothesis: Déjà Vu?", in Muysken and Smith, eds, 1986.

Goodman, Morris. Review of Bickerton's *Roots of Language*. *International Journal of American Linguistics* 51,1, January 1985:109-137.

Hill, Kenneth C., ed. *The Genesis of Language*. Ann Arbor: Karoma, 1979.

Hoenigswald, Harry M. "Language history and creole studies" in Hymes, 1971.

Keller, Rudi. "Invisible-hand Theory and Language Evolution". *Lingua* 77, 1989:113-127.

Mintz, Sidney W. "The socio-historical background to Pidginization and Creolization" in Hymes, 1971.

Muysken, Pieter, and Norval Smith, eds. *Substrata versus universals in creole genesis*. Papers from the Amsterdam Creole Workshop, April 1985. Amsterdam: John Benjamins, 1986.

Polomé, Edgar. "Creolization and Language Change", in Woolford and Washabaugh, 1983.

Singler, John Victor. "The homogeneity of the substrate as a factor in pidgin/creole genesis". *Language* 64,1, 1988:27-51.

Theory

Brousseau, Anne-Marie, Sandra Filipovich, Claire Lefebvre. "Morphological Processes in Haitian Creole". *Journal of Pidgin and Creole Languages* 4:1, 1989:1-36.

Byrne, Francis. *Grammatical relations in a Radical Creole: Verb complementation in Saramaccan*. John Benjamins, 1987.

Carden, Guy and William A. Stewart. "Binding theory, bioprogram and creolization: evidence from Haitian Creole". *Journal of Pidgin and Creole Languages* 3 (1), 1988:1-67.

Fournier, Robert. "Pu en créole haïtien". *Revue Québecoise de Linguistique Théorique et Appliquée* 6:2:107-126.

Givón, Talmy. "Prolegomena to any sane creology", in Hancock, 1979.

Hancock, Ian F., ed. *Readings in Creole Studies*. E Storia Scientia, 1979.

Howe, Kate. "Réanalyse des Pronoms Personels Pluriels du Créole Haïtien." Paper presented at the VIe Colloque International des Etudes Créoles, 29 September - 6 October 1989, Cayenne, French Guiana.

------ . "Haitian Creole and Papiamentu: Relative Pronouns or Complementizers?". Paper to be presented at the 1990 meeting of the Society for Pidgin and Creole Linguistics, Jan 4-6, 1991, Chicago, Ill.

Koopman, Hilda and Claire Lefebvre. "Haitian Creole Pu", in Muysken, 1981.

Lefebvre, C., Magloire-Holly, H. and Pion, N. (eds.). *Syntaxe de l'Haïtien*. Ann Arbor: Karoma, 1982.

Lefebvre, Claire and Diane Massam. "Haitian Creole Syntax: A Case for *DET* as Head". *Journal of Pidgin and Creole Languages* 3, 1988:213-243.

Mufwene, Salikoko. "Equivocal structures in some Gullah complex sentences". *American Speech* 64.4. 1989:05-326.

Taylor, Douglas. "Some Dominican Creole Descendants of the French Definite Article" in LePage, 1961.

Van Name, Addison. "Contributions to Creole Grammar". *Transactions of the American Philological Association* 1, 1869-70:123-167.

Verbs

Brinton, Laurel J. "The aspectual nature of states and habits". *Folia Linguistica* XXI/2-4, 1987:195-214.

Bruce, Les. "Serialization: from Syntax to Lexicon". *Studies in Language* 12-1, 1988:19-49.

Fauchois, Anne. *Nature et Fonction des Monèmes "se" en Créole Haïtien*. Port-au-Prince: Centre de Linguistique, Université d'Etat d'Haïti. Impressions Magiques, 1985.

Givón, Talmy. "Serial Verbs and Syntactic Change: Niger-Congo", in Li, 1975.

Kiefer, Ferenc. "On defining modality". *Folia Linguistica* XXI/1, 1987:67-94.

Lord, Carol. "Serial Verbs in Transition". *Studies in African Linguistics* 4,3, December 1973:269-295.

Muysken, Pieter. "Creole tense/mood/aspect systems: the unmarked case?", in Muysken 1981.

Schachter, Paul. "A non-transformational account of serial verbs". *Studies in African Linguistics* Supplement 5, Oct 1974:253-282.

Sebba, Mark. *The Syntax of Serial Verbs: An investigation into serialization in Sranan and other languages*. John Benjamins, 1987.

Singler, John Victor, ed. *Pidgin and Creole Tense-Mood-Aspect systems.* Creole Language Library, Volume 6. John Benjamins, 1990.

Spears, Arthur K. "Tense, Mood, and Aspect in the Haitian Creole Preverbal Marker System" in Singler, 1990.

Stahlke, Herbert. "Serial Verbs". *Studies in African Linguistics* 1.1. 1970: 60-99.

Williams, Wayne R. "Serial Verb Constructions in Krio". *Studies in African Linguistics* Supplement 2, Oct 1971:47-65.

Wierzbicka, Anna. "The semantics of modality". *Folia Linguistica* XXI/1 1987:25-43.

Winford, Donald. "Stativity and other aspects of the creole passive". *Lingua* 76 (1988) 271-297.

Wingerd, Judy. "Serial Verbs in Haitian Creole" in P. Kotey and H. Der Houssikian, 1977:452-466.

Wingerd, Judy. *A Partial grammar of the Haitian Creole Verb System: Forms, Function and Syntax*. PhD Dissertation. Suny, Buffalo, 1983.

Sociolinguistics

Britto, Francis. *Diglossia: a study of the theory with application to Tamil.* Washington, D.C., Georgetown University Press, 1986.

Chaudenson, Robert. *Créoles et enseignement du français.* L'Harmattan, 1989.

DeCamp, David. "Toward a generative analysis of a post-creole speech community" in Hymes 1971.

Fishman, Joshua A., ed. *Readings in the Sociology of Language.* Mouton, 1968.

Herman, Simon R. "Explorations in the Social Psychology of Language Choice", in Fishman, 1968.

Howe, Kate. "Haitian Creole as the Medium of Education in Haiti." Paper presented at the 1989 meeting of the Society for Pidgin and Creole Linguistics, 27-30 December 1989, Washington, DC.

Rickford, John R. *Dimensions of a creole continuum : History, texts and linguistic analysis of Guyanese creole.* Stanford University Press, 1987.

Woolford, Ellen and William Washabaugh, eds. *The Social Context of Creolization.* Karoma, 1983.

Haiti

Bellegarde-Smith, Patrick. *Haiti: The Breached Citadel.* Westview Press, 1990.

Boodhoo, Ken I. "Realism vs. Idealism in U.S.-Haitian Relations: Why is Washington Indifferent?". *Carribean Affairs* 1 (4), Oct-Dec 1988.

Danner, Mark. "A Reporter at Large: Beyond the Mountains - I, II, III". *The New Yorker*, November 27, December 4, December 11, 1989.

Deren, Maya. *Divine Horsemen: The Voodoo Gods of Haiti.* London: Thames and Hudson, 1953.

Dupuy, Alex. *Haiti in the World Economy: Class, Race, and Underdevelopment Since 1700.* Westview Press, 1989.

Ferguson, James. *Papa Doc, Baby Doc: Haiti and the Duvaliers.* Basil Blackwell, 1988.

Foreign Area Studies, The American University. *Haiti: a country study.* United States Government, 1982.

Freeman, Bryant C. *Haitian Medical Anthropology: Some Folk Beliefs and Practices.* Port-au-Prince: La Presse Evangélique, 1990.

Hurbon, Laënnec. *Comprendre Haïti: Essai sur l'Etat, la nation, la culture.* Port-au-Prince: Henri Deschamps, 1987.

Jeanty, Edner A. and O. Carl Brown. *Parol Granmoun: 999 Haitian Proverbs in Creole and English.* Port-au-Prince: Editions Learning Center, 1976.

Lemoine, Maurice. Translated by Andrea Johnston. *Bitter Sugar: Slaves Today in the Caribbean.* Banner Press, 1985.

Métraux, Alfred. Translated by Hugo Charteris. *Voodoo in Haiti.* Schocken Books, 1972.

Smith, Keith. "Sooner or later, another bloody chapter is going to be written in Haiti." *Caribbean Affairs,* 1 (4), Oct-Dec 1988.

Wilentz, Amy. *The Rainy Season: Haiti since Duvalier.* Simon and Schuster, 1989.

Novels

Buch, Hans Christoph. *The Wedding at Port-au-Prince: a Novel.* Translated by Ralph Manheim. Harcourt Brace Jovanovich, 1986.

Carpentier, Alejo. *El reino de este mundo.* Editorial Seix Barral, 1969.

Davis, Wade. *The serpent and the rainbow.* Warner Books, 1987.

Greene, Graham. *The Comedians.* Viking Press, 1965.

Roumain, Jacques. *Les Gouverneurs de la Rosée.* Messidor, n.d.

Glossary

A

a	at, to
a*	the
ab de Nwèl	Christmas tree
aba	down with
abi	abuse (n.)
abitrèman	arbitrarily
abitye + vb.	usually + vb., be in the habit of + vb.
abòde	approach (vb.)
abrite	shelter (vb.)
absan	absent
achevèk	archbishop
achte	buy (vb.)
adjektif	adjective
adjwen	assistant
adopte	adopt
adrese	address (vb.)
afè	matter, business
afèpabon	with problems, in trouble (financial)
afyo	arracacha
agrikilti	agriculture
agwonòm	agronomist
agwopwofesyonèl	agroprofessional
aji	act (vb.)
ak	act (n.)
ak	and
akademi	academy
akize	accuse
akò	agreement
akòde	grant (vb.)
akolit	acolyte
akonpaye	accompany
akòz de	because of
aksepte	accept
aksidan	accident
aksidante	injured in an accident
aktivite	activity
ala*	emphatic marker
alawonnbadè	all together
ale	go
ale atè	fall through, fail
ale bwa chat	bite the dust, die
ale lan peyi san chapo	to die
alfabetizasyon	literacy
alò	so
alòs	so
alòske	whereas, while
ame	arm (vb.)
amelyore	improve
Amerik Latin	Latin America
amwaz	mugwort
an	in (followed by language name)
an	year
an*	the
an menm tan	at the same time
an releng	penniless
anachi	anarchy
anba	below, under, underneath
anbachal	clandestine, secret
anbakasyon	craft, vessel
anbake	embark
anbasad	embassy
anbochaj	recruiting (var. of **anbochay**)
anbochay	recruiting, hiring
andemon	on edge (person)
andeyò	countryside (as opposed to town)
andidan	in
ane	year
anflamasyon	swelling, inflamation
angaje	pledge, involve
angle	English
anivèsè	anniversary
ankèt	inquiry
ankò	again, also, in addition
ankò	still (adv.)
anlè	in the air
anmè	bitter
anmwe	help (as exclamation)
anndan	inside
anne	year

annik*	just (+ vb.)
annou*	let's (+ vb.)
anpeche	prevent
anpil	many
anplis de	in addition to
anplwaye	employee
anplwaye	use (vb.)
anraje	madden, enrage
anrejistre	record, register (vb.)
ansanm	together
ansasen	assassin
ansasinay	assassination
ansasinen	asassinate
ansent	pregnant
answit	next, afterwards
ansyen	former
ant	between
antan	while
antere	bury
antèt	head, leader
Antiy	Antilles
antrave	in a tight spot
antre	go in, enter
antreprann	undertake
antrepriz	company, business
anvan	before
anviwon	about, approximately
anviwonman	environment
anyen*	nothing, not ... anything
ap*	verb marker [+progressive]
aparèy	facility, apparatus
apati	starting from
apèl	call, appeal (n.)
apeti	appetite
apiye	support, back (vb.)
aplike	apply
apostwòf	apostrophe
apral*	be going
aprann	learn
apre	after
apremidi	afternoon
apreyande	apprehend
apwofondi	get deeper
arebò	on the side of
arestasyon	arrest (n.)
arete	arrest (vb.)
arete	decree (n.)
arive	manage (to do sth.)
asanble	assembly
asasen	assassin
asasinay	assassination
asosi	balsam apple
asosyasyon	association
atache	attaché
atansyon	attention
atè	on the ground
aticho	artichoke
atik	article
atire	draw, attract
atis	artist
atitid	attitude
ave	garlic weed
avè	with
avèk	with
avi	notice (n.)
avili	degrade
avni	future
avril	April
avwa	savings, fortune
awondisman	ward (administrative district)
ayisyen	Haitian
ayisyèn*	Haitian (fem.)
Ayiti	Haiti
azil	asylum

B

ba	low
Baamas	Bahamas
baboukèt	makeshift bridle, muzzle
bagay	thing
bagay la mare	things are difficult
bakaloreya	baccalaureate
bal	bullet
ban*	give
banbile	rejoice

bandi	bandit
bann	group
bann (always with **yon**)	many
bat	churn, beat
batay	battle (n.); fight (vb.)
batèy	sugarcane workers' camp
bati	build
batize	baptize
bato	boat
baton	stick (n.)
bawon	baron
bay*	give
ba w sa sou 2 chèz	solve your problems in a jiffy
bayawonn	mesquite
bè	butter
bèbè	mute
bèbèl	decorations
bèkèkè	idiot
bèl	pretty, good
bèlte	beauty
benediksyon	blessing
benefis	benefit (n.)
berejenn	eggplant
bès	decrease (n.)
bese	lower (vb.)
bèt	animal
betiz	prank, absurdity
pase youn moun nan betiz	make fun of someone
bezwen*	need, want (vb.)
bilan	balance sheet, score
bileng	bilingual
bilten	ballot
bis	bus
biwo	office
biwod vòt	polling station
blan	white (person), foreigner
blese	wound, injure
blije*	be obliged (to do something)
bliye	forget
blòk	neighborhood, block
bloke	block (vb.)
bò kote	as for, on the part of, from, near
bon	good
Bondye	God
bonè	early
bouji	candle
boujon	bud (n.)
boujonnen	bud, blossom (vb.)
bouk	small town
bouke	fed up, tired
bouke	stop (vb.)
boule	burn (vb.)
boule ak	deal with
boure	stuff (vb.)
bous	scholarship, grant
bout	piece of, length of
boutèy	bottle
bradsou bradsa	arm in arm
branch	area, branch
brasewos	braceros (Sp.) (sugarcane cutters)
brave	face, brave
bri	noise, rumor
brid	bridle
brili	burn (n.)
brize	break (vb.)
bwa	arm (of body) (var. of **bra**)
bwa	wood
bwa fouye	dugout (boat)
bwè	drink (vb.)
bwè san	exploit to death
bwòdè	fancy, elegant
byen	good (n.), wellbeing
byen antandi	of course

C

chabon	coal, charcoal
chache	try (to do); seek
chaje	full, busy
chak	every, each
chan	field
chand batay	battle field
chanje	change (vb.)
chanjman	change (n.)

chans	chance, luck
chante	sing
chante	song
chapo	hat
charite	charity
chay	weight, cargo
chè	flesh
chèche	seek, look for
chèf	head, leader
chèf de bann	ringleader
chèf seksyon	section chief
chen	dog
chèz	chair
chita	sit, stay; be situated
cho	hot; in a hurry, worked up (person)
chofè	driver
chomay	unemployment, idleness
chomè	unemployed person
chwa	choice
chwazi	choose

D

dabitid	usually
dabò	at first
dakò	agree, be in agreement
daktilografi	typing
dal (with yon)	many
damou	of love
danje	danger
danse	dance (vb.)
daou	of August
dapre	according to
dat	date, day
Dayiti	of Haiti
de	from, in
de	two
de twa (2 -3)	a few
de*	some
debake	arrive, disembark
deblozay	violent quarrel
dechèpiye	tear to pieces
dechouke	uproot
defann	defend; prevent
defans	defense
defason	so that
defen	dead
defini	definite
defisi	deficit
dega	damage (n.)
degre	degree
degrenngole	rush down
deja	already
deklarasyon	statement
deklare	declare
dekonfiti	ruin (n.)
dekrete	declare, decree (vb.)
demach	steps (to achieve sth.), attempt
demanti	deny
demen	tomorrow
demere	live, inhabit
demi	half
demi ma	half mast, half staff
demisyon	resignation
demisyone	resign
demokrasi	democracy
demokrat	democrat
demokratik	democratic
denonse	denounce, inform on
denpi	from, since
denye	devoid of
dènye	last (adj.)
dènye a	the latter
dènyèman	recently, lately
depafini	ruin (vb.)
depanse	spend (money)
depatman	department (geographical division)
depatya	destroy (with rage)
depi	for (period of time in past), since, from (in time expressions)
deplase	move (vb.)
deplasman	transportation
depòtasyon	deportation
depòte	deport

derape	leave, depart
derasinen	uproot
deraye	derail
desanm	December
desann	get down, go down; stay (overnight)
deside	decide
desizyon	decision
detanzantan	from time to time
detay	detail
detèminan	determiner (grammatical)
detèminasyon	determination
detounen	turn away
devan	lead (position)
devlope	develop
devni	become
devwa	duty
dewoule	happen
dèy	mourning
dèyè	behind
deyò a	outside (loc. phrase)
dezame	disarm
dezyèm	second (adj.)
dezyèmman	secondly
di	say
di	ten
dife	fire
diferan	different
diferans	difference
difikilte	difficulty
difteri	diphtheria
digdal (always with **yon**)	many
dikdantan	a long time
diktatè	dictator
diktati	dictatorship
dikte	dictate
dimanch	Sunday
dimaten	in the morning (after time of day)
diminye	diminished
diplòm	diploma
dirèk	direct
direksyon	direction; leadership, management
direktè	director
dirèkteman	directly
dirijan	leader
dirije	lead, direct
dis	ten
disèt	seventeen
disipline	discipline (vb.)
diskite	discuss
diskou	speech
disparèt	disappear
dispozisyon	preparation
distribisyon	distribution
diswa	evening (attr.)
ditou	at all
divalyeris	duvalierist
diven	wine
divès	different,various
dizuit	eighteen
djob	job
dlo	water
do	back (n.)
do*	should, must
doktè	doctor
dola	dollar
domaj	pity, shame
dòmi	sleep
dominiken	Dominican, of the Dominican Republic
donk	for, in that case
douvan	before, faced with
dòz	dose
drapo	flag
drese	draw up
drive	drift (vb.)
dwa	right (n.)
dwa dazil	right of asylum
dwa moun	human rights
dwe*	should, must
dwèt	finger
dyalog	dialogue

E

e	and
eben	well (introducing sentence)
ebyen	well (interj.)
ede	help (vb.)
edikasyon	education
efè	effect
an efè	indeed, in fact
efektif	size
efritman	unravelling
egalman	equally
egzakteman	exactly
egzamen	examination
egzanp	example
egzije	demand (vb.)
egzistans	existence
egziste	exist
ekimenik	ecumenical
ekip	team
eklèsisman	clarification
ekonomik	economic
ekri	write
ekriti	writing
ekritman	writing
eks.	etc.
eksplwatasyon	exploitation
eksplwatè	exploiter
eksteryè	foreign, exterior
ekstradisyon	extradition
ekstrèm	furthest, extreme
ekzakteman	exactly
ekzanp	example
ekzekitif	executive
ekziste	exist
ekzòd	exodus
eleksyon	election
elèv	pupil
eli	elect (vb.)
elimine	eliminate
emisyon	program, broadcast
en	one (numeral)
endisiplin	lack of discipline
endistriyèl	industrial; industrialist
enfimyè	nurse
enfliyans	influence (n.)
enfòmasyon	information
engra	ungrateful
enjenyè	engineer
enkapab	incompetent, incapable
enkonpetans	incompetence
enpas	dead-end street
enperyalis	imperialist
enpi	and
enpòtans	importance
ensekirite	lack of security
enskri	register (vb.)
enspirasyon	inspiration
enstiti	institute (n.)
enstitisyon	institution
entènasyonal	international
enterè	interest (n.)
enterese	concerned (in, with)
enteryè	interior
entèvni	intervene, intercede
envite	invite
epi	and
episkopal	episcopal
epoutan	and yet
erè	mistake (n.)
eseye	try (vb.)
èske*	question marker
esklav	slave
esklavaj	slavery
espas	space
espesyal	special
espesyalman	especially
espirityèl	spiritual
esplwatè	exploiter
esprè	purposely
espwa	hope (n.)
estabilize	stabilize
estasyon	station
estime	estimate (vb.)
etan done	given (that)
etann	spread (vb.)
Etazini	United States

etidyan	student
etone	surprise (vb.)
etranje	foreign
evalwe	evaluate
evèk	bishop
evenman	event
evite	avoid
Ewòp	Europe
ewozyon	erosion

F

fakilte	faculty (university)
faktori	factory
fanm	woman
fanmi	family
fann	split, crack (vb.)
fasil	easy
fasilite	make easy, facilitate
fason	way, manner
fatra	trash
favè	favor
fè	do, make
fè eksprès	jump, hitch a ride
fè kado	give a gift
fè kò ansasinay	assassinate as a group (i.e. death squad assassinations).
fè labab	shave
fè lachte	behave like a coward
fè manti	lie, tell untruths
fè nwa	darkness
fè on jan pou	solve the problem for, do something for, help
fè prèv li	prove oneself
fè soti*	put out, publish (causative)
fè vwèl pou peyi san chapo	die
fèb	weak
felisite	congratulate
fèm	firm (adj.)
fèmen	close (vb.)
fèt pou *	should
fèt*	made
fèy	leaf
fi	woman
figi	face
fin*	have + vb. (perfective)
fin*	have just
fini ak	ruin (vb.)
finisman	end (n.)
fò	good (at doing sth.)
fò	strong
fò (+ subj. + vb.)*	be necessary, must
fòk	it is necessary
fòk (+ subj.+vb.)*	subj. + must/should + vb.
fòm	form (n.)
fòmasyon	training
fòme	form (vb.)
fomil	form (paper)
fon	bottom, depths
fon	fund
fondalnatal	profound, basic
fondatè	founding, founder
fondman	foundation
fonksyonè	civil servant
fonksyone	function (vb.)
fontyè	border, frontier
fòs	force, strength
fot	mistake (n.)
founi	supply (vb.)
fouye	dig
Frans	France
franse	French
frape	knock (vb.)
fratènèl	brotherly
fratènite	fraternity
fraz	sentence (n.)
frè	brother
frechè	freshness
fwa	faith
fwa	time, occasion
fyèl	stamina, bile

G

gad	guard (n.)
gade	concern (vb.), be (someone's) business
gade	look at
gagari	gargle
gagòt	mess, disorder
galope	gallop, run around
galri	veranda
garanti	guarantee (n.)
gason	man
gate	spoil, waste (vb.)
gaya	healthy
gen*	have
genyen ... a revwa ak	to have to do with
gen dwa	can, be able
genyen rezon	be right, be correct
genlè*	seem
gentan	already
genyen*	have
Giyàn	French Guiana
gonfle	swell (vb.)
goud	gourde (Haitian currency)
gouden	one quarter of a gourde
goumen	fight (vb.)
gouvènman	government
gramè	grammar
grandon	big landowner
grangou	hunger, hungry
granmèsi	thanks to
granmoun	adult
grann	grandmother
grannèg	bigshot
gras	pardon, grace
de gras	please
gras a	thanks to
grate	scratch (vb.)
grav	serious, seriously
grenn	single unit
grèv	strike (n.)
grimèl	woman of light complexion
gwo	big, important
gwo chabrak	bigshot
gwo palto	big guy, powerful person
gwo zouzoun	bigwig
gwosi	swell, grow larger
gwoup	group
gwoupman	group

I

idantifikasyon	identification
ijans	urgence
ilegal	illegal
inakseptab	unacceptable
inite	unit
inivèsite	university
inogire	inaugurate
inondasyon	flood (n.)
inosan	innocent
inyon	union
isit	here
istorik	historic
itilize	use (vb.)

J

jaden	garden, field
jan	kind, type
jan	way
bon jan	decent, adequate
jan (with **yon**)	a little
ki jan*	how
janbe	cross (vb.)
jandam	policeman
janm*	never, not ... ever
janmen	never
janvye	January
je	eye
jèm	germ
jèn	young
jeneral	general
jeneralman	generally
jenès	youth, young people

Jenèv	Geneva
jennen	embarrass
jete	throw
Jezi	Jesus
ji	juice
jidisyè	judiciary
jije	judge (vb.)
jijman	trial
jis	just, fair; just, merely
jiska	up to, until
jistis	justice
jodi a	today
jòn	yellow
jou	day
jouk	until
jounal	newspaper
jounalis	journalist, journalism
jouskaprezan	up to the present
jouskaske	until (conj.)
jwe	play (vb.)
jwenn	find (vb.)
jwi	enjoy

K

k*	which
ka	case
ka	quarter
ka*	be able, can
kaba	end (vb.)
kabann	bed
kabare	tray
kache	hide (vb.)
kado	present, gift
kafe	coffee; brothel
kakachat	catshit
kalandrye	calendar
kalbas	gourd
kale	beat, whip
kalite	kind (n.)
kalte	kind (n.)
kamyon	truck
kamyonèt	small truck (for interurban public transportation)
kan	camp (n.)
Kanada	Canada
kanmenm	all the same
kann	sugarcane
kannòt	rowboat
kanntè	small sea craft, "boat-people" boat
kanpe	stand (still); stand up
kanson	pants
kantite	quantity
kap*	be able, can
kapab*	be able, can
kapital	capital
kaprina	old spinster
karant	forty
Karayib	Caribbean
kareman	openly
kase	break (vb.)
kat	card
kat	four
katolik	catholic
katòz	fourteen
katrè*	four o'clock
katreven	eighty
katreven di	ninety
katreven kenz	ninety five
katryèm	fourth
katryèmman	fourthly
katye jeneral	headquarters
gran katye jeneral	general headquarters
kayiman	cayman, alligator
kazèn	barracks
kè	chorus
an kè	together
kè	heart
kè sote	fear (n.)
ke	that (compl.)
kèk	some
keksyon	question
kèlke	some
kèlkeswa	whatever

kenbe	stand; endure, stay firm; hold, support; keep; capture
kenz	fifteen
kesyon	question
ki*	who (rel. pro.)
Kiba	Cuba
kidonk	so; alias; to wit
kilomèt	kilometer
kilti	culture
kit ... ou byen	whether ... or else
kite	leave
kite*	let, allow
klè	clear (adj.)
klèman	clearly
klere	light up, clear
klima	climate
kliyan	client
kò	body; corps
kòb	100th of a goud (Haitian currency); money (in general)
50 kòb ak 2 gouden kole	one and the same thing
kochon	pig
kochon grimèl	pink pig (as opposed to creole pig)
kòd	rope
kokiy	shell (n.)
koklich	whooping cough
kokobe	crippled
kolaborasyon	collaboration
kolaboratè	colleague, workmate
kole	stick (vb.)
kolik	abdominal cramps
Kolonbi	Columbia
kòm	like, as
kòm dabitid	as usual
kòm kwa dire	supposedly, that is to say
kòm sa dwa	as it should, properly
kòman	how; what (asking for repetition)
kòmande	order (vb.)
kòmanse	begin
kòmansman	beginning (n.)
kòmantè	comment (n.)
komen	common
an komen	in common, public
kòmès	trade, commerce
komèsan	merchant, shopkeeper
komin	commune (administrative district)
kominal	of a commune
kominike	statement
kominote	community
komisè	prosecutor
komite	committee
kòmsadwatèt	as is fitting, in the right way
kòmsi	as if
konbit	collective work group
konbyen*	how much, how many
kondane	condemn
kondisyon	condition
kondwi	lead (vb.)
kònen	sound (vb.)
konesè	connoisseur
konferans	conference
konfli	conflict (n.)
konfrè	colleague
konfyans	confidence
konjonkti	juncture
konn + vb.*	vb. + usually, often
konn*	know
konnen*	know
konpa	rythm
konpatriyòt	compatriot
konpayèl	companion
konpetan	qualified
konpetans	proficiency
konpleman	complement (n.) (grammatical)
konplo	plot (n.)
konpòtman	behavior
konpoze	compose
konpwomèt	compromise (vb.)
konsa	thus, like this
konsa (following number)	about, approximately
konsakre	devote
konsekan	thoughtful, aware
konsène	responsible (for sth.)
konsètasyon	unity, concert
konsèvatè	conservative

konsève	keep, conserve
konsèy	advice
konsidere	consider
konsil	consul
konsilte	consult
konstate	find, ascertain
konstipe	constipate
konstitisyon	constitution
konstitiye	constitute
konsyan	aware
konsyans	awareness
konsyantizasyon	consciousness-raising
konsyantize	raise (someone's) consciousness
kont	account
kont	against
kontabilite	accounting
kontak	contact (n.)
kontakte	contact (vb.)
kontamine	contaminate
kontan	happy, pleased
konte	count (vb.)
kontinye	continue
kontre	meet
kontrebann	contraband
konvansyon	convention
konwè l ye la	right now
kopi	copy (n.)
kore	secure, support (vb.)
korespondan	correspondent
kòripsyon	corruption
Kosta Rica	Costa Rica (DOKA: Kostarica)
kòt	coast
kote	place (n.)
kote*	where
kou	blow (n.)
kou	course, class
kou	like (prep.)
kou	neck
kou	when
kou wèl ye la	right now
kouche	lie (down)
koudeta	coup d'etat
koukouy	firefly
koule	flow
kouman	as, how
koumanse	begin
kounye a	now (var. of **kounyeya**)
kounye an	now (var. of **kounyeya**)
kounyeya	now
koupab	guilty
koupe	cut (vb.)
kouray	courage
kouri	run (vb.), spread (vb.) (of rumor)
kout	denotes action involving following noun
koute	listen
koutmen	hand (help)
kouwè	like, as
kouwè l li ye a	right now
kouwèl ye la a	right now
kowòdinasyon	coordination
kowoperasyon	cooperation
kòz	reason, cause
kozman	talk (n.)
kraze	smash
kraze brize	destructive
kretyen	Christian
kretyen vivan	person, human being
kreye	create
kreyòl	Creole
kreyon	pencil
krible	riddle with holes
krik	peep (utterance)
kriminèl	criminal
kriye	weep
krochi	crooked, winding
kroup	croup
kwè	think, believe
kwen	corner

L

la	there (loc.)
labab	beard
lachanm	= House of Representatives

lacharite	charity
lachte	cowardliness
ladan	among, in, inside
lafanmi	family
lafwa	time (instance)
lafyèv	fever
lage	give up, let go, let out, release; leave, go away
lagè	war
lagras	grace
Lagwadloup	Guadaloupe
laj	age
lajan	money, wages
lajistis	justice
lajounen	day, daytime
lajwa	joy
lakay	at home, in the house of
lakomin	commune (administrative district)
lakòz	cause (n.)
lalibète	liberty
lalwa	law
lamanjay	food
lame	army
lamizè	poverty
lan*	in (var. of **nan***)
lan*	the
lanati	nature
lanfè	hell
lang	language
langchat	cat tongue
lanmò	death
lanmou	love (n.)
lanne	year
lannwit	night
lanp	lamp
lanse	issue (vb.)
lapenn	pain, sorrow
laperèz	fear (n.)
lapli	rain (n.)
lapolis	police
laprès	media, press
lari	street
larivyè	river
laroujòl	rubella, German measles
laswenyay	treatment, care
Laswis	Switzerland
lasyans	science
latitid	latitude
latriye	rest, remains
e latriye	et cetera
lavalas	torrent
laverite	truth
lavi	living, livelihood, life
laviktwa	victory
lavil	downtown (n. and loc.)
layite	display, show off
lè	time
lè	when, during, at the time of
a lè	per hour
ki lè*	when (interr.)
lèd	ugly
legliz	church
lejislatif	legislative
lekòl	school
lekti	reading
lemonn	world
lendi	Monday
lenjistis	injustice
lenmi	enemy
lennmi	enemy
leplisouvan	most often
lès	east
lesklavaj	slavery
lespri	spirit
lestonmak	chest
lèt	letter
leta	state (n.)
levanjil	gospel
leve	raise
lèzòd	the orders
lezòt (pl. only)	others
li	read
li*	3s personal marker
liberasyon	liberation
libreri	bookstore
lide	idea
lidè	leader
lig	league

Lik	Luke
lil	island
limen	light (vb.)
limyè	light (n.)
lit	fight, struggle (n.)
lite	fight, struggle (vb.)
liv	book
lò	when
lòbèy	quarrel, disagreement
loje	lodge (vb.), lodging (n.)
lojman	lodging
lokal	premises, headquarters
lokalite	place (n.)
lokalize	locate
lokomosyon	transportation
lonè	honor
lonje	hold out, stretch out
lonje dwèt sou	to point a finger at
lonjitid	longitude
lontan	a long time, before
lopital	hospital
lòt	other
lòtre jou	the other day
lou	heavy
louvri	open
lwa	law
lwa	vodou spirit
lwès	west
lwil	oil (n.)
lye	connect, join

M

m*	1s personal marker
ma	mast
mach	march, walk (n.)
machann	vendor
mache	market
mache	walk ; work, function (vb.)
mache ak	go with
machin	vehicle, car
madi	Tuesday
mafreze	wretched, rotten
magazen	store
majistra	mayor
majorite	majority
makòn (always with **yon**)	many
makònen	tie together
makout	macoute (n. and attr.)
makristi	castor oil plant, palma christi
mal gòj	sore throat
maladi	disease, illness
maladi chabon	anthrax
malatchong	false
malè	misfortune
malere	poor man
malerèz	poor woman
malgre	in spite of
malmouton	mumps
malouk	awful
maltrete	mistreat
manbre	have members
manchèt	machete
mande	ask (for), beg
mangonmen	complicate
manipile	manipulate
manje	eat
manje vach anraje	not be able to make ends meet
manje	food
manm	member
manman	mother
manti	lie (n.)
mare	arrest, tie up; tie, attach
mare gwo mago	make big money
maryaj	marriage
maryaj enterè	marriage of convenience
marye	go with, match
mas	March
mas	mass (quantity)
masak	massacre (n.)
maspinen	to beat (someone) up
materyèl	material
mati	martyrdom, martyr
matine	morning
matirite	maturity

matirize torture, make a martyr of
matyè matter, subject
mayèt power
mazora toothless person
me May (month)
medikal medical
Meksik Mexico
meksiken Mexican
melanje mix (vb.)
memwa memory
men but
men hand (n.)
men here is
menm even (adv.)
menm* emphatic marker with personal marker.
menmman parèyman exactly the same
menmsi even if
mennen take, lead, conduct (vb.)
meprize despise
meri townhall
meriken (North) American
merite deserve
mès custom
mesaj message
mèsenè mercenary
mèsi thanks, thank you
mesye (pl.) men, Messrs.
mesyedam people
mèt Master (title for lawyer)
mèt* may
met* put
mete put
 mete ak join, put together
 mete dife set fire
 mete kakachat deyò expose the truth
 mete kanpe erect (vb.)
 met kò + personal marker + deyò leave, depart
 mete sou add to
 mete sou pye set up (vb.)
metòd method
metye profession
mezanmi goodness (interj.)
mezi measure
 mezi + n. every single + n.
mil thousand
militè military; soldier
milite militate
milye environment, surroundings
minidyaz group (of musicians)
minis minister
ministè ministry
mis muscle
misyon mission
mitan midst, middle
miyèt crumb
 an miyèt moso in tiny pieces
mizè poverty, misery
mizik music
mizik song
mizisyen musician
mò dead
mobilize mobilize
mòde bite (vb.)
modòd watchword, call (to do something)
moman moment
mòn hill, mountain
monseyè bishop
monte go up, get in (vehicle)
montre show (vb.)
moral moral
mòso bit, piece
moso piece
mouch fly (n.)
moun person
mouri die
moute raise (vb.)
mouvman movement
 nan 2 tan 3 mouvman in a jiffy
move bad
move je scoundrel
movèz fwa bad faith, insincerity
msye man; Mr; 3s pronoun
mwa month
mwayèn average (n.)

mwayen	means (n.)
mwens	less

N

n*	1/2p personal marker
nan ka	in trouble
nan*	in, to
nanm	substance, soul
nannwit	(at) night
nanpwen	there is/are no/none ...
nasyon	nation
nasyonal	national
natif natal	native
natirèl	natural
nèf	nine
nèg	guy
nenpòt	any, whatever
nesesè	necessary
nesesite	need, necessity
nèt	totally, completely
nètalkole	definitively, totally
netwayaj	cleaning, clean-up
neye	drown
ni	nor
ni ... ni	and, both ... and
nimewo	number
nò	north
Nodès	Northeast
nòdwès	northwest
nòmalman	normally
non	name
non	no
nòt	note
nou*	1/2p personal marker
nouvèl	news
nouvo	new
novanm	November
nwa	black
Nwèl	Christmas
nwit	night

O

ò	now, but, well
o ralanti	at a slow pace
obeyi	obey
oblije*	have to
obsèvatè	observer
obsève	observe
ochan	hymn, anthem
odè	smell, odor
ofisyèl	official
òganizasyon	organization
òganize	organise
ogmante	increase, augment
okazyon	occasion
òkès	orchestra
okou	in the course of, during
oksilyè	assistant
olandèz	Dutch
olye	instead of
on*	a
onè	honor
onèt	honest
onon	in the name of
onz	eleven
operasyon	operation
opinyon	opinion
orè	timetable
oserye	seriously
osid	to/in the south
otèl	hotel
oto	auto (car)
òtograf	spelling, orthography
otomatik	automatic
otorite	authority
ou*	2s personal marker
oubyen	or
ougan	vodou priest
oun*	a
ousnon	otherwise
ouvè	open (adj.)
ouvèti	opening
ouvri	open

ouvriye	worker
ozanviwon	surrounding; around, at about

P

pa	by; per
pa bò isit	here
pa ekzanp	for example
pa malè	by misfortune
pa mwa	per month
pa*	emphatic possessive
pa*	not (verb negation)
pa ... ankenn*	no + n., not ... any
pa ... ankò*	no longer, not ... any more
pa ... ditou	not ... at all
pa ... ni ... ni*	not ... either ... or
pa ... okenn*	none, not ... any
pa ... pèsonn*	not anybody, nobody
pa fin kòdyòm	not to be right, the way it should be
pak	park
pakèt (after yon)	a lot, many
pale	speak, talk
palè	palace
palidis	malaria
palto	jacket
pami	among
pàn	breakdown (vehicle, machine)
an pàn	broken down
pandansetan	meanwhile
pandye	hang down
pannan	while
panse	think
Panyòl	Dominican Republic
panyòl	Spanish (language); person from Dominican Republic
pap*	negative marker + verb marker [+ progressive]
papa	father
papye	paper
paraf	mark, signature
paralize	paralyze
paran	parent
parapò a	compared to
pare	deflect
parèt	be published, appear
pase	because (var. of **paske**)
pasè	ferryman
pase	happen
pase	more than (+ number)
pase	pass (vb.)
an pasan pa	passing by, via
pase*	than (in comparative construction)
pasifik	peaceful
paske	because
paspò	passport
pat*	negative + verb marker [+anterior]
pati	leave (vb.)
pati	part
pati	party (political)
patikilyèman	particularly, especially
patisipasyon	participation
patisipe	participate
patripòch	pun on **patriyòt** and **pòch**, *pocket*
patriyòt	patriot
patwon	owner, boss
patwouy	patrol (n.)
pave	street, paving stone
pawòl	word, lyrics
pazapa	apace
pè	be afraid, fear
pè	priest, father (in church)
peche	sin
pèdi	lose, waste
pèdi tan	waste time
pèlen	trap (n.)
pèmanan	permanent
pèmèt	allow, permit
pèn	effort
penpennen	struggle (vb.)
pèp	people (vs. élite)
peryòd	period, menses
pèsonèl	personal
pete	break out, burst
peye	pay (vb.)

peyi	country
Peyi Ba	Holland
peyizan	peasant
pi (+ adj.)*	more (= adj.), adj. + -er
pi ba	below (in text)
pi fò	majority
pi piti	less
piblik	public
pibliye	publish
piki	injection
pil	pile (n.)
pile	crush, step on
pinèz	bug
pinga*	emphatic negative for imperative form
mache sou pinga-yo	be very careful
pini	punish
pisans	power
pise	pee, urinate
piske	as, since
pitit	child (offspring)
plak	record, disk
plant	plant (n.)
plante	plant (vb.)
plas	place, space
plè	wound (n.)
plenn	plain (flat land); rural area not far from the city
plenyen	complain
plezi	pleasure
pli de	more than
plis	(the) more
an plis	more, in addition
plizyè	several
pòch	pocket
poko*	still not
polis	policeman
politik	political
politik	politics
polivalan	general
polyo	polio
ponko*	not yet
ponyen	handful
ponyèt	wrist

popilasyon	population
popilè	popular
pòs	position, post
posesif	possessive
posib	possible
posibilite	possibility
pòsyon	portion
pòt	door
pote	bring, carry
pote kole	join together, stick together
Pòto Riko	Puerto Rico (DOKA: Pòtoriko)
pou	for
pou granmèsi	for nothing, in vain
pou kont kò pa yo	on their own
pou kont yo	on their own
pou pi piti	at least
pou pi rèd	more severely, stubbornly
pou pwòp kò pa yo	on their own
pou san	percent
pou ti krik ti krak	for any reason at all
pou*	[complementizer]
poud	powder, (by extension) drugs
poukisa	why
pouswiv	follow
poutèt	because of (prep.)
poutèt ke	because
pouvwa	power
pòv	poor
pòz	pose (n.)
poze	put
poze oun kesyon	ask a question
pozisyon	position
pral*	be going
prale*	be going
pran	take
pran dispozisyon	make preparations
pran konsyans	become aware
pran kontak	make contact
pran plezi	take pleasure, have fun
pran wòl	play a role
prans chans	take the/a chance

pratik	practice (n.)
pratikman	practically
pre	near
prejije	prejudice (n.)
prekosyon	precaution
premye	first
premyèman	firstly
prensipalman	mainly, mostly
preokipasyon	concern, worry (n.)
près	press (n.)
presbitè	rectory
prese	in a hurry
prese prese*	as quickly as possible
presize	say, clarify
presizeman	precisely
presizyon	clarification
prèske	almost
preskil	peninsula
prevansyon	prevention
prevni	prevent
prevwa	foresee
prezan	present (time)
prezidan	chairman, president
pri	price
primè	elementary (school)
prive	private
prizon	prison
prizonye	prisonner
pwason	fish (n.)
pwatann	green bean (lit. 'tender bean')
pwen	point
pwoblèm	problem
pwofesè	teacher
pwofesyonèl	professional
pwofitab	advantageous, profitable
pwofite	take the opportunity
pwogram	program
pwogrè	progress
pwogresis	progressive
pwojè	project
pwomès	promise (n.)
pwomèt	promise (vb.)
pwomosyon	advancement, promotion
pwonon	pronoun
pwononse	make a pronouncement
pwòp	own (adj.)
pwopoze	propose
pwopriyetè	owner
pwosesis	process (n.)
pwosesyon	procession
pwoteje	protect
pwoteksyon	protection
pwotestan	protestant
pwoteste	protest
pwovèb	proverb
pwovens	province
pye	foot
a pye	on foot
pye bwa	tree

R

rache	cut to pieces, kill with machete or axe
radyo	radio
rafal	burst (n.)
rakwen	corner
randevou	appointment, rendez-vous
rankontre	find
ranmase	gather
ranplase	replace
ransèyman	information
rantre	go in
ranvèse	overthrow (vb.)
ranyon	ruin, rag
an ranyon	in ruins
raple	recall
raple alòd	call to order
rapò	report (n.)
rapousib	continue
rasanble	gather
rasin	root
rasis	racism
ravaje	ravage
rayi	hate (vb.)
rebwazman	reforestation
rechèch	investigation

rèd	stiff; severe, stubborn
redi	stiffen
refèt	done again
refize	refuse
reflechi	reflect
règ	rule (n.)
an règ	in order
regle	settle
rejim	regime
rejyon	region
reklame	demand
rekonèt	admit, recognize
rekonsilyasyon	reconciliation
rekonstwi	rebuild
rekòt	harvest
rèl	shout (n.)
rele	call (vb.)
relèvman	recovery
relijyèz	religious
relye	connect, link
remake	notice (vb.)
remèd	remedy (n.)
remèsiman	thanks
remèsye	thank (vb.)
remèt	give back
renmen	like (vb.)
renmèt	deliver
reparasyon	repairs
repare	repair (vb.)
Repiblik Dominikèn	Dominican Republic
repo	rest
reponn	answer (vb.)
repotaj	report, article
repoze	rest (vb.)
repran	take (on) again, start again
repran chè	get bigger
represyon	repression
reprezantan	representative (n.)
resepsyonis	receptionist
resevwa	receive
resi	manage (to do something), succeed (in doing something)
reskonsab	responsible
respè	respect (n.)
respekte	respect (vb.)
responsablite	responsability
restavèk	unpaid servant (child)
ret*	stay (vb.)
rete	stay, remain; still have
retire	take from, take off, remove
retounen	return (vb.)
retresi	postposed
revandikasyon	demand (n.)
revany	revenge
revoke	fire, dismiss
revolisyonè	revolutionary
reyabilitasyon	rehabilitation
reyafime	reaffirm, confirm
reyalite	reality
reyalize	realize, make real, hold (event)
reyini	meet
reyinyon	meeting
reyisi	make success of, be successful
reyisit	success
reyòganize	reorganize
reziste	resist
rezo	network
rezon	reason (n.)
ri	street
rich	rich
richès	wealth
ride	help (vb.)
rim	cold (illness)
riral	rural
riske	risk (vb.)
rit	rythm
rive	arrive; happen; manage (to do sth.), succeed in (doing something)
rive*	including, up to (vb. used with prep. function)
rivyè	river
riyèl	little street

S

sa	that, those (pronoun)
sa a*	this
sa k(i)*	those who
sa k*	what
sak	bag
sakre	holy
sakrifye	sacrifice
sal	dirty
sali	salvation
samdi	Saturday
san	blood
san	hundred
san	without
sanble*	seem
sanitasyon	sanitation
sanmanman	outlaw
sans	sense, meaning
sant	center
sante	health
santral	center, central
sant vil	town center, downtown
sapen	fir tree
saranpyon	measles
sasina	assassination
satisfè	satisfy
save	knowledgeable, scientific, scholarly
sè	sister
se + vb.*	have to + vb.
se*	be
segondè	secondary
sèjan	sergeant
sekirite	security
sekou	help, aid (n.)
sekretarya	secretariat
seksyon	section, subdivision
sektè	sector
sèl	only (adj.)
selebre	celebrate
sèlman	only (adv.)
selon	according to
semèn	week
semèn pase an wo	week before last
seminè	seminar
sen	holy
sèn	stage (theater)
Sen Domeng	Dominican Republic
Sen Maten	St Martin
senbòl	symbol
sendika	union (labour)
senk	five
senkant	fifty
senkantsèt	fifty seven
senp	simple, mere
senpatizan	sympathizer
sentetik	synthetic, artificial
sepandan	however
separe	divide, separate
septanm	September
seremoni	ceremony
seri	series, some
serye	serious
sèt	seven
sètadi	that is (to say)
sèten	certain
sètoblije + vb.*	have to + vb.
sèvi	serve
sèvi	use (vb.)
sèvi avè yon bagay	to use something
sèz	sixteen
sezi	seize, grasp
si	if
sibi	undergo, suffer
sida	AIDS
sidès	southeast
sidwès	southwest
sijè	subject (n.)
sijere	suggest
sikile	move around
siklòn	hurricane
sikwi	route, circuit
sila a*	this, that
silans	silence (n.)
silvouplè	please
siman	surely

simaye	sow, scatter
siperyè	higher
sipèstisye	superstitious
siprann	surprise (vb.)
sis	six
sispann	stop (vb.)
sistèm	system
sistematik	systematic
site	cite
site	housing development; in Haiti, often slum areas
sitirasyon	situation
sitou	especially
sitwayen	citizen
sivik	civic
siy	sign (n.)
siyati	signature
siyen	sign (vb.)
siyifye	signal (vb.)
sòf	except
sòlda	soldier
solèy	sun
solid	solid
solidarite	solidarity
solisite	ask for
solisyon	solution
son	sound (n.)
sonje	remember
sosyete	society
sòt*	have just
sot*	leave, go out, come out
sote	jump (vb.)
sòti	go out, come out, leave
sòti X (pou) rive X*	from X to X
sou kote	on the side of, next to
sou*	about, on
soufrans	suffering (n.)
soufri	suffer
soupe	supper
souple	please
sous	source
soutàn	cassock
souvni	memory (of event)
sovaj	wild
sove	save
stad	stage, point
swa	evening
swa ... swa ...	either ... or ...
sware	evening
swasant	sixty
swasant katòz	seventy four
swen	care (n.)
swiv	follow
syèj	head office

T

ta*	verb marker [+anterior+irrealis]
tab	table
tabli	establish
taks	tax
taksi	taxi
talè a	a short time ago, just now
talon	heel
talon kikit	high heels (of shoes)
tan	time
tandans	tendency
tande	hear
tankou	such as, like
tann	expect, wait for
tanpèt	storm
tanpri	please
tansyon	bood pressure, tension
tap*	verb marker [+anterior +progressive]
taptap	covered pickup or van, with set route and price, for urban public transportation
taye	cut, trim (vb.)
taye banda	show off
tchotcho	money (small amount, earned with difficulty)
tè	land (n.)
te*	verb marker [+anterior]
teknisyen	technician
Teksas	Texas
telefonnen	telephone (vb.)

televizyon	television
tèlke	such as
temwayaj	evidence, proof
tenèb	darkness, evil
tep	tape (n.)
teren	field
teritwa	territory
tèt	head
tètanba	with head down, upside down
tèt fè mal	headache
tetanòs	tetanus
ti	little
ti kras	little, a bit
tibebe	baby
timidman	timidly
timoun	child
tirè	hyphen
tire	shooting, shots; shoot
tire revany	take revenge
tisi	fabric, material
tit	title
tonbe	fall (vb.)
tonèl	bower
totalkapital	first-rate
tou	also, too
touche	earn
toude	both
toufe	suffocate
toujou	still (adv.)
tounen	return
tounen	trip (n.)
tounen	turn (into), become
toupatou	everywhere
toupizi	spin, run around
touswit	right away
tout	all
tout bon vre	truly
tout kote	everywhere
tout moun	everyone
toutotan	as long as
touye	kill
tradisyon	tradition
trafik	traffic
trann	thirty
transpò	transportation
travay	work (n. and vb.)
travayè	worker
travèse	cross (vb.)
tray	suffering
trayi	betray
tren	train (n.)
trennen	take, lead
trete	treat (n.)
tribinal	court, tribunal
tribòbabò	everywhere
trimen	slave away
tristès	sadness
twa	three
twazyèm	third
twazyèmman	thirdly
twò (+ adj. or adv.)	too (+ adj. or adv.)
twonpèt	trumpet
twòp + n.	too much + n.
twouve	find (vb.)
tyè	third (fraction)

U

uit	eight

V

va*	verb marker [+irrealis]
vach	cow
vaksen	vaccine
vaksinasyon	vaccination
vaksinen	vaccinate
valab	valuable
vale	swallow
valè	value
van	wind
vann	sell
vant	stomach
vant mòde	stomach ache

vanyan	courageous
varyete	kind, variety
vè	maggot
vèb	verb
vekse	annoy, upset
venteyen	twenty one
ventnèf	twenty nine
verite	truth
veyatif	watchful, careful
vijilan	watchful, vigilant
viktim	victim
vil	town
vin*	become
vin*	come
vini	come
vire	drive around, stroll around
vire	tour (n.)
vis	vice, deputy (prefix)
vit	quickly
vitès	speed
viv	live (vb.)
vivan	alive
vize	aim (vb.)
vle	want
vle di	mean (vb.)
vodouyizan	vodou practicing
volonte	will, desire, willingness
vòt	vote (n.)
votan	voter
vote	vote (vb.)
voye	send
voye je sou	glance at
voye moute	present (vb.) (on radio and television)
vrè	real, true
vrèman	really
vwa	way
vwal	sail (n.)
vwayaj	travel, journey
vwayaje	travel (vb.)
vwazen	neighbor
vwèl	sail (n.)
vyann	flesh, meat
vye	horrible, ugly
Vyetnam	Vietnam
vyolans	violence
vyolasyon	violation, breach
vyole	break (the law), violate

W

w*	2s personal marker
wè	see
wè nan boutèy nwa	be deceived, taken in
wi	yes
wòl	role
wouj	red
wout	road
wòwòt	immature

Y

y*	3p personal marker
yè	yesterday
ye*	be
yo*	3p personal marker
yon*	a
yonn	one (pron.)
you*	a
youn*	a
younn	one (pron.)

Z

zafè	matter, affair
zafra	sugar harvest
zak	act (n.)
zam	weapon, arm
zam fann fwa	sophisticated weapon
zanmi	friend
zannimo	animal
zantray	womb
zèv	works
zewo	zero

zing	tiny bit
zo	bone
zòn	area, zone
zòrèy	ear
zòt	others
zòtèy	toe
zotobre	bigshot
zouti	tool
zye	eye